T0383060

NEW WORKS
IN ACCOUNTING
HISTORY

Richard P. Brief, *Series Editor*

Leonard N. Stern School of Business
New York University

A Garland Series

PROFESSIONAL ACCOUNTING AND AUDIT IN AUSTRALIA, 1880-1900

Edited by
Garry D. Carnegie
and
Robert H. Parker

Garland Publishing, Inc.
A member of the Taylor & Francis Group
New York & London 1999

Published in 1999 by
Garland Publishing Inc.
A Member of the Taylor & Francis Group
19 Union Square West
New York, NY 10003

10   9   8   7   6   5   4   3   2   1

Library of Congress Cataloging-in-Publication Data

Professional accounting and audit in Australia, 1880–1900 / edited by Garry D.
    Carnegie and Robert H. Parker.
        p. cm. — (New works in accounting history)
        Includes bibliographical references.
        ISBN 0-8153-3446-X (alk. paper)
        1. Accounting—Australia—History. 2. Auditing—Australia—History.
    I. Carnegie, Garry D. II. Parker, Robert H., 1932– . III. Series.
HF5616.A8P76 1999
657'.0994'09034—dc21   99-33042

Printed on acid-free, 250-year-life paper
Manufactured in the United States of America

ACKNOWLEDGEMENTS

The editors are most grateful for the assistance provided by Jill Bright, Gwyneth Dickens, Zlatica Kovac, Denise Patterson and Trissia Waddingham in the preparation of this volume. Special thanks are also extended to the library staff at Deakin University for their assistance in obtaining copies of many of the articles reproduced herein.

CONTENTS

Introduction by the Editors   1

Professional Accounting

Argus, 31 May 1883, p.5. 27

"Accountants and Clerks' Association," *Argus,* 23 June 1883,
p.10. 28

"A Sad Case," *Melbourne Bulletin,* Vol.5, No.222, 16 January
1885, p.1. 31

"Accountants," *AIBR,* Vol.IX, No.4, 14 April 1885, p.205. 33

COOPER, Chas.A., "The Society of Accountants," *Argus,*
10 March 1886, p.4. (Letter to the Editor). 34

CRELLIN, William, "The Society of Accountants," *Argus,*
16 March 1886, p.11. (Letter to the Editor). 36

"Chartered Accountants," *AIBR,* Vol. X, No 7, 14 July 1886,
p.380. 39

"PROFESSIONAL ACCOUNTANT," "Unchartered Accountants,"
AIBR, Vol.X, No.8, 14 August 1886, p.446.
(Letter to the Editor). 40

"Incorporated Institute of Accountants, Victoria," *AIBR,* Vol.XI,
No.3, 15 March 1887, p.156. 41

CRELLIN, William, "Incorporated Institute of Accountants, Victoria," *AIBR*, Vol.XI, No.4, 15 April 1887, p.200. (Letter to the Editor and Editor's response). 44

CRELLIN, William, "Incorporated Institute of Accountants, Victoria," *AIBR*, Vol.XI, No.5, 14 May 1887, p.271 (Letter to the Editor and Editor's response). 47

"Incorporated Institute of Accountants," *Argus*, 16 June 1887, p.10. 49

"Incorporated Institute of Accountants (Victoria)," *AIBR*, Vol.XI, No.7, 14 July 1887, pp.403-4. 52

"The Incorporated Institute of Accountants, Victoria," *AIBR*, Vol.XII, No.2, 16 February, 1888, p.99. 54

"The Institute of Accountants," *Journal of Commerce*, 28 June 1889, pp.4-5. 55

"PHILO", "What is an Accountant?," *Argus*, 5 August 1890, p.6. (Letter to the Editor). 59

"Accountants and Actuaries," *AIBR*, Vol.XIV, No.8, 16 August 1890, pp.592-3. 63

CRELLIN, William and FLACK, Joseph H., "Accountants and Auditors," *AIBR*, Vol.XIV, No.11, 17 November 1890, p.794. 66

"Incorporated Accountants," *Journal of Commerce*, 21 June 1892, pp.4-5. 67

"Accountants and Auditors," *Journal of Commerce*, 4 July 1893, p.5. 69

"Institutes of Accountants," *AIBR*, Vol.XVII, No.7, 19 July 1893, p.668. 71

"The Status of Accountants," *AIBR*, Vol.XVII, No.11, 20 November 1893, p.1014.[1] 72

"Chartered Accountants," *AIBR*, Vol.XVIII, No.6, 19 June 1894, p.374. 74

"The Accountants' Institute," *Journal of Commerce*, 17 July 1894, pp.5-6. 76

"Auditors and their Associations," *Journal of Commerce*, 12 February 1895, p.5-6. 78

"Institutes of Accountants," *AIBR*, Vol.XX, No.10, 19 October 1896, pp.717-8. 81

YARWOOD, F.N., *A Public Accountant's Work and Duties* (Sydney: The Sydney Institute of Public Accountants, June 1898) 21 pp. 82

"The Incorporated Institute of Accountants, Victoria," *AIBR*, Vol.XXII, No.7, 19 July 1898, p.430. 102

BRENTNALL, Thomas, "Interesting Address to Young Accountants," *BMA*, Vol.XII, No.4, 15 November 1898, pp.242-7 and *BMA*, Vol.XII, No.5, 15 December 1898, pp.328-31. 104

"Regulating the Profession of Public Accountants," *BMA*, Vol.13, No.3, 31 October 1899, pp.179-81. 116

OEHR, R.J., "How to Become a Skilled Accountant," *BMA*, Vol.13, No.5, 29 December 1899, pp.291-300. 120

HOWDEN, J. McA., "The Legalising of the Profession of Accountants," *BMA*, Vol.14, No.1, 29 August 1900, pp.14-9. 133

Audit

"A Definition of Bank Audit," *AIBR*, Vol.X, No.3, 15 March 1886, pp.124-5.[2] 143

"Second-Class Audit," *AIBR*, Vol.IV, No.6, 9 June 1880, pp.184-5. 146

"Continuous Audit," *AIBR*, Vol.IV, No.12, 8 December 1880, pp.406-7. 148

"The Auditor-General of Queensland on Banking Returns,"
AIBR, Vol.VI, No.8, 10 August 1882, pp.274-5. _____ 150

"Bank Audit," *AIBR*, Vol.X, No.3, 15 March 1886, pp.117-8. _____ 153

"The New Banking and Trading Companies Bill," *AIBR*, Vol.X,
No.7, 14 July 1886, pp.371-2. _____ 155

"Examples of Auditors' Certificates," *AIBR*, Vol.X, No.7,
14 July 1886, pp.382-3. _____ 158

BIGGS, St. John A., "Bank Audit," *JBIA*, Vol.1, No.4,
December 1886, pp.12-6.[3] _____ 162

TAYLOR, Henry D'Esterre, "Bank Audit: Causes of its
Inefficiency, and Suggestions for its Improvement," *AIBR*,
Vol.XI, No.3, 15 March 1887, pp.152-5.[4] _____ 168

"Duties of Auditors," *AIBR*, Vol.XI, No.10, 15 October 1887,
pp.607-8. _____ 174

"The Duties of Auditors - The Anglo-Australian Bank," *AIBR*,
Vol.XV, No.5, 18 May 1891, pp.314-5. _____ 176

"Audit," *AIBR*, Vol.XVI, No.1, 18 January 1892, p.7. _____ 179

"The Audit of Insurance Companies Accounts," *AIBR*, Vol.XVI,
No.2, 18 February 1892, pp.136-7. _____ 180

"Audit," *AIBR*, Vol. XVI, No.2, 18 February 1892, pp. 81-2 and
No.3, 18 March 1892, pp.169-70. _____ 182

DAVIS, C.H., "Audit," *AIBR,* Vol.XVI, No.4, 18 April 1892,
p.260. _____ 188

"Auditors: Their Responsibilities and Duties," *BMJBIA*,
Vol.VII, No.4, November 1893, pp.219-23. _____ 189

BRENTNALL, Thomas, "Address to Members of the
Incorporated Institute of Accountants, Victoria," *Supplement
to AIBR*, Vol.XVII, No.11, 20 November 1893, pp.1-3.[5] _____ 194

"Liability of Directors and Auditors," *AIBR*, Vol.XIX, No.3, 19 March 1895, pp.151-2. 200

"Auditors and Their Certificates," *Journal of Commerce*, reprinted *BMA*, Vol.VIII, No.10, May 1895, pp.663-5. 203

MILES, John B.C., *Concerning Auditing* (Sydney: The Sydney Institute of Public Accountants, 28 November 1895) 21pp. 207

HOLT, William, "The Companies Act, 1890, Further Amendment Bill. As Affecting Auditors, with Observation on Their Functions and Future Scope," *BMA*, Vol.X, No.4, November 1896, pp.284-90. (Letter to the Editor.) 227

"The Victorian Companies Act 1896," *AIBR*, Vol.XXI, No.1, 19 January 1897, pp.3-5. 234

"Inadequate Audit," *AIBR*, Vol.XXIII, No. 4, 19 April 1899, pp.227-8. 238

Miscellaneous

"Uniformity in Stating Accounts," *AIBR*, Vol.VII, No.2, 12 February 1883, pp.58-9. 243

"Accounts of Trading Companies," *AIBR*, Vol.VII, No.10, 12 October 1883, p.390. 246

"What Are Profits for Distribution?," *AIBR*, Vol.X, No.5, 13 May 1886, p.245. 248

"Goodwill as an Asset," *AIBR*, Vol.X, No.6, 14 June 1886, p.316. 250

"Company Law in Victoria," *AIBR*, Vol.XV, No.11, 18 November 1891, pp.818-9. 251

"The Formation and Presentation of Bank Balance-Sheets", *AIBR*, Vol.XVII, No.6, 19 June 1894, pp.370-1. 256

"'Reserve Fund' and 'Reserves'," *AIBR*, Vol.XIX, No.1,
19 January 1895, pp.5-7. 259

"The Item Depreciation," *AIBR*, Vol.XXIII, No.6, 19 June 1899,
p.387. 262

STRANGWARD, W.O., "Accountants and Auditors," *BMA*,
Vol.13, No.4, 30 November 1899, pp.218-26. 263

HOLMES, C.M., "Bankers' Books as Compared with Traders,"
BMA, Vol.14, No.4, 29 November 1900, pp.210-16,
No.5, 20 December 1900, p.273. 272

LIST OF ABBREVIATIONS

AIBR	=	The Australasian Insurance and Banking Record
BMA	=	The Bankers' Magazine of Australasia
BMJBIA	=	The Banker's Magazine and Journal of the Bankers']Institute of Australasia
JBIA	=	Journal of the Bankers' Institute of Australasia

Endnotes

[1] The November 1893 issue was incorrectly numbered as Vol.XVIII, No.10.

[2] This article also appeared in *AIBR*, Vol.IV, No.5, 8 May 1880, pp.143-5.

[3] This article also appeared in *AIBR*, Vol.X, No.12, 14 December 1886, pp.732-4.

[4] This article also appeared in *JBIA*, Vol.1, No.7, March 1887, pp.9-14.

[5] This article was reprinted in part as "Functions of Auditors," *BMJBIA*, Vol.VII, No. 5, December 1893, pp.392-4.

INDEX OF AUTHORS

Biggs, St.John A., 1886

Brentnall*, Thomas, 1893, 1898

Cooper, Chas. A., 1886

Crellin*, William, 1886, 1887, 1890

Davis, C.H., 1892

Flack*, J.H. 1890

Holmes*, C.M., 1900

Holt, William, 1896

Howden*, J.McA., 1900

Miles, John B.C., 1895

Oehr, R.J., 1899

"Philo", 1890

"Professional Accountant", 1886

Strangward, W.O., 1899

Taylor, Henry D'Esterre, 1887

Yarwood, F.N., 1898

* Founding member of the IIAV

INTRODUCTION

This volume of reproductions of writings on professional accounting and audit published in Australia between 1880 and 1900 is dedicated to the memory of Professor Louis ("Lou") Goldberg (1908-1997), a member of the Commonwealth Institute of Accountants (established as the Incorporated Institute of Accountants, Victoria, in 1886) from 1931, the first full-time teacher of accounting in an Australian university, the first full-time professor of accounting in Australia and, above all, an accounting historian and a lover of history. He was a life-long collector of books and pamphlets on accounting, donating a valuable accounting collection to Deakin University (Carnegie, 1997).

Accounting, Lou once wrote (Goldberg, 1949, p.3), has both a short history and a long history. The history of accounting in Australia is sufficiently short and Lou's life was sufficiently long for him to know personally some of the writers on accounting whose pre-federation contributions are reprinted here.

For most of Lou's life, Melbourne was the financial capital of Australia. In the late nineteenth century it was more than that. As Richard Twopeny (1883, pp.1-2) explained:

> Although Sydney is the older town, Melbourne is justly entitled to be considered to be the metropolis of the Southern Hemisphere ... it is in the Victorian city that the trade and capital, the business and pleasure of Australia chiefly centre ... . The headquarters of nearly all the large commercial institutions which extend their operation beyond the limits of any one colony are to be found there. If you wish to transact business well and quickly, to organise a new enterprise ... you must go to Melbourne and not to Sydney ... . There is a bustle and life about Melbourne which you altogether miss in Sydney. The Melbourne man is always on the look-out for business, the Sydney man waits for business to come to him.

The period covered by this volume ends on 1 January 1901 with the establishment of a federal Commonwealth of Australia and the transformation of the six colonies of Victoria, New South Wales, South Australia, Queensland, Tasmania and Western Australia into states. The colonies and their capital cities of Melbourne, Sydney, Adelaide,

Brisbane, Hobart and Perth experienced fluctuating and varied fortunes during the two decades as illustrated by the population figures in Table 1. The 1880s was the decade of "Marvellous Melbourne" and the other eastern colonies also boomed, but the South Australian economy faltered and Western Australia still stagnated. In the 1890s there was severe recession in the eastern colonies but Western Australia boomed as gold was discovered in Kalgoorlie and Coolgardie.

Table: Population (000s) of the Australian Capital Cities, 1881-1901

	Melbourne	Sydney	Adelaide	Brisbane	Perth	Hobart
1881	268	225	92	31	9	27
1891	473	400	117	94	16	33
1901	478	496	141	119	61	35

Source: McCarty (1978, p.21)

Both boom and bust brought work for accountants. Although the IIAV was founded during the boom years, its members were not short of work during the recession. Indeed, Davison (1978, p.110) suggests that accountants, as well as lawyers, "like black-feathered birds of prey, enjoyed a carrion feast throughout the depression years."

It is not surprising, therefore, that much of the history of professional accounting and audit in the 1880s and 1890s, and of the literature concerning it, comes from Melbourne. This literature was the creation more of commentators on accounting than of the accountants themselves. It is to be found especially in three Melbourne based journals: the *Australasian Insurance and Banking Record* (*AIBR*); the journal of the Bankers' Institute of Australasia; and the *Journal of Commerce*. The *AIBR*, founded in 1877, quickly established itself as a journal of importance. Its "standards of accuracy in statistical collection and objectivity in reporting" made it a "major influence in Australian affairs" during this period (Hall, 1968, p.239). Until 1885 it was edited by Robert Wallen (1831-1893) who was not only a financial journalist but also a successful stockbroker; the first secretary and later chairman of the Melbourne Stock Exchange; and chairman of the Stock Exchange of

Melbourne in 1885 and 1886 (Hall, 1976). The bankers' journal (which changed its name several times) commenced publication in 1886. The *Journal of Commerce* was established in 1854. Its editor and proprietor, G.W. Walmsley, closely identified the journal with the IIAV (Macdonald, 1936, p.36) and the journal was much more sympathetic to the nascent profession than was the *AIBR*.

For more technical reading, contemporary Australian accountants relied mainly on UK sources, including the professional journals, especially *The Accountant,* to which some of them contributed. Members of the Queensland Institute of Accountants (1891), small though that body was (see Gynther, 1985), were the most frequent contributors, notably Herbert Priestley, whose 1898 paper on profits and dividends was published both in *The Accountant* and in *The Incorporated Accountants Journal.* Other contributors were George Matheson (1897) and Thomas Welsby (1898). Priestley was also the author of an 1894 book on bankrupts' accounts in New South Wales. Two papers by F.N. Yarwood of the Sydney Institute of Public Accountants were published in *The Accountant* in 1899. The Australian version of one of them is included in the present volume. Accountants in Victoria appear not to have sought publication in the UK during this period and in the absence of local professional journals, many papers went unpublished, including, for example, the paper on audit read by C.H. Holmes to an IIAV meeting in 1888 (see below).

Most of the pieces reproduced here were published anonymously; of the named authors all were Melbourne based except Miles and Yarwood. Five of them (Brentnall, Crellin, Flack, Holmes and Howden) were founding members of the IIAV; another, Oehr, was its registrar from 1909 to 1938.

We have been selective in our choice of what to reproduce and have endeavoured, sometimes with difficulty, to reproduce articles of acceptable quality. In particular we have excluded articles published by Australian authors only in the UK, as these tend not to deal with matters of specifically Australian interest. We have also excluded material on bookkeeping (e.g. the books and pamphlets of Dimelow, Scouller, Wild and Yaldwyn, on which see Carnegie and Parker, 1994; Goldberg, 1977, 1984; Carnegie and Varker, 1995; and Carnegie and Parker, 1996, respectively); and on accounting for special areas such as mining companies, pastoralists, solicitors, bankrupts, and the public sector. A fairly complete list of books, pamphlets, chapters and articles on accounting published in Australia from 1871 to 1900 can be found in Parker (1990, pp.447-452).

PROFESSIONAL ACCOUNTING

Within the accounting world of colonial Victoria, the last two decades of the nineteenth century witnessed the formation of occupational associations beginning with that of accountants and clerks in 1883. Subsequently, associations were formed for accountants alone based on the British model of the accounting profession (Parker, 1989, pp.12-9; Chua and Poullaos, 1993, p.700; Carnegie and Parker, 1999, pp.77-80). Victoria's first association of accountants was formed in 1886 and emerged in response to attempts to constitute a branch of a British accountancy association as the local accountancy profession in Melbourne. By 1900, Victoria was served by four professional accountancy associations while legal recognition for their members was sought during the closing months of the century. The articles in this section deal largely with actors, events, rationales, conflicts and outcomes associated with this push for professionalisation. They illustrate the mobilisation of an occupational collective in a colonial context.

A letter to the editor published in the Melbourne *Argus* on 26 May 1883 titled "A Mercantile Clerks' Society" by "Ledger" spawned a series of letters approving of the suggestion to form such a society. The *Argus* of 31 May contained a story on the subject which appears as the first article in this section. While advocates of a mercantile clerks' society were not calling for the formation of an accountancy association of the kind already in place in Britain since 1853 (Johnson and Caygill, 1971, p.156; Walker, 1995), such calls for a local occupational association led to the formation in Victoria of the United Accountants and Clerks' Association soon after (Carnegie and Edwards, 1998). The *Argus* of 23 June 1883 reported on a meeting called to initiate the association and elucidated its objects, which included "the procuring of employment for those in want of same." The consequences of unemployment among accountants and clerks were dramatically illustrated in the front page story in the *Melbourne Bulletin* of 16 January 1885 which reported on the death, by suicide, of an accountant named Newell. Newell was having difficulties finding a job. The report referred to difficult employment conditions for accountants and clerks stating that they "are a drug in the market. An advertisement for one calls forth hundreds of answers."

The earliest professional accountancy association established in Australia was the Adelaide Society of Accountants, formed in South

Australia in November 1885 (Parker, 1961). A few months before the formation of this body, the *AIBR* of 14 April 1885 discussed the formation of the Institute of Chartered Accountants in England and Wales (ICAEW) and published a letter, signed "Accountant," dated January 1885, which supported the formation in Britain of an alternative association of accountants. The correspondent was presumably referring to the Society of Accountants which soon after formation became the Society of Accountants and Auditors (Incorporated) (SAA) (Garrett, 1961, pp.1-2). The *AIBR* did not support the attempts of a "few energetic accountants" to monopolise public accountancy work and argued against the recognition of accountancy as a profession stating that "accountancy in its ordinary practice is a trade in which empirical knowledge is almost the sole qualification, and this species of knowledge is precisely that which is the most difficult to grade and label."

The Institute of Accountants in Victoria was formed in Melbourne on 12 April 1886 with an all-male foundation membership of 45. The body was incorporated under the Companies Statute 1864 on 1 March 1887 with the name Incorporated Institute of Accountants, Victoria (IIAV) (Macdonald, 1936; Edwards *et al*, 1997; Carnegie and Edwards, 1998). Prior to the formation of this body, Charles Alfred Cooper, in the capacity as "Commissioner for Australia" of the SAA, had attempted to establish a branch in Melbourne under that association's "British Empire" policy (Garrett, 1961, p.14; Parker, 1989, pp.16-7; Edwards *et al*, 1997, pp.50-3). Cooper placed on the public record his disappointment with the decision taken to form a "purely local society" rather than to consolidate the unorganised profession in Victoria into an SAA branch (*Argus*, 10 March 1886), while William Crellin, the IIAV's inaugural president, defended the decision in responding to the criticisms made (*Argus*, 16 March 1886). Cooper proceeded to establish in Victoria the first branch of the SAA but was unable to make the Society the nucleus of the organised accountancy profession in Australia (Smith, 1903, p.398; Garrett, 1961, p.14; Carnegie and Parker, 1999, p.92).

In reporting on the fifth annual report of the ICAEW, the *AIBR* of 14 July 1886 maintained its stance on attempts to monopolise public accountancy work, stating its support of accountancy associations formed on a voluntary basis but opposing "arrogant pretension" manifest in "the tacitly-expressed right to drive out of the profession those who do not care to be gregarious, or those who will not submit to their qualifications being tested by their fellows." In response, a correspondent, "Professional Accountant," drew attention to a fault in the method of appointing public auditors enabling "unqualified free-lances" to accept audit engagements. The correspondent noted that "all other trades and professions are properly jealous of their rights, and if the projected Society of Accountants can gain for us the protection extended to other professional men, the public must benefit considerably." Following the incorporation of the IIAV on 1 March 1887, the *AIBR* of 15 March 1887 examined the objects of the body and stated "we are not altogether sanguine that the new society will make better accountants." In a letter to the editor published in the 15 April 1887 issue, Crellin responded to the criticisms made. Not convinced by Crellin's letter, the editor replied querying, among other things, whether the founders would "aid in the promotion of the public welfare in preference to seeking their own advantage?" Crellin responded again in a letter published in the 14 May 1887 issue. However, he was unable to change the *AIBR*'s view on the public interest question, which was stated thus: "we are unconvinced that the Institute is established for any other purpose than the promotion of the interests of those who may join it, and that therefore it has no special claim on the favour of the public."

The *Argus* of 16 June 1887 reported on the IIAV's first annual general meeting held on 15 June. Among other things, the first annual report recognised the role played by Cooper in giving impetus to the formation of a local independent association. It also referred to the opening of IIAV membership to "members of the profession, whether in public or private practice, connected with Government departments, banks, insurance and other incorporated companies, or in mercantile houses." While pointing out its disapproval of any tendency to monopolise public accountancy work, the *AIBR* of 14 July 1887 challenged the widening of the IIAV's membership to include accountants not in public practice, stating that the move was "likely to impair its public usefulness."

The *AIBR* of 16 February 1888 reported on the first IIAV "occasional" meeting. Such meetings were held for the purpose of reading papers on subjects of interest to members. At the first occasional meeting C.H. Holmes read a paper titled "The Scope and Limits of the Duties of the Public Auditor" which remained unpublished. The paper drew animated discussion necessitating the adjournment of the meeting. The acquisition by J.H. Flack, the IIAV's secretary, of between fifty and sixty books and pamphlets on a visit to London for the association's professional library was also reported upon.

A report in the *Journal of Commerce* of 28 June 1889 opened with the statement "there is perhaps no word in the mercantile vocabulary which is so frequently misused as that of 'Accountant.'" The report pointed to the wide usage of the term, including its "use of by a great army of clerks out of work," and noted that the IIAV's formation some three years earlier had afforded some guarantee to the public that audits and like accountancy work would be properly conducted. Posing the question "What is an Accountant?," "Philo" in a letter to the editor argued that a "skilled [double-entry] bookkeeper" was qualified to undertake public accountancy work (*Argus*, 5 August 1890). The *AIBR* of 16 August 1890 challenged "Philo's" views stating that "the really competent public accountant regards the process of bookkeeping by double entry as a very elementary affair." Crellin and Flack of the IIAV responded to a comment made in this article about certain accountants advertising themselves as actuaries. Their letter and the editor's response appeared in the *AIBR* of 17 November 1890.

The sixth annual report of the Council of the IIAV was reviewed in the *Journal of Commerce* of 21 June 1892. The article claimed that "there is no question but that as the Society grows older so does its sphere of usefulness extend, its necessity become greater, and its power and possibilities for good increase." It was pointed out that the members generally should participate to a greater extent in the various meetings held for the discussion of matters relating to their work. The article also referred to the Council's success in gaining recognition for members in connection with municipal audits (Carnegie and Parker, 1999, p.95) and commented upon the desirability of a proposal put by Agar Wynne, a member of the Legislative Council (see "Miscellaneous" section), to recognise members under the companies legislation.

The *Journal of Commerce* of 4 July 1893 referred to the high level of public interest in bookkeeping and auditing resulting from the fallout from the early 1890s economic depression in Eastern Australia. High levels of corporate and personal financial failure were experienced during this depression. For example, 120 companies ceased operating in the eight months to March 1892 while 1,374 company directors filed for bankruptcy during 1890 to 1892 (Wright, 1992, p.97). The article commented favourably on the increase in the IIAV's membership and the greater interest being displayed in its administration and stated that the IIAV was "the leading society of accountants in Victoria." The report also expressed a desire for all accountants in Victoria to be "really clever experts in accountancy work."

A New Zealand correspondent had made enquiries of the *AIBR* about whether there was any precedent to proposals in that country to form an accounting association where accountants not in public practice were eligible for selection. The correspondent believed that only practising public accountants should be admitted. While agreeing with this contention, the *AIBR* noted that admission to an Institute at its inception "is not necessarily a guarantee of ability, or even much knowledge, while outside the ranks there are a great number of able men." Nevertheless, the article was somewhat complimentary of the IIAV in its efforts to raise the standard of the qualification stating that "its examining work is very good."

The 20 November 1893 issue of the *AIBR* referred to the comments on the status of the profession of accountancy made by Thomas Brentnall, President of the IIAV, at the association's annual meeting held on 13 October. The article addressed the status of accountants in the context of efforts being made in Britain to obtain legal recognition of their status. The *AIBR* was not complimentary about the quality of public auditing in Melbourne and claimed that "public accountancy is not an occupation that ought to enjoy the status of a mediaeval guild." Alleged political problems within the IIAV in connection with proposed changes to its articles of association were discussed in the *Journal of Commerce* of 17 July 1894. On explaining in some detail the machinations involved, the article warned the association "it would be a grievous pity indeed, as well as a public loss, if through desire for personal aggrandisement or from other motives, the Council of the Institute proceeding in an unconstitutional matter, creates dissensions amongst members, alienates public sympathy, and wrecks the work of a decade."

Auditors' responsibilities were examined in the 19 June 1894 issue of the *AIBR*. The reported considered comments made by the prominent British accountant, Edwin Waterhouse, and argued that the ICAEW was disinclined on account of fear to discipline its members and that the majority of chartered accountants were, among other deficiencies identified, devoid of real mercantile experience. The qualifications and responsibilities of auditors were discussed in the *Journal of Commerce* of 12 February 1895. The article called upon accountancy associations generally to take more decisive action concerning the qualifications and responsibilities of their members. It was also critical of the IIAV for an apparent focus on increasing membership rather than concentrating on raising the status of the qualification and questioned what actions were being taken by the association in relation to the Companies Act Further Amendment Bill. This bill proposed certain requirements to be met for a person to be licensed as an auditor. Subsequently, members of the IIAV, the Victorian branch of the SAA, the ICAEW, the Australian Institute of Incorporated Accountants (AIIA) (1892) and the Federal Institute of Accountants (FIA) (1894) were, among others, eligible for licensing by the Companies Auditors' Board (Waugh, 1992, p.382; Carnegie, 1993, pp.67-9; Chua and Poullaos, 1998, pp.175-8).

Following a statement contained in the report of the Incorporated Institute of Accountants of New Zealand that the Institute did "not include in its membership all the able and trustworthy accountants of the colony," the *AIBR* once again took up the issue of the monopolising of public accountancy work in its 19 October 1896 issue. While recognising that the public was entitled to professional services by competent practitioners, the *AIBR* claimed that the public ought not to encourage the monopolising of the profession in efforts to enhance the quality of such services. Such concerns were reported yet again in the *AIBR* of 19 July 1898 in the context of attempts by the IIAV to register its members as practising accountants. Subsequently, The Public Accountants Bill, a private members bill, was introduced (see *Bankers' Magazine of Australasia,* 31 October 1899 and 29 August 1900). The bill sought legal recognition of members of the IIAV, the AIIV, the FIA and the local branch of the SAA but later lapsed (Seabrook, 1929, p.100; Macdonald, 1936, p.25; Maskell, 1944; Carnegie, 1993, pp.69-71 and Chua and Poullaos, 1998, pp.178-82).

Yarwood's paper on "A Public Accountant's Work and Duties" was presented to members of the Sydney Institute of Public Accountants on 9 June 1898 and provides perspectives on public accountancy work in New South Wales at that time. Brentnall's inaugural address to members of the Incorporated Accountants Students' Society (Victoria) of 12 October 1898 was published in two parts in the *Bankers' Magazine of Australasia* (BMA) and contains a diversity of advice for students of accountancy and some reflections on certain issues affecting the accountancy profession at the time. Oehr's lecture titled "How to Become a Skilled Accountant" was published in the *BMA* of 29 December 1899. Oehr regarded a "skilled accountant" as one who combined theoretical knowledge with much practical experience (p.299). In delivering and publishing these lectures, Yarwood, Brentnall and Oehr were contributing to the development of a local literature on professional accountancy at the end of the colonial era.

In the absence in Australia of an accountancy journal during the period to Federation on 1 January 1901, it is not surprising to find articles on the emerging organised accountancy profession and other accountancy matters in periodicals such as the *AIBR, BMA* and the *Journal of Commerce.* The *AIBR,* while supportive of raising standards of competence and enhancing the quality of auditing, did not support attempts to monopolise public accountancy work. It did not believe competence was enhanced by joining an association that was established to promote its members' interests. On the other hand, the *Journal of Commerce* was more sympathetic to the cause. According to Macdonald (1936, p.36), "this Journal had been closely identified with the Institute [IIAV] from the outset, and its editor and proprietor, Mr G.W. Walmsley, had reported, very fully and accurately, the Institute's meetings and its activities." Such congenial relations led, in 1909, to an arrangement whereby a section in the *Journal of Commerce* was reserved as the official organ of the IIAV and copies were distributed to its members (Macdonald, 1936, p.36).

AUDIT

The last two decades of the nineteenth century in Australia saw not only the beginnings of an organised accountancy profession but also an increase in the number of public companies, especially in Victoria. In 1880 only 35 new companies were registered in Victoria, of which one was a land and property company and 13 were manufacturing companies. In 1888, the peak year, the number reached 345, of which 150 were land and property companies and 99 manufacturing companies. By 1893 the numbers fell to 76, one and 56 respectively (Butlin, 1964, p.413). The fall was, of course, a result of the collapse of the land boom. The twelve largest companies listed on the Stock Exchange of Melbourne in 1890 comprised eight mining companies, three banks and one public utility. There were no railways since these were government owned. There was no audit requirement in the Victorian Mining Companies Act of 1871 (although audit had been briefly required between 1858 and 1860: see Morris, 1997). Similarly there was no audit requirement in legislation relating to banks and public utilities. There was no compulsory audit until 1896 for companies generally in Victoria (later in other states) but audit was probably required for many companies by their articles of association, as illustrated by Ma and Morris (1980, pp.26, 28-31, 75 and 115) in the case of banks.

The financial scandals in Victoria which preceded and followed the collapse of the land boom have been well documented (Cannon, 1966; Sykes 1988), but Victoria was not alone. There were similar scandals in South Australia and Western Australia (Sykes, 1988, ch.7 and 10) in the 1880s and in the UK (Pegler, 1909; Rosenblum, 1933; French, 1985) in the last quarter of the century. The scandals were a severe test for the new profession and although it is Davison's (1978, p.112) view that "a popular fear of bad bookkeeping ... gave accountants their new professional status," auditors came in for much criticism of a kind which is still familiar a century later. As Humphrey *et al.* (1992) suggest there has probably always been an audit expectations gap.

Compared with their colleagues in the UK, Australian accountants published comparatively little on audit in the 1880s and 1890s. Most of what they wrote is included in the present volume. Publication understates the amount of debate since not all the lectures delivered on auditing were published, or if they were they have not survived. Those that have are very rare and hard to track down. An example is an 1892 lecture by Lyell which was not published in an Australian journal (as was Brentnall's address of 1893) or an English journal (as was Yarwood's lecture of 1898). Lyell, Brentnall and Yarwood were all leading practitioners of the time. There were no equivalents of the pioneering UK texts by Pixley and Dicksee. Thus, the audit literature of the 1880s and 1890s reproduced in this book contains little in the way of student and reference material written by and for auditors but comprises mainly the reactions of financial journalists, bankers and other non-accountants to the audit implications of the financial scandals. The papers on audit in this volume are perhaps best seen in the context of and against the background of both the scandals and the rise of the accountancy profession.

The earliest substantial article on audit written in Australia appeared in the *AIBR* of 8 May, 1880. Entitled "A Definition of Bank Audit," it was unsigned but was probably written by Robert Wallen. It was motivated by the collapse of the City of Glasgow Bank in Scotland in 1878 and the proposed banking legislation it gave rise to in the UK, although there is also a reference to the collapse of the relatively small Provincial and Suburban Bank in Melbourne in 1879 (Sykes, 1988, ch.6). The article came down strongly in favour of the prevention of fraud as the main object of an audit and of what would now be called a systems audit:

> If the auditors, as the result of their examination, are able unreservedly to certify that the system of accounts is perfect in conception and accurate in its working; that the checks between the various departments (especially the accountant's and the cashier's) are sufficient, and regularly tested; that the inspections are frequent and thorough; that the several books submitted for their examination are kept by the properly appointed officers, having an intelligent knowledge of the nature of the entries they pass; that no manipulation of the advances could be worked

even by the manager without the knowledge and concurrence of at least one senior officer; and that the cash, bills and securities are under such custody as would render any single-handed dealing with them all but impossible – then, *plus* the customary verifications, they have fully discharged their duty, and the shareholders have good grounds for believing themselves free from danger by "fraud."

Wallen did not believe that external auditors had either the competence or the time to examine the value of a bank's securities and advances. Furthermore, he warned against over dependence by shareholders on audit:

It is far better that the limited functions of audit should be clearly defined than that there should be mistaken dependence upon any false safeguard.

It followed from this, the *AIBR* argued in its next issue (9 June, 1880), that there was no reason why the same auditor should not act for rival banks. Such an auditor was likely to be both more expert and more independent. Nevertheless, as late as 1893 the Bank of Victoria adopted articles of association which disqualified any person acting as auditor who was at the same time an auditor of any other bank in Melbourne (Ma and Morris, 1980, p.29).

The themes of the 1880 article were to be repeated many times and it was reprinted in its entirety by the *AIBR* itself in its March 1886 issue. The reason for the reprint was linked to the failure of the Commercial Bank of South Australia (Sykes, 1988, ch.7). Whilst Victoria and Melbourne boomed during the 1880s, South Australia and Adelaide, which had been very successful in the 1860s and 1870s, were faced in the early 1880s with bad wheat harvests, falling copper prices and the collapse of a land boom. The Permanent Equitable Building Society collapsed after systematic embezzlement by its secretary. This had not been discovered by its auditors who "signed the society's accounts, even though many of the relevant records did not exist" (Sykes, 1988, p.552).

The failure of the Commercial Bank of South Australia was a greater disaster. Its funds had been embezzled for many years by its manager and its accountant. The auditors (J. Storrie and H.F. Yuill, the latter a founding member in 1885 of the Adelaide Society of Accountants) did not check the value of the bank's securities. The *AIBR*, however, reiterated its view that auditors should not be required to value securities, but only to confirm their existence. The task of valuation should be performed by a bank's own inspectors. The *AIBR* also argued that the appointment of government auditors instead of professional auditors "would be a fatal mistake" (15 March 1886).

The City of Glasgow Bank failure in the UK resulted in 1879 in the introduction of bank audit provisions in UK company law. Similar provisions were proposed in the 1886 Victorian Banking and Trading Companies Bill. These were welcomed by the *AIBR* (14 July, 1886) which further suggested that a form of audit certificate should also be enacted to bring to an end the "inharmonious variety" as exhibited in the certificates it reprinted relating to Australasian and UK banks. The Bill did not become law.

In similar vein, the *AIBR* in its 15 October 1887 issue called for an authoritative statement from the recently formed Incorporated Institute of Accountants, Victoria to "give greater definiteness to the status of auditors, and form a guide to directors and others," and expressed a preference for professional auditors, although not necessarily those of the IIAV.

Much of the discussion of auditing and related matters was in the form of lectures which were not preserved. Fortunately two lectures on bank audit given by St. John A. Biggs and Henry D'Esterre Taylor to the Bankers' Institute of Australasia were reprinted in the December 1886 and March 1887 issues of the *AIBR*.

Biggs regarded the objects of audit as twofold: to see that no frauds had been committed and that the balance-sheet was made out so as to "rightly represent the true position of affairs." Unlike Wallen he deemed it "absolutely necessary that every transaction should be examined and checked, the cash counted, bills and other securities examined, and due allowance made for bad and doubtful debts." This needed to be done by two separate and distinct persons: the permanent officials of the bank checking and supervising all the work done in the bank, the auditor making sure that the books balanced properly, that the securities were all in the possession of the bank, and that the balance sheet rightly represented the true position. No audit of a bank could be thoroughly efficient without a continuous audit. In the discussion on the paper, George D. Meudell (auditor of the Savings Bank) claimed that Biggs had confused inspection and audit. Meudell recommended continuous audit by public auditors.

Taylor (from the Savings Bank) set forth radical proposals, which included security of tenure for auditors, adequate remuneration, and exhaustive and continuous check aimed at the prevention as well the detection of fraud. These were regarded as neither expedient nor practicable by the discussants, who included Meudell and Henry Gyles Turner, general manager of the Commercial Bank of Australia, and both a participant in and a historian of the events in Victoria in the 1880s and 1890s (Turner, 1904, Vol.II, chapters 8-10).

The greatest disasters and biggest financial scandals were those of the 1890s in Victoria. Between April and August 1893 thirteen banks closed their doors, although all but one re-opened (Sykes, 1988, p.177). Even before the bank closures, the *AIBR* (17 December 1892, p.866) had pointed out that:

> the declared suspensions affected assets amounting to about £26,000,000, a sum which, for a city like Melbourne, with a mediocre foreign trade and financial standing, must be considered a large portion of its wealth ... the falling of blow after blow, the discovery of grave abuses in handling funds, the shattering of reputations, so bewildered the public that confidence and credit became seriously affected.

One of the earliest casualties was the Anglo-Australian Bank which suspended operations in August 1891. The sad story of this bank has been recounted by a number of writers: by the *AIBR* in its 18 September 1891 issue; by Turner (1904, p.306); by Coghlan (1918, p.1718), Government Statistician of New South Wales, 1886-1905; and much more recently by Cannon (1966, ch.11) and Sykes (1988, pp.150-1). In the present context it is notable for the dispute, before suspension, between the bank's directors and its auditors, Langton, Holmes and McCrindle (the first two founder members of the Incorporated Institute of Accountants, Victoria). The auditors' stand was welcomed by the *AIBR* which praised them as a "leading firm, which is not afraid to discharge all the duties of auditors." It is not referred to, however, by Turner, Coghlan, Cannon or Sykes, although the last two are very critical of auditors in general.

The auditors had opposed the directors on three issues. Firstly, they refused to accept shares as being "paid up" where the shareholder was still in debt to the company for the consideration. Turner (1904, p.306) explained the circumstances thus:

> The Anglo-Australian Bank in its balance-sheet of August, 1891, stated shareholders' capital at £110,000. In the criminal prosecution which followed its suspension, it was proved that the only amount actually paid up was £37 10s. The remainder of the "capital" was represented by an overdraft in the British Bank of Australia, its foster parent, for the

amount assumed to be paid for the shares by an official, who intended to unload them on the public. In the British Bank itself, the uncalled capital, which stood at £350,000, produced less than £10,000, all the large holdings of shares being in the names of insolvent kindred companies or their penniless nominees.

Secondly, the auditors refused to recognise a balance of cash at Anglo-Australian's banks made up mainly "by paying in two cheques on two current accounts in the company itself on 30th September, which were retired the next morning by the company's cheque upon its bank." Thirdly, they refused to accept the inclusion of interest in the valuation of freehold properties.

The extent of the collapse is apparent from the *AIBR*'s report in its 29 June 1893 issue (p.600). The total assets realised amounted to £4,475, against outstanding liabilities of £437,428. The expenses of liquidation were estimated at £2,500. A call of £4 per share, amounting to £153,964 had realised £600 and not more than an additional £2,000 was expected to be realised.

Another dispute between auditors and directors concerned the Guardian Accident and Guarantee Insurance Company and its auditors, Swain and Dangerfield. The dispute was commented on by the *AIBR* in its February 1892 issue and by *The Age* newspaper on 29 January 1892. *The Age* congratulated Swain on fearlessly performing an unpleasant duty and called for a change in the law to make auditors more independent.

The AIBR's considered views on the auditing aspects of the financial crisis of the 1890s are contained in a two-part article in its February and March 1892 issues. It explained that:

> The disasters which have recently overtaken some of the financial institutions doing business in Melbourne and Sydney, have caused the subject of audit to be brought more prominently before the public than has hitherto been the case. At some of the meetings of shareholders it has been more than hinted that collapse could have been averted had the auditors appointed to examine and certify to the correctness of accounts performed their duties in a less perfunctory manner.

Auditors were being accused of inability to discover frauds committed by managers and secretaries and contributory negligence to such frauds. The *AIBR* called attention again to the uncertainty as to the duties of auditors. It defined an audit as:

a complete examination and verification of the whole of the transactions of a public company for a given period by a person or persons totally independent of the company, and not subject to the control of the directors or officials

whilst recognising that in practice many auditors had an inferior status and were regarded as being responsible to the directors rather than to the shareholders.

The *AIBR* summed up its proposals as:

(1)   An enactment that the status of auditors is equal, so far as their special duties are concerned, to that of directors.

(2)   Compulsory rotation of auditors.

(3)   Definition by enactment of the specific duties of directors and auditors respectively.

(4)   The inauguration of a system of continuous audit, or audit at irregular periods, as well as at the half-yearly rests.

(5)   The adoption of a general printed form, giving particulars as to the information required of auditors and the best means of obtaining it.

(6)   The establishment of an Institute of Auditors.

(7)   An improved method of election of auditors in the case of companies taking deposits and not holding gold reserve.

In 1893, however, the *AIBR*, reacting to Brentnall's address to members of the IIAV, expressed more radical views:

With respect to the quality of the public auditing in Melbourne, we can speak from a lengthened [sic] experience in the critical examination of balance-sheets, and we are compelled to come to the conclusion that public audit is so often a mere farce that it would be better if it were altogether abolished ... . The public have frequently been lulled to sleep by an auditor's certificate, when without it they would have felt the need for inquiry (20 November 1893, p.1014).

There was no legislation on company auditing in Australia before the Victorian Companies Act of 1896. The *AIBR* of 19 January, 1897 objected to the provisions of the Act that required auditors to "sit in judgment upon the legality of the acts of the management," and argued that the "whole of the provisions regarding the qualifications of auditors should have been struck out" since membership of a professional body did not ensure quality.

For the remainder of the decade, the *AIBR* limited itself to commenting on the audit aspects of UK scandals. In its March 1895 issue, it discussed the London and General Bank case, noting in passing that it was by no means a rare thing, either in London, Melbourne or Sydney for an auditor to take "a very low view of his functions." In its 19 April 1899 issue, it discussed the Milliwall Dock scandal, returning to a favourite theme:

> while we hold little belief in the efficiency of audit from outside, we are profoundly convinced that every considerable establishment should have its own internal audit department, conducted by men who are independent of managers of the operations which furnish the material for the bookkeeping.

The journal of the *Bankers' Institute of Australasia* in its November 1893 issue quoted not only the standard UK authors, Dicksee and Pixley, but also "Mr. A. Lyell, the eminent Melbourne auditor" as calling for recognised standards of practice to guide members of the IIAV, and for fees adequate enough to ensure that sufficient work was done.

Miles's 1895 lecture to the SIPA, "Concerning Auditing," begins with an acknowledgement of the influence of English textbooks and English cases. The "elementary articles of our professional faith" were to be found "in the authentic gospels according to those eminent evangelists of our sect, Saint Dicksee and Saint Pixley." Lengthy quotations were provided from two recent English auditing cases. He is as scathing as the *AIBR* on standards of accounting and audit. In New South Wales in his opinion, many auditors were neither competent nor independent, being "utterly incapable of writing up an ordinary cash book, and of constructing a proper balance-sheet," and the "acquiescent minions" of company directors.

Brentnall, Lyell and Yarwood all used their lectures to give advice to young accountants. None of these authors wrote a textbook. The only examples of this by members of Australian accounting bodies during this period are Priestley's *Bankrupts' Accounts N.S.Wales* (1894) and Vigars, *Station Bookkeeping* (1900), both of which dealt with topics on which there was, unlike auditing, no suitable UK textbook.

MISCELLANEOUS

The ten articles in this section are discussed under four subject headings: preparation and presentation of accounts; company law; bookkeeping and books of account; and accountancy issues.

Preparation and presentation of accounts

The *AIBR* of 12 February 1883 examined an address given by Edwin Guthrie, a prominent British accountant (Kitchen and Parker, 1980, pp.8-22), read before the Manchester Society of Chartered Accountants on 20 October 1882. Guthrie drew attention to the lack of uniformity displayed in the accounts of 124 insurance companies published in the *Post Magazine*. His main focus was on matters of disclosure in bringing about greater uniformity in stating accounts. The *AIBR* commented upon the importance of the nature of the business and the capacity of the reader of the accounts in prescribing the contents of accounts. The report also stressed the importance of valuation of "stock, properties, risks, etc.," in preparing accounts, suggesting that Guthrie's concerns about disclosure were not the only matters of relevance to enhancing uniformity. The report closed thus "on the whole we expect the improvements will come from the accountants of business concerns rather than from professionals."

The 12 October 1883 issue of *AIBR* outlined concerns about the lack of information observed in certain profit and loss accounts. Rather than stating details of gross receipts and expenditure, some companies were showing only the balance of the working or manufacturing account in the profit and loss account. While some companies were concerned to "conserve the interests of shareholders by withholding information," the *AIBR* argued gross figures should be stated under the Companies Statute. Using a case illustration, the report also opposed the practice of not publishing a balance sheet on the grounds that publication was not in the interests of the company.

The preparation and presentation of bank balance sheets was discussed with the aid of case illustrations in the 19 June 1894 issue of *AIBR*. The article examined the treatment of deposits and lendings and also made a case for the reporting lag from balance date to be generally shortened.

Company law

"What are Profits for Distribution?" was addressed by *AIBR* in its 13 May 1886 issue. The article examined Stringer's Case and suggested a need for further legal guidance on the question. In conclusion, the *AIBR* argued the case for frequent revaluations to be undertaken in preparing accounts. Another paper on the subject by Herbert Priestley was read to members of the Queensland Institute of Accountants in Brisbane on 14 December 1897. The paper entitled "Profits and Dividends," was also read *in absentia* to the Incorporated Accountants Students Society of London and was published in both *The Accountant* and *The Incorporated Accountants Journal* (Parker, 1990, p.439).

The *AIBR* of 18 November 1891 examined the key provisions of a private members bill brought to the Legislative Council by Agar Wynne to amend the Victorian Companies Act (Gibson, 1971, pp.40-1). While acknowledging the need for significant legislative reform and noting the various Companies Acts which had been passed in England since the passing of the principal Act of 1862 on which the Victorian Act was based, the *AIBR* argued that the reforms proposed were untimely due to the difficult circumstances prevailing and, because of their comprehensiveness, should be dealt with by a Ministry. The reforms proposed included the application of the no liability principle to trading companies, the filing of annual statements of accounts in a prescribed format and the prohibiting of companies using the word "bank" from dealing in land.

Bookkeeping and books of account

The *BMA* published a summary of a lecture delivered by W.O. Strangward in its 30 November 1899 issue. It was presented before the Bank Officer's Student Society. The lecture was concerned with single and double entry bookkeeping, different types of books of account, key financial statements and with the audit of accounts. The *BMA* also published a lecture by C.M. Holmes on the differences between bankers' and traders' books of account. In the address, Holmes discussed the merits and features of the "Jones' System" of bookkeeping introduced by Edward Thomas Jones in 1796 (Yamey, 1956). Holmes and Strangward were both fellows of the IIAV.

Accountancy issues

Accounting for goodwill, reserves and reserve funds, and depreciation were other issues addressed by the *AIBR*. The issue of 14 June 1886 reported on an article appearing in *The Economist* of 3 April on business goodwill and agreed with the view therein expressed that goodwill should not appear as an asset in balance sheets. A discussion of the meaning of "reserve" and "reserve fund" which took place between correspondents in the London *Times* was reported upon and further discussed in the *AIBR* of 19 January 1895. The 19 June 1899 issue argued against the habit of ignoring the charging of depreciation or deferring the charge and insisted that the charge ought to be made against profits and not as a deduction after profit has been ascertained. The report stated that a charge "ought to be made for ordinary wear and tear" of the designated property.

CONCLUSION

We hope that this volume of 65 writings on professional accounting and audit increases awareness of accounting issues, problems and debates in Australia in the last two decades of the nineteenth century. Whilst a potentially useful resource for researchers and others interested in accounting's past, we suggest that the volume's availability should not diminish efforts to study accounting development through other sources of information, including surviving business records.

Fittingly, a copy of this volume will be placed in "The Louis Goldberg Collection" at Deakin University, Geelong Woolstores campus. Thanks to Lou, this wonderful accounting collection is available for enjoyment and study by students, academics, practitioners and others with an interest in accounting history.

Garry D. Carnegie
Robert H. Parker
March, 1999

REFERENCES

Butlin, N.G., (1964), *Investment in Australian Economic Development, 1861-1900* (Cambridge: Cambridge University Press).

Cannon, M., (1966), *The Land Boomers* (Melbourne: Melbourne University Press).

Carnegie, G.D., (1993), "The Australian Institute of Incorporated Accountants (1892-1938)," *Accounting, Business and Financial History,* Vol.3, No.1, March, pp.61-80.

Carnegie, G.D., (1997), "Vale Louis Goldberg," *Accounting History,* NS Vol.2, No.2, November, pp.7-8.

Carnegie, G.D. and Edwards, J.R., (1998), "The Construction of the Professional Accountant: The Case of the Incorporated Institute of Accountants Victoria (1886)." Paper presented at the *Second Asian Pacific Interdisciplinary Research in Accounting Conference,* Osaka City University, Japan.

Carnegie, G.D. and Parker, R.H., (1994), "The First Australian Book on Accounting: James Dimelow's 'Practical Book-Keeping Made Easy,'" *Abacus,* Vol.30, No.1, March, pp.78-97.

Carnegie, G.D. and Parker, R.H., (1996), "The Transfer of Accounting Technology to the Southern Hemisphere: The Case of William Butler Yaldwyn," *Accounting, Business and Financial History,* Vol.6, No.1, March, pp.23-49.

Carnegie, G.D. and Parker, R.H., (1999), "Accountants and Empire: The Case of Co-Membership of Australian and British Accountancy Bodies, 1885 to 1914," *Accounting, Business and Financial History,* Vol.9, No.1, March, pp.77-102.

Carnegie, G.D. and Varker, S.A., (1995), "Edward Wild: Advocate of Simplification and an Organised Profession in Colonial Australia," *The Accounting Historians Journal,* Vol.22, No.2, December, pp.131-49.

Carnegie, G.D. and Wolnizer, P.W. (eds.) (1996), *Accounting History Newsletter 1980-1989 and Accounting History 1989-1994: A Tribute to Robert William Gibson* (New York and London: Garland Publishing).

Chua, W.F. and Poullaos, C., (1993), "Rethinking the Profession-State Dynamic: The Case of the Victorian Charter Attempt, 1885-1906," *Accounting, Organizations and Society,* Vol.18, No.7/8, pp.691-728.

Chua, W.F. and Poullaos, C., (1998), "The Dynamics of 'Closure' Amidst the Construction of Market, Profession, Empire and Nationhood: An Historical Analysis of an Australian Accounting Association, 1886-1903," *Accounting, Organizations and Society*, Vol.23, No.2, pp.155-87.

Coghlan, T.A., (1918), *Labour and Industry in Australia* (Melbourne: Oxford University Press).

Cooke, T.E. and Nobes, C.W. (eds.), (1997), *The Development of Accounting in an International Context: A Festschrift in Honour of R.H. Parker* (London: Routledge).

Davison, G., (1978), *The Rise and Fall of Marvellous Melbourne* (Melbourne: Melbourne University Press).

Edwards, J.R., Carnegie, G.D. and Cauberg, J., (1997), "The Incorporated Institute of Accountants, Victoria (1886): A Study of Founders' Backgrounds" in Cooke and Nobes.

French, E.A., (1985), *Unlimited Liability: the Case of the City of Glasgow Bank* (London: Certified Accountant Publications).

Garrett, A.A., (1961), *History of the Society of Incorporated Accountants 1885-1957* (Oxford: Oxford University Press).

Gibson, R.W., (1971), *Disclosure by Australian Companies* (Melbourne: Melbourne University Press).

Goldberg, L., (1949), "The Development of Accounting," *Australian Accountancy Student,* reprinted in Gibson, C.J., Meredith, G.G. and Peterson, R., *Accounting Concepts. Readings* (Melbourne: Cassell Australia).

Goldberg, L., (1977), "The Search for Scouller: An Interim Report," *Accounting and Business Research*, Vol.7, No.3, Summer, pp.221-35.

Goldberg, L., (1984), "The Rest of John Scouller," *Accounting History Newsletter*, No.8, Winter, pp.17-38, partly reprinted in Parker (1990).

Gynther, M.M., (1985), "The Accounting Profession in Queensland up to 1905: A Progress Report," *Accounting History Newsletter*, No.10, Winter, pp.21-34, reprinted in Carnegie and Wolnizer (1996).

Hall, A.R., (1968), *The Stock Exchange of Melbourne and the Victorian Economy 1852-1900* (Canberra: Australian National University Press).

Hall, A.R., (1976), "Robert Elias Wallen (1831-1893)," *Australian Dictionary of Biography,* Vol.6 (Melbourne: Melbourne University Press).

Humphrey, C., Moizer, P. and Turley, S., (1992), "The Audit Expectations Gap - Plus Ca Change, Plus C'est la Même Chose?," *Critical Perspectives on Accounting*, Vol.3, No. 2, pp.137-61.

Johnson, T.J. and Caygill, M., (1971), "The Development of Accountancy Links in the Commonwealth," *Accounting and Business Research*, Vol.1, Spring, pp.155-73.

Kitchen, J. and Parker, R.H., (1980), *Accounting Thought and Education: Six English Pioneers* (London: Institute of Chartered Accountants in England and Wales, reprinted Garland Publishing, New York and London, 1984).

Ma, R. and Morris, R.D., (1980), *Disclosure Practices of British and Australian Banks in the Nineteenth Century* (Kensington, NSW: University of New South Wales).

Macdonald, O.R., (1936), "Historical Survey 1887-1936" in *The Commonwealth Accountants' Year Book 1936*, pp.5-55 (Melbourne: Commonwealth Institute of Accountants), reprinted in Parker (1990).

Maskell, R.E., (1944), "Fifty Years of Progress: The History of the Federal Institute of Accountants 1984-1944," *The Federal Accountant*, 25 July, pp.201-51.

Matheson, G.C., (1897), "Accountants and Accounting," *Accountant*, 18 September, pp.896-8.

McCarty, J.W., (1978), "Australian Capital Cities in the Nineteenth Century" in McCarty, J.W. and Schedvin, C.B. (eds.), *Australian Capital Cities* (Sydney: Sydney University Press).

Morris, R.D. (1997), "The Origins of the No-Liability Mining Company and its Accounting Regulations" in Cooke and Nobes.

Parker, R.H., (1961), "Australia's First Accountancy Body—The Adelaide Society of Accountants," *The Chartered Accountant in Australia,* December, pp.337-40.

Parker, R.H., (1989), "Importing and Exporting Accounting: The British Experience" in Hopwood, A.G. (ed.), *International Pressures for Accounting Change*, pp.7-29 (Hemel Hempstead: Prentice-Hall International).

Parker, R.H., (ed.), (1990), *Accounting in Australia: Historical Essays* (New York and London: Garland Publishing).

Parker, R.H., (1990), "Australian Writings on Accounting, 1871-1900," in Parker.

Pegler, E.C., (1909), "Some Notable Frauds in Accounts," *Accountant*, 15 May, pp.687-96, reprinted in Stamp, E., Dean, G.W. and Wolnizer, P.W. (eds.), *Notable Financial Causes Célèbres* (New York: Arno Press, 1980).

Priestley, H., (1894), *Bankrupts' Accountants, N.S. Wales* (Sydney: A.A. Wall).

Priestley, H., (1898), "Profits and Dividends," *Incorporated Accountants Journal*, May; *Accountant*, 27 August, pp.822-8 and 3 September, pp.841-6.

Rosenblum, L., (1933), "The Failure of the City of Glasgow Bank," *The Accounting Review*, Vol.8, No.4, pp.285-91, reprinted in Stamp, E., Dean, G.W. and Wolnizer, P.W. (eds.), *Notable Financial Causes Célèbres* (New York: Arno Press, 1980).

Seabrook, G.K., (1929), "Regarding the Granting of a Charter to the Australasian Corporation of Public Accountants," *The Federal Accountant*, November, pp.99-109.

Smith, J., (ed.), (1903), *The Cyclopaedia of Victoria: An Historical and Commercial Review, Descriptive and Biographical Facts, Figures and Illustrations, an Epitome of Progress*, Vol.1 (Melbourne: The Cyclopaedia Company).

Sykes, T., (1988), *Two Centuries of Panic. A History of Corporate Collapses in Australia* (Sydney: Allen & Unwin).

Turner, H.G., (1904), *A History of the Colony of Victoria* (London: Longmans, Green, and Co.), Vol.II.

Twopeny, R., (1883), *Town Life in Australia* (London: Elliot Stock; reprinted 1973 as a Penguin Colonial Facsimile).

Vigars, F.E., (1900), *Station Book-Keeping. A Treatise on Double Entry Book-Keeping for Pastoralists* (Sydney: William Brooks & Co.).

Walker, S.P., (1995), "The Genesis of Professional Organization in Scotland: A Contextual Analysis," *Accounting, Organizations and Society*, Vol.20, No.4, pp.285-310.

Waugh, J., (1992), "Company Law and the Crash of the 1890s in Victoria," *UNSW Law Journal*, Vol.15, No.2, pp.356-88.

Welsby, T., (1898), "Duties of a Secretary in Connection with Limited Liability Companies," *Accountant*, 17 September, pp.887-91 and 24 September, pp.914-6.

Wright, R., (1992), *A People's Counsel. A History of the Parliament of Victoria 1856-1990* (Melbourne: Oxford University Press).

Yamey, B.S., (1956), "Edward Jones and the Reform of Book-Keeping, 1795-1810," in Littleton, A.C. and Yamey, B.S. (eds.), *Studies in the History of Accounting*, pp.313-24 (London: Sweet and Maxwell).

Yarwood, F.N., (1899), "Public Accountants' Work and Duties," *Accountant*, 11 March, pp.285-92.

Yarwood, F.N., (1899), "Random Notes," *Accountant*, 6 September, pp.954-8.

PROFESSIONAL ACCOUNTING

We have received and published several letters approving of a suggestion to form a mercantile clerks' society, for the mutual aid and assistance of those engaged in commercial offices. The idea was first submitted through our columns by a correspondent signing himself "Ledger." He pointed out that the position of a clerk is very precarious; that as a rule salaries are extremely small, and that dismissals sometimes take place for no other reason than that trade is temporarily dull, owing to the season or some passing depression. A society, such as he contemplates, would provide a registry office for those turned adrift; would give them a place in which to meet ["such as the various trades "have"], where information likely to be of service to them might be obtained, and would grant small loans for short periods to those in want of assistance. Another correspondent mentions other matters as properly coming within the scope of the proposed association, such as "an interchange of information and the formation of pleasant business relations between the members, also a full discussion of and concerted action with regard to any obnoxious regulations that may be made." Another gentleman would have it do all this and much besides. We think that a friendly society of this sort might be formed with advantage to all concerned. If the commercial travellers can manage to act together, and find it advisable to do so, why should not accountants, bookkeepers, and office-assistants generally do the same, and reap whatever benefit is to be derived from union? It appears to us doubtful whether such a league would exercise much influence over the general relations between employer and employed, as unfortunately the number of youths and men seeking situations as clerks is always considerably in excess of the vacancies, but probably it would occasionally do good by seasonable support and assistance. If it could in any way discourage the rush after half-starved clerkships, and direct some of the youthful energy of the colony into those channels of mechanical industry which lead to comfort and independence, it would accomplish a charitable work. However, apart from attempts at interference or dissuasion a mercantile clerks' society might do much good. If it were to answer no other purposes than to provide a registry for its members, to give unemployed clerks a place of meeting apart from the public house, and to afford that timely relief which has frequently kept men from despair and degradation, it would have ample justification for its existence, and undeniable claims to support.

ACCOUNTANTS AND CLERKS' ASSOCIATION

A meeting for the initiation of an Accountants and Clerks' Association for Victoria was held last evening in the Coffee Palace, Collins-street. Mr. C.J. Lucas was called to the chair. About 30 attended.

The CHAIRMAN said that the small attendance was no indication of the interest taken in the movement. There had been letters received from various parts of the colony expressing pleasure that such an association was being established. A circular had been drawn up by the provisional committee for despatch to employers. It was as follows:—

The committee have much pleasure in bringing under your notice the initiation of the above association, and would draw your particular attention to two of the objects for which it is proposed to be formed: — 1. The procuring of employment for those in want of same; and, 2. The supplying to employers the requisite information for obtaining respectable and efficient assistance, for which purpose a register will be kept with complete references as to each case. The committee therefore kindly ask your assistance in the formation of the association by bringing it under the notice of your employes, so that it may secure the success which it deserves. It is also intended to give monetary aid in necessitous cases, at the discretion of the committee. And as most of the work connected with the association will be gratuitously performed it is hoped that the association will meet with your approval and support.

He had not the slightest doubt that if the association was properly managed it would be a great success. Many good movements like that had been spoilt by too much verbosity instead of work. He trusted they would not start by encouraging a lot of useless talk, and he intended, so far as he was concerned, to set a good example. There must be giving and taking among men who were starting anything of this sort, and he was sorry, therefore, to mention that one member of the provisional committee had retired in dudgeon at this early stage, because everything had not gone his way. He would read the rules which the provisional committee proposed for adoption. These provided that those present at the first meeting should be members without nomination, but others would have to be duly proposed, seconded, and balloted for, three black balls to exclude. The entrance fee for all members should be 2s. 6d., and the subscription be quarterly. The rules had been based on the model of those of the Victorian United Law Clerks' Society, which society was working well, and was in a satisfactory financial condition. He suggested that the rules should now be adopted *in globo*, so that they could get to work at once. Should any of them prove unsuitable, they could be altered afterwards.

Mr. PETHERICK moved the adoption of the rules as proposed.

Mr. ELLIS seconded the motion, and it was agreed to.

The CHAIRMAN said that the idea would be to get a number of influential employers to support the association as patrons.

On the question of election of officers, which was next proceeded with,

Mr. PRINCE objected to what he said was an attempt to rule on the part of a clique. The chairman evidently wanted to stifle discussion — ("No, no") — by having the rules adopted at once *in globo*.

Mr. HILES said he was the member of the provisional committee who had been alluded to by the chairman. He objected to the latter's remarks that he (the speaker) had resigned because he could not have everything his own way. He had retired because he did not think the association as constituted by the rules would meet the requirements of clerks, and secondly because he objected to two members of the committee being from one establishment.

Mr. ELLIS said he also objected to that, but pointed out that the committee had not yet been appointed. What had hitherto acted had only been a provisional committee.

Mr. MUNRO — If we get into squabbles we shall kill the association. (Applause.) Let us elect the committee.

The following were subsequently elected officers: — Chairman of the committee, Mr. C.J. Lucas; hon. treasurer, Mr. J.T. McNaughton; other members of the committee, Mr. A. Ellis, Melbourne Gas Company; Mr. J.D. Munro, Dress Supply Association; Mr. J.D. Dowdle, at Mr. Currie's, wine and spirit merchant; Mr. H.M. Cullagh, at Lange and Thoneman's; Mr. C.J.

Haynes, United Australian Mutual Fire and Marine Insurance Company; Mr. A.H. Burton, Victorian Clothing Company (secretary *pro tem*); and Mr. J.G. Hook, Universal Building Society.

It was decided that the temporary office should be 17 Templecourt.

A SAD CASE

There perished by his own hand in one of the suburbs, the other day, an accountant named Newell. The circumstances of his death disclosed a sad state of affairs. He had been in a desponding state, as he had not been able to obtain employment for the past six months. He had a wife and family, and his failure to gain work, coupled with the thoughts of these, un-hinged his mind. One night he took a revolver from a drawer, went quietly into the parlour, and put an end to his miserable existence. Which of you will dare to judge him? Not you, oh, clergyman, with the cosy manse and the comfortable stipend—not you, oh, layman, with vast ventures or with steady income paid for your weekly toil! Can any of us picture the blank, heart-breaking, brain-maddening despair of that husband and father as he heard the Christmas bells pealing from the churches or saw other husbands and fathers taking their wives and families to seaside, to sports, to theatres. What a world this must have seemed to the hopeless wretch who, with a wife and four children at home, went out seeking employment and receiving, oh bitter, cruel mockery! the compliments of the season. God! What a stab it must have been to that breaking heart to have the casual acquaintance wish him, "A Happy New Year!" He had not been able to obtain employment for six months. Think of that, and then picture this man, on the threshold of the new year, when others were eating, and drinking, and making merry—picture him stealing away from his wife, taking a revolver, going quietly and despairingly into another room and placing upon his soul the terrible sin of self-slaughter. Shall we judge him, gentle reader? No—rather let us say softly, "his sins lie lightly on him," and thank God that it was not our lot to know such great, such over-powering temptation.

The sad death of poor Newell, pathetic as its surroundings were, has still a practical moral to be drawn from it. He was an accountant, and it is, therefore, no surprise to learn that he had a difficulty in obtaining employment. Accountants and clerks are a drug in the market. An advertisement for one calls forth hundreds of answers. Such men, out of employment, swarm in our streets. Some do as Newell did, others sink into taproom loafers and die in our hospitals, whilst others again, under pressure of a wolfish necessity, become our forgers, valueless-cheque passers, and obtainers of goods and money under false pretences. Most of

31

them were willing to work, but could find none. The false pride of their parents fitted them for "gentlemanly occupations"—trade was low! Look around and see if, within your knowledge, you can count ten tradesmen, sober and willing to work, who cannot find employment. Ten! Can you think of one! This is a serious consideration for parents when educating their children. One who has learnt a trade can always live honestly—the man who has a "genteel occupation" may rise to position and affluence, but very frequently chance, not folly, decides whether he may not be forced to accept the bitter alternative of a glutted employment market—the felon's cell or the suicide's dishonoured grave.

ACCOUNTANTS

ACCOUNTANTS.

As was to be foreseen, the establishment of the Institute of Chartered Accountants in England has not proved to be an unmixed benefit to accountants at large. The principal object of such an organisation could only be the monopolising of the work of public accountancy by its members. The adoption of an imposing title would influence that considerable section of the public which is inclined to take the name for the thing. Thus membership in the Institute would naturally lead to the advantage of the few, to the detriment of the many not in membership. If accountancy were a profession in which profound theoretic knowledge and severe mental training (as in the actuarial profession) are requisites, and were the Institute of Chartered Accountants founded on the recognition of these requisites, the result could hardly be cavilled at. But accountancy in its ordinary practice is a trade in which empirical knowledge is almost the sole qualification, and this species of knowledge is precisely that which is the most difficult to grade and label. It would be unreasonable to demur at attempts to raise the status of accountants. But the encouragement of a healthier spirit of independence amongst accountants is one thing; an attempt made by a few energetic accountants to exclude others from employment by the adoption of a high sounding title is another thing. It is, therefore, not surprising to find that a new society is projected in England, concerning which the following communication has been made to the press :—

"Sir,—I herewith enclose you a paper in relation to an effort that is being made to form a society, the chief object of which seems to be the defence of the weak against the strong. The Institute of Chartered Accountants, at the moment composed almost entirely of principals in the profession, is evidently bent upon becoming a most powerful trades union; and if the rumour is correct that an endeavour will soon ·be made to pass a law whereby all accountancy work will by compulsion drift into the hands of the select few, a monstrous piece of injustice will be done to thousands of accountants and accountants' clerks. Many of the latter as a result will be compelled to remain servants for the rest of their days. All must be pleased at the efforts that have of late been made to raise the tone of the profession, which undoubtedly a short time ago was at a very low ebb; but at the same time care must be taken that in the way of reform no wrong is done. If the Institute shuts its doors against able and experienced men, it is high time that a new society should be formed; and I wish every success to this one, especially as another of its objects is the association of members in the profession for their mutual improvement, an aim which, from what we have seen or heard of the Institute up to the present time, seems hardly within the way of its ideas of usefulness.

"ACCOUNTANT,"

"January, 1885."

THE SOCIETY OF ACCOUNTANTS

TO THE EDITOR OF THE ARGUS

Sir,—With reference to the leading articles that have lately appeared in your valuable paper respecting the above, I shall esteem it a great favour if you will allow me to make a personal explanation, so that no misunderstanding may arise in the future.

In accordance with instructions received from the council of the Society of Accountants (London), I convened a meeting of the members of the profession in Melbourne, which was held on 4th December last, at the Duke of Rothsay Hotel, and there laid my views before the gentlemen present as to the desirability of establishing a branch of the English society in Victoria. A committee was appointed to consider my proposals, and a resolution was subsequently passed by the committee to the effect that it was desirable to establish a Society of Accountants in Victoria, with the view of some future connexion with my society. With this resolution I agreed, and understood that the Victorian society would be formed on that basis. A general meeting was, however, convened by one of the members of the committee, and the same was held during my absence in Sydney, and I was informed on my return that the meeting in question had resolved to form a purely local society, with no reference to any future connexion with the one to which I am attached. Such being the case, I could not do otherwise than retire from the scene. But it is a matter of great satisfaction to me that some of the professional accountants in Melbourne has signified their intention of becoming members of the Society of Accountants, whose headquarters are in London, with over 400 subscribers, the objects of which are comprehensive, rather than be associated with a local body whose adherents must necessarily be small, and whose views are exclusive. In the case of the society I have the honour of representing, diplomas will only be granted by the council in London, on the recommendation of the Australian executive, and as the examinations for admission of members will be of a most rigid character, none but the names of the most competent men will appear on our roll.

I here leave the matter with your readers. It is for them to judge whether a certificate of competency, granted by the English Society, having the special licence of the Board of Trade, will not have more weight in the commercial world than a certificate granted by such a society as the one now being formed on a purely local basis, and of narrow views.—I am, &c.,

CHAS A. COOPER, A.S.A.,
Commissioner of the Society of
Accountants by Appointment.
Melbourne. March 9.

THE SOCIETY OF ACCOUNTANTS

*TO THE EDITOR OF THE
ARGUS*

Sir,—The provisional committee of this society desires me to reply to the letter of Mr. C.A. Cooper, which appeared in your paper of the 10th inst., because for the time being I have custody of all the documents, and also because I have personal knowledge of every step taken since its inception.

The material statements in Mr. Cooper's letter are two:— That a change of front has taken place since the committee framed its report, and that the public would not have so much confidence in a local accountants' society as they would have in a local branch of an English society. With your permission, I wish to contest both these statements.

Mr. Cooper's charge under the first head is contained in the following sentences in his letter:—"A resolution was passed by the committee to the effect that it was desirable to establish a society of accountants in Victoria with the view of some future connexion with my society," and "the meeting (subsequently held) had resolved to form a purely local society, with no reference to any future connexion with the one to which I am attached." Neither of these statements is accurate.

The resolution passed by the committee is contained in the 4th clause of its report, which I quote:—

"After hearing Mr. Cooper's explanations, your committee is unable at present to see any advantage to be gained by forming a branch society, and recommends that the question of the relationship of a local society with this (i.e., Mr. Cooper's) or any other society in Great Britain, whether by affiliation or by correspondence only, be left to the council of the Victorian society, if one be formed."

This clause of the report was adopted by the meeting without the alteration of a single word.

Before Mr. Cooper went to Sydney I read to him the whole report which had been prepared, and subsequently sent him a notice convening the meeting, to which it was to be presented, and in reply received the following:—

"January 29, 1886

"Wm. Crellin, Esq.

"Dear Sir,—

"Society of Accountants.

"Your circular duly to hand. I leave for Sydney to-morrow. I regret that I shall not be able to be present at the meeting. I have informed both Messrs. Lyell and Holmes that I shall be most happy to become the secretary of the Victorian Society, as owing to the resolutions arrived at by the committee, I feel I can do so without 'infra dig.'

"CHAS. A. COOPER."

On his return from Sydney I showed him the report as adopted, with the few immaterial alterations made by the meeting in some of the other clauses, and in reply to his question, "What had been done about a secretary?" told him that the appointment of officers was to be left to those who might hereafter found the society. I added, as the expression merely of my own views, that I hoped it might be possible to get the requisite work of the first year or two done by honorary officers. Mr. Cooper left me without expressing any disappointment or dissatisfaction with what had been done, and I heard nothing of his having "retired from the scene" until I read his letter in your paper. I cannot understand why Mr. Cooper has changed his mind since the 29th of January.

The other material statement of his letter is, "that a certificate of competency granted by the (his) English society would have more weight with the commercial world than a certificate granted by the (our) local society now proposed to be formed," and he adduces as the reason "that the English diplomas will only be granted by the council in London on the recommendation of the Australian executive." So we are asked to believe that examinations conducted by and the recommendations of A, B, C, D, and E—acting as the "Australian executive" of a society domiciled in London—will carry more weight with local professional and commercial men than examinations by and the recommendations of the same persons if acting for a local society.

Of course, if Mr. Cooper succeeds in persuading the cream of the profession to join his local branch, leaving only the skimmed milk to the local society, then his prediction may come true. But as to that, *nous verrons*.

I am sorry to take up a controversial position towards Mr. Cooper, because all are agreed in admitting that by his well-timed movement he has given an impe-

tus to a project which has often
been mooted, and has often been
allowed to drop. But surely those
who have spent the best years of
their life in the colony may be
pardoned if they feel somewhat
indisposed to sanction the idea
that no good thing can be done
here unless it bears the seal of a
body of gentlemen sitting in London who are unknown to us, and
to whom we are mostly unknown.

Thanking you by anticipation
for inserting this letter.—I am,
&c.,

March 15.   WILLIAM CRELLIN.

CHARTERED ACCOUNTANTS

We have been favoured with a sight of the report of the Council of the Institute of Chartered Accountants in England and Wales, presented to the fifth annual meeting of the Institute held in London on 5th May last. This report we have carefully perused. While we are prepared to uphold as strenuously as anyone the desirability of accountants being properly qualified for the duties they undertake, it is yet clear that the primary object of the Institute is to form a strong and exclusive professional organisation. In short, the English accountants aspire to occupy a position which is not granted to any other lay profession or calling. Persons desiring to become solicitors are articled for three to five years under provisions which virtually are under the control, not of solicitors, but of an outside power behind which again is the Master of the Rolls. But the Institute of Chartered Accountants aims at prescribing who shall enjoy the *status* of an accountant, and at prescribing aspirants who do not conform to its regulations. Its constitution to all intents and purposes is that of a trade union of the most exclusive pattern. To aid it in the carrying out of its pretensions the Institute has obtained a charter, and its members are thus able to flourish a cabalistic "C.," and to call themselves "chartered." In point of fact they are not chartered, but their society as an organisation merely is chartered. So far as we can see there is no reason why, apart perhaps from irreverence, there should not be "chartered carpenters," or "instituted bankers," as well as "chartered accountants." If it is considered desirable as a measure of public utility that the State should see that accountants are properly qualified, then let them be trained in the same manner as solicitors, that is, by a method prescribed by the law of the land, and by examinations conducted by an examining body outside their own ranks. Not only does the Institute elect its members for proficiency, it has also a "property qualification." Thus from the income and expenditure account we observe that the entrance fees go as high as twenty guineas, and that there are also certificate fees. The excessive fees levied (amounting to £4683 for the year 1885) are not required to meet the expenditure, for while the total income was £5508, the expenditure was only £3228, leaving £2280 to the good.

We notice that bankruptcy law engages a great deal of the time of the Council of the Institute, and that sundry recommendations are made with the object of improving the last English Bankruptcy Act. Now it is possible that the proposed amendments are sound enough, but the public cannot realise too clearly that it is no more the interest of accountants to labour for the enactment of simple and inexpensive bankruptcy laws, than it is the interest of solicitors to agitate for the simplification of the machinery of the law generally, and the consequent diminishing of fees. The chief end of accountants is to obtain fees, and, with a few noteworthy exceptions, the "chartered accountants," say of London, will advise nothing likely to frustrate the object of their professional existence. We certainly do not complain, or think it a just cause of complaint, that accountants care principally for their own interests, but this necessary solicitude for self certainly impairs the value of their advice on the methods to be adopted in the legal adjustment of the affairs of insolvents.

Apart from these general strictures the Institute does good work. Without doubt it has "elevated the profession," although it may also have cast down and injured many worthy accountants who have preferred to maintain their independence, or have objected to pay heavy fees.

In the practical work of examination, 286 candidates have been tested during the year, of whom 191 have passed. Of these 50 passed the preliminary, 43 the intermediate, and 98 the final examination. The number of members is now 1371, of whom 530 are fellows, 583 associates in practice, 215 associates not in practice, and 43 not in England and Wales. A Chartered Accountants' Benevolent Association has recently been formed in connection with the Institute, and already has received a substantial amount of support.

In the remarks we have made, we have only desired to show that anything like arrogant pretension is undesirable. If the accountants in any country or district choose to form a society or institute, no one can object, but rather applaud so long as such an organisation rests on a voluntary basis, but when it assumes the tacitly-expressed right to drive out of the profession those who do not care to be gregarious, or those who will not submit to their qualifications being tested by their fellows, then it seeks to fill a position to which the law should certainly not give a special sanction. The adjective "chartered" might very well be dropped. As a term it is applied illogically, it is ugly, and it is calculated only to impose on the imagination of the vulgar.

UNCHARTERED ACCOUNTANTS

UNCHARTERED ACCOUNTANTS.

SIR,—The thanks of the profession are due to you for the judicious article on "Chartered Accountants" in your last impression. Knowing your readiness to promote the perfection of our financial system, an apology is scarcely necessary for calling attention to a fault in the present method of appointing public auditors. I refer to the competition to which we are subjected by employees in banks, building societies, and insurance companies. Many of these gentlemen holding permanent appointments, with fixed salaries, undertake the duties of public auditors, which cannot be done properly without wasting the time and labour for which they are already paid. Apart from any consideration of ⅃tness, it is surely unfair to ask professional accountants, who have devoted time and money to the study of the literature and law of their profession, and who maintain expensive offices and staffs, to share with these unqualified free-lances the limited sum disbursed in auditors' fees by the banks and public companies. All other trades and professions are properly jealous of their rights, and if the projected Society of Accountants can gain for us the protection extended to other professional men, the public must benefit considerably. Directors of banks and insurance companies may then be prompted to admonish their clerks to adhere to the strict letter of their bonds, " not to engage in any other business whatever." An auditor's certificate may then be accepted without hesitation by a shareholder, with the knowledge that the examination has been made by a skilled accountant whose very existence depends on his care and vigilance.—Yours faithfully,

PROFESSIONAL ACCOUNTANT.

INCORPORATED INSTITUTE OF ACCOUNTANTS, VICTORIA

On 1st inst., the Incorporated Institute of Accountants, Victoria, received its license from the Attorney-General in pursuance of the conditions of an Act to provide for the incorporation of literary, scientific, and other associations and institutions.

We have been favoured with an advance copy of the memorandum and articles of association of the Institute. From the memorandum we learn that the objects for which the institute is established are stated in the memorandum of association to be as follows:—

(a) To aim at the elevation of the profession of accountants by the dissemination of professional knowledge, and the inculcation of sound practice.

(b) To increase the confidence of the banking, mercantile, and general community in the employment of recognised accountants and auditors, by admitting to the institute such persons only as shall in future, save as hereinafter provided, pass satisfactory examinations in the theory and practice of the work, and by the prevention of illegal and dishonourable practices.

(c) To afford means of reference for the amicable settlement of professional differences, and to decide upon questions of professional urgent etiquette.

(d) To promote good feeling and friendly intercourse amongst the members.

(e) To watch over and promote the interests of the profession generally.

There are some things which are commendable, others which invite criticism in this programme. Generally, so far as the institute is the counterpart of what artizans know as a trades union, it cannot justly be criticised. A profession has as much right to form an organisation for self-help as a trade. But the aim of the founders of the Incorporated Institute of Accountants is more ambitious, for, judging from article *(b)* they desire to indicate to the public who shall be recognised as accountants and auditors.

It need hardly be said that for any self-constituted society to seek to determine who shall take a recognised position in the industrial or the professional world is a serious matter. An institute which seeks to control the right of *entrée* into a profession can receive its justification only from the existence of irregularities which cannot otherwise be dealt with. The memorandum of association suggests this justification. Articles *(a) (b) (c)* in their retrospective application, imply that the profession of accountants needed elevation; that accountants have been deficient in professional knowledge, and require instruction in sound practice; that they have indulged in illegal and dishonourable practices, and that education in professional usage and etiquette will be a good thing for them.

The articles of association of the institute relate to the qualification of future members, the admission of members, the council, meetings, &c. The provisions relating to the qualification of future members are framed in such a manner that up to the end of December, 1890, admission may be obtained without examination. But after that date it will be necessary for applicants to pass certain examinations. Candidates are eligible who "have held the position of principal accountant to a corporation, registered or incorporated public company, in a Government department, or in public, mercantile, or professional employment." This provision is unquestionably liberal. The scale of fees is a moderate one, and is free from the objection of being prohibitive. One article (No. 46) regulates the use of designations of which the following is a list:—

A.I.A.V. Incorporated.
F.I.A.V. Incorporated.
H.M.I.A.V. Incorporated.
C.M.I.A.V. Incorporated.

This is rather a formidable list of titles, but it must be admitted that the accountants have as much right as the Oddfellows, Good Templars and others, to add a string of mystical initials to their signatures.

We are not altogether sanguine that the new society will make better accountants. Accountancy, like many other occupations, has a *technique* of its own, and the acquisition of this will doubtless be promoted by the institute. But to make an able accountant, an extensive knowledge of business, a sagacious grasp of affairs, firmness and rectitude of purpose, are requisites which membership in no institute can confer.

So far as the Incorporated Institute of Accountants in Victoria is likely to be useful to the public, we cordially wish it success. We do not admit that it has a just claim to dictate who shall be employed as public accountants, but it can discipline its own members, and require them to become fully qualified for such employment.

INCORPORATED INSTITUTE OF ACCOUNTANTS, VICTORIA

LETTER TO THE EDITOR AND THE EDITOR'S RESPONSE

SIR,—It is, I am sure, gratifying to those who at the cost of much time and labour, have succeeded in establishing the Institute of Accountants, to learn that in your deliberate judgment its aims are commendable, its provision for the admission of future members liberal, and its scale of fees moderate. Three other things are needed to make it an assured success—a large accession of members, wise and prudent methods of working, and steadfast perseverance in the prosecution of its aims. The first has begun, the council having, since the institute was incorporated, admitted and having before it applications for admission from several gentlemen of good standing in the profession. The second and third are in the hands of the members themselves.

If, as you seem to fear, it may not be found able fully to accomplish all it aims at, it will not differ in that respect from many other praiseworthy organisations.

That "it will not make better accountants" is a proposition, the acceptance of which must depend on the scope given to the words I quote. It certainly cannot be expected to implant in its members the mental and moral qualities which you so properly describe as essentials to the making of an accountant of the first rank; but it may do much to strengthen and cultivate these natural gifts where they exist, especially in those who, in the future, join its ranks as "students;" for whom special provision is made in its scheme, and I hope will before long be made in its working arrangements. But is it not a contradiction to say that it may promote the acquisition of the *technique* of accountancy, and yet cannot make better accountants than would grow up without its aid?

There is a serious misapprehension of the aim of the society running through several paragraphs of your otherwise appreciative notice, which it seems to me to be desirable to correct. In one, you speak of the institute as ambitious to indicate to the public who shall be recognised as accountants and auditors. In another, it is inferentially described as seeking to control the right of *entrée* into the profession; and in a third, you protest against its (supposed) claim to dictate who shall be employed as public accountants. The clause *(b)* in the memorandum of association, which is the text on which these comments are based, relates to the *admission to the Institute* of such persons only (with some temporary exceptions) as shall pass examinations in the theory and practice of accountancy. The right to control admission to *its own ranks* can hardly be disputed. You recognise that its provisions in this respect are liberal, but even if it were to exercise this power in a narrow and exclusive spirit, the injury would fall not on those competent persons who might be shut out, but on the institute itself. It neither seeks nor claims either to control admission *to the profession,* or to dictate who shall be employed, but it does undoubtedly seek, and hopes by its examinations and the exercise of its disciplinary functions, to make membership of the society a passport to public confidence. But this will not detract from the professional standing of any equally trustworthy persons who for various reasons may not join the body.

I assume it to be a slip of the pen when you justify the forming of the institute by the analogy of a trades union. Truer analogies are to be found in the institutes of actuaries, architects, and civil engineers. Then there is nothing "mystical" in a Fellow of the Institute of Accountants, Victoria, using after his name—in lieu of this long title—the initial letters F.I.A.V., a practice common to all like societies. We do not designate our executive officers "Worshipful Grands," nor do we decorate them with badges, aprons, and sashes, as do the Oddfellows and Good Templars, with whom you compare us. These slight slips, however, do not materially detract from the value of your sympathetic notice, for which I thank you.—

Yours, &c.,

WILLIAM CRELLIN.

Melbourne, 2nd April, 1887.

[We are not convinced by Mr. Crellin's letter that we have misapprehended the aim of the Incorporated Institute of Accountants, Victoria. The institute, as we understand it, is formed for what is usually called the "protection" of the interests of those who join its ranks, and not for the benefit of those who remain outside, but who may be equally competent accountants. That is, it is a professional union as much as a society of stone masons in a trades' union. The founders of the institute profess to have the benefit of the public at heart, in recommending themselves and those they may receive into fellowship, as the pure unadulterated elect of accountancy. Will they, in order to sustain the *rôle* they adopt, help in the reform of the insolvency laws of the colony of Victoria, although such reform may result in the reduction of their own emoluments, and the diminution of a large aggregate of unclaimed dividends? That is, will they aid in the promotion of the public welfare in preference to seeking their own advantage? We have no right to expect they will, but it is then the more obvious that their association is confined by the narrow bounds of a professionalism, which is not entitled to the sympathy of those who stand outside it. The incorporation of the institute is not so important a matter as it may ap-pear to be, as it confers nothing more than a common legal status. That the desire to monopolise accountancy work is not always realised, is evidenced by what has occurred in England, where there are now two powerful rival organisations, besides a large number of accountants who find the mere description, "public accountant," quite sufficient, in addition to their qualifications, to recommend them to the public. As regards to titles which admission to the institute confers, they may be ornamental and imposing, but we cannot perceive any intrinsic value in them, notwithstanding that their owners stop short, as Mr. Crellin puts it, at personally decorating themselves with badges, aprons, and sashes.—ED. *Banking Record.*]

INCORPORATED INSTITUTE OF ACCOUNTANTS, VICTORIA

LETTER TO THE EDITOR AND THE EDITOR'S RESPONSE

SIR,— In my letter of the 2nd instant I tried to show that the Institute is not justly chargeable with an endeavour to control the right of entry into the profession of accountancy, or with seeking to dictate who shall be employed as public accountants. If I failed, it must be due to my own inaptitude, and not to any inherent difficulty in the task, because, in the whole of the memorandum and articles of association there is not one clause which, fairly interpreted, will support such charges.

It is now said that it seeks the "protection" of the interests of those who join its ranks, and not the benefit of those equally competent accountants who remain outside. But, when a society makes admittedly liberal provision for the admission of new members—openly proclaims its desire that they shall join its ranks, and has already given proof of its *bona fides* by the admission of all who, so far, have applied—it is entitled to be credited with something better than an intention to create a monopoly. Such benefits as may be derived from belonging to the Institute are open to be secured by all who come within the broad and liberal conditions laid down in the articles, and even those competent gentlemen who, for reasons of their own, may ultimately elect to remain outside its ranks, cannot fail to be advantaged if the profession be advanced in public estimation by its labours.

But to test its claim to be in some degree actuated by public spirit, you ask whether it will help in the reform of the Insolvency Laws of the colony, although such reform may result in the reduction of the emoluments of its members. To this I reply:—*(a)*. That since the Institute got into working order, no opportunity for giving such help has arisen. *(b)*. I am informed on good authority that when these laws were some time since under the consideration of the Chamber of Commerce, with a view to their amendment, three members of the Institute at least (two of whom are members of the council of the Institute), did, in fact, give their assistance with that object; what other members may have done, I have no present means of learning. *(c)*. At a meeting of the council of the Institute, held some time prior to the publication of your comments, the necessity for amendments in the Insolvency Laws was recognised, and being informed that a Bill for that purpose is likely to be introduced during the coming session of Parliament, it was agreed to seek an opportunity to take part in promoting it.

You proceed to speak of the reform of the Insolvency Laws resulting in the diminution of a large aggregate (?) of unclaimed dividends, and imply that this is a reason why the Institute should be adverse to such reform. I fail to understand the pertinency of the reference. Unclaimed dividends, like unclaimed bank balances, are trust monies, and are not the property of their custodians. When such dividends accrue from an insolvent estate, they are, after the lapse of a given time, payable into the Treasury, and when from an assigned estate, they remain in one of the banks to the credit of a trust account waiting claimants. When an estate is realised, and all lawful claims adjusted, the sooner the dividends are claimed and

paid the better pleased is the assignee. This, at all events, was my experience when a member of a firm doing, at that time, the largest business of the kind in Melbourne, and I have no reason to think that it is otherwise now.

WILLIAM CRELLIN.
Melbourne, 26th April, 1887.

[The Incorporated Institute of Accountants, Victoria, has a sturdy champion in Mr. Crellin. Without retraversing the ground, we content ourselves with saying that we are unconvinced that the Institute is established for any other purpose than the promotion of the interests of those who may join it, and that therefore it has no special claim on the favour of the public. A professional accountant, carrying on his business as such, will not we fancy suffer because he does not attach a tail of cacophonous initials to his name. As regards the insolvency laws, we are pleased to hear that the members of the Institute are helping in the cause of reform and lessening of emoluments, and heartily wish them success.—ED. *Banking Record*.]

INCORPORATED INSTITUTE OF ACCOUNTANTS

The first annual meeting of the Incorporated Institute of Accountants of Victoria was held last evening at the Cathedral Hotel, Swanston-street, Mr. W. Crellin in the chair.

Mr. A. GILMOUR, one of the hon. secretaries, read the report.

It pointed out that the institute arose out of a meeting of public accountants, convened in December, 1885, by Mr. Chas A. Cooper, A.S.A., to which he submitted proposals for the establishment in Melbourne of a branch of the Society of Accountants, London. Although Mr. Cooper's proposals were, after careful consideration, set aside in favour of a local independent society, it was due to that gentleman to place on record the service he rendered at the initial state of the society. On April 12, 1886, 45 gentlemen having in the meantime agreed to join the proposed society, a meeting was held, when the institute was founded, and the first council constituted. Since that date there had been held three general meetings of members, nine meetings of council, and five meetings of committees of the council, with the following results:—The memorandum and articles of association had been prepared and adopted, the institute had been registered as a company limited by guarantee under the Companies Statute 1864 and Act No. 764; 11 new members had been admitted resident in Victoria, South Australia, New Zealand, and Fiji; an examining committee had been appointed, and a scheme for the examination of candidates adopted, printed, and circulated. Steps had been taken to open up communication with similar societies in Great Britain through the instrumentality of Mr. E. Langton and Mr. J.H. Flack, members of the council, who were on a visit to the old country. Authority had been given to select in London a few standard works on subjects related to accountancy to form the nucleus of a technical library. It was hoped that during the coming year members of the profession, whether in public or private practice, connected with Government departments, banks, insurance and other incorporated companies, or in mercantile houses, would largely join the ranks of the institute. The council had not overlooked the important subject of providing for the dissemination of professional knowledge amongst members and students by the reading of papers and delivering lectures, but nothing had been accomplished calling for report. It was commended to the careful consideration of the new council. It was probable that during the current year the Parliament of Victoria would deal with the important question of a reform of the insolvency law. Should such be the case, the institute might be able to render some assistance in that direction. During the year the institute had lost Mr. Robt. McCaskie, one of its founders, by death, and a letter of condolence had been forwarded to Mr. McCaskie's family. In resigning into the hands of members the functions with which it was entrusted, the council had much pleasure in congratulating members on the measure of success attained, and the fair prospects of usefulness in the future.

The scheme for the examination of candidates referred to in the report embraced the following subjects: — Bookkeeping, auditing, the adjustment of partnership and executorship accounts, the rights and duties of liquidators, trustees, and receivers, principles of the law of insolvency, principles of the law of joint stock companies and mercantile law, and the law of arbitration and awards.

The CHAIRMAN, in opening the business of the meeting, stated that the council had elected as honorary members Messrs. T.W. Jackson and J.W. Fosbery, audit commissioners, and Mr. R. Gudeman, the under-treasurer. Colonel Templeton, the chairman of the Public Service Board, would have been present at the meeting but for another engagement. He expressed the warmest sympathy with the institute, and said that it would have been well if it had been formed years ago.

Mr. J.C. Tyler, the honorary treasurer, was unable to attend, but the accounts read by Mr. Gilmour showed a credit balance of £255.

In moving the adoption of the report and balance-sheet, the Chairman said that the institute had 58 members. There were a great many more accountants in the city who might join, and would be an acquisition to them, and he suggested that efforts should be made with a view to bringing them in. As an educational means, he suggested the delivery of a course of lectures, which might be attended by non-members. He mentioned that there would have been a larger attendance at the meeting but for the fact that several were sick. Some had been in the Windsor railway accident, and after apparently feeling better were now in their rooms again.

Mr. A. LYELL seconded the motion, and in doing so expressed the opinion that the institute would be most valuable in connection with the financial developments that were taking place between the colonies and the home country. To be able to certify to accounts as members of that institute would lend greater value to their certificates.

Mr. H.G. TURNER, president of the Bankers' Institute, was invited to say a few words. He was heartily welcomed, and mentioned that the Accountants' Institute was in advance of the Bankers' Institute in the adoption of an examination scheme. He found from the evidence which had been taken by the Banking Commission recently that bank managers were unanimous in expressing an opinion that bank auditing, as conducted at present, was most unsatisfactory, and it would be a fine field for the Accountants' Institute to establish a system which would give satisfaction to both shareholders and bank officials.

Mr. C. SALTER, president of the Insurance Institute, also offered a few congratulatory remarks, and the motion was then agreed to.

The following were re-elected members of council:— Messrs. James H. Cole, William Crellin, H.W. Danby, Thos. J. Davey, C.W. Ellis, J.H. Flack, I.C. Foden, Edward Langton, C.J. Lucas, Andrew Lyell, A.C. McDonald, C.J. Richardson, A.F.W. Saunders, G.W. Selby, jun., and J.C. Tyler.

Mr. J. McDonald was re-appointed auditor.

A hearty vote of thanks having been passed to Mr. Crellin, the rest of the evening was spent in a social manner.

INCORPORATED INSTITUTE OF ACCOUNTANTS (VICTORIA)

Incorporated Institute of Accountants (Victoria).

A REPORT of the proceedings at the first annual meeting of the Incorporated Institute of Accountants (Victoria), held on 15th June, appears on another page, and will be found interesting. The annual report adopted by the meeting, and the scheme for the examination of candidates for admission, indicate that the Council takes a proper view of its duties and its responsibilities. The aims of the Institute, as shadowed forth in this report, are such as, if attained, will certainly raise the standard of efficiency in accountancy to the public advantage.

We have not scrupled in former issues to express disapproval of any tendency to a disposition on the part of the Institute to monopolise for its members, to the exclusion of other public accountants, who may be as well qualified as themselves, a business which, if occasionally overrated in some of its aspects, is yet one of the highest commercial importance. But we have now to ask whether it is advisable to open the ranks of the Institute to the extent suggested in the annual report. A prevalent view is that the Institute of Accountants occupies a position exactly analogous to that of the Insurance Institute or the Institute of Bankers. A little reflection, however, will show that this view is hardly correct. If the question be asked —What are the relations of the three Institutes named to the general public? the answer must be that accountants—of course we are speaking of public accountants—are directly employed by the public, and are answerable to the public ; whilst on the other hand, insurance men and bankers, even when occupying the highest positions, are the permanent officials of individual concerns. In short, the accountants take the status of a professional class more distinctly than do the officials of banking and insurance companies. The Insurance Institute and the Institute of Bankers, by their lectures, discussions, libraries, and prize essays, offer academic advantages to their members. The Institute of Accountants while not neglecting these things, must also seek to charge itself in some measure with the discipline of its members as professional men.

If our view be correct, then the desire expressed by the Council that private accountants, who are regular paid servants in banks, insurance companies, mercantile firms, &c., should be received into the Institute is scarcely a judicious one. Wishing to avoid exclusiveness, the Council has gone to the opposite extreme, and proposes a step which, as it appears to us, is likely to impair its public usefulness. It would be better that the Incorporated Institute of Accountants should stand before the public as a responsible professional body answerable, within reasonable bounds, for the professional conduct of its members. Accountants and bookkeepers in salaried employment might still be allowed to take advantage of the Institute's scheme of examination, although it can hardly be advanced that the Institute is called upon to provide for the mental improvement of any but its own members and their articled clerks.

Somewhat foreign as it may be to the special subject of this article, it may be appropriate at this point to throw out the suggestion that either in connection with the University of Melbourne, or independently, an examining body might be constituted, the function of which should be to draw up a scheme of annual examinations in a variety of subjects, directly or indirectly connected with commerce in its broadest sense, which would satisfy the needs of employés in banks and other joint-stock companies, as well as of those in private employment. The admirable schemes of the Society of Arts and of the City of London College might be studied and imitated in Melbourne with advantage. Any one who has witnessed the work of the City of London College will know how great are the services which it renders to the mercantile community at large, and how conducive its efforts have been to the welfare of its industrious students. The whole subject of commercial education in Melbourne is one which might worthily engage the attention of the Chamber of Commerce, of merchants, and of bankers.

Passing from this digression, the details of the scheme of examination of candidates for admission to the Institute of Accountants merit notice. The subjects are:— Book-keeping, auditing, the adjustment of partnership and executorship accounts, the rights and duties of liquidators, trustees, and receivers, principles of the law of insolvency, principles of the law of joint-stock companies and mercantile law, and the law of arbitration and awards. This is, beyond all doubt, a first-class curriculum, deserving of all praise. One highly important subject is, however, omitted, viz., that of the principles of the valuation of assets. Accountants are constantly appealed to for information as to what method should be adopted for valuing stock, for in large manufacturing concerns the question is often more perplexing than the uninitiated might think possible. In the conversion of private concerns into joint-stock companies, also, an accountant may be called upon for a professional opinion as to the soundness of the principles upon which the valuation of the property in its many forms has been conducted,

and this opinion carries weight with the investing public. The correct valuation of assets in a balance-sheet dwarfs every other point in importance. Doubtless, the Council will hold elementary intermediate and advanced examinations in each of the subjects it has adopted, but, even within the three years which will thus be engaged, the closest application to the text books will be necessary, so comprehensive and thorough is the course. A sound education in the science of accountancy will thus be provided for, and any candidate who may succeed in passing successfully from stage to stage through the whole course of study should become thoroughly equipped, so far as mental attainments are concerned, for the work of his profession. Acuteness of observation in practice, and sound experience on a wide and varied field, will then make him an accomplished accountant.

It was pleasing to notice at the meeting the cordiality of feeling existing between the Institute of Accountants and the Insurance Institute and the Bankers' Institute. The establishment of harmonious relations between these bodies is a sensible step.

————◆————

THE INCORPORATED INSTITUTE OF ACCOUNTANTS, VICTORIA

THE INCORPORATED INSTITUTE OF ACCOUNTANTS, VICTORIA.

ONE part of the scheme of the Incorporated Institute of Accountants recently established, is the holding of occasional meetings of the members for reading papers on subjects of interest to the profession, to be followed by discussion of any questions of principle or practice raised in such papers. The first of such meetings was held in September last year, when eighteen members were present, and Mr. C. M. Holmes (Messrs. Langton and Holmes) read an interesting and instructive essay on "The Scope and Limits of the Duties of a Public Auditor." This was followed by an animated discussion in which Messrs. Saunders, Davey, Crellin and Meudell (a visitor) took part, when the meeting was adjourned.

The adjourned meeting was held on 19th January, at which forty-one persons were present, including several visitors to whom special cards of invitation had been sent, and who were chiefly gentlemen employed in the offices of members. Mr. Andrew Lyell re-opened the subject, and was followed by Messrs. Flack, Howden, Saunders, A. C. M'Donald, Davey, Jackman (a visitor) and the President. Mr. Lyell replied to the remarks made by the various speakers. At the close it was urged by several members that the subject was far from being exhausted, and it is probable that another meeting will soon be held.

Before calling on Mr. Lyell, the president reported that Mr. Flack (honorary secretary) had recently returned from Great Britain where he had interviewed the officials of the Institute of Chartered Accountants of England and Wales, London, the Societies of Accountants of Edinburgh and Glasgow, and the Manchester Accountants Students' Society, by whom he had been well received and who had expressed much interest in the account Mr. Flack was able to give them of the progress of the new Institute on this side of the globe. He further reported that Mr. Flack had purchased in London, or had received as presents to the library, between fifty and sixty volumes and pamphlets on various branches of an accountant's work ; these embrace standard works on book-keeping, auditing, arbitrations, bankruptcy, duties of trustees and executors, the Companies' Acts, promoting and winding up of companies, which would be useful to members as works of reference, and will be available for that purpose as soon as the Council can make arrangements for their custody. He also called attention to the advertisement in the daily papers and in the January number of the *Journal* of the proposal to provide a course of lectures in accountancy in all branches, and expressed a hope that before long the Council would receive overtures from gentlemen competent to undertake the work.

The president informs us that since the meeting, Messrs. Davey Flack and Co. have presented the Institute with nineteen volumes of books chiefly relating to systems of book-keeping selected by Mr. J. H. Flack in London, of the value of about £5 10s.

THE INSTITUTE OF ACCOUNTANTS

There is perhaps no word in the mercantile vocabulary which is so frequently misused as that of "Accountant." This applies frequently to distinguish those skilled in commercial and financial bookkeeping, and likewise to those whose special duty it is to check the arithmetical work of others, but it is also made use of by a great army of clerks out of work, or persons who have no particular vocation who are to be found on the fringe of the commercial circle, existing by means best known to themselves. It need hardly be said that between the two former and the latter classes there is no affinity. For want of a system in this, a comparatively young community, it has happened that the incompetent are employed in duties where skill should be a desideratum. This is more particularly the case in regard to audits and certificates given for purposes intended to satisfy the public mind as to the genuineness of the particulars. It hardly requires a word from us to say that auditors should be professional men of known ability, and yet in very many instances, particularly in connection with that important work of supervising municipal accounts, laymen are engaged, who, although frequently possessing ability, are without other necessary qualifications. Again, of late it has not been a novelty to find numerous prospectuses in which certain facts are certified to, or deductions made, by persons of no special knowledge, but who call themselves accountants. An instance of this was recently afforded us when an accountant, so self-styled, certified that the profits of a business were equal to paying a certain dividend on the capital. As collateral figures did not support this view, he was requested to explain, when it appeared that he had intended to convey the meaning that the profits in the past had been equal to paying a certain interest on the capital—an infinitesimal sum—then employed, whereas he had practically stated that those profits were equal to a certain dividend upon the capital proposed to be paid up! No more dangerous statement could well be made, and except for the condemnation of a newspaper article a great wrong might have been done. Innumerable instances of such curious certificates, and more glaring examples of doubtful auditing might be given, but as the general fact is well known, it only requires calling to mind. It was with much pleasure, therefore, that some three years ago we noticed the formulating of a scheme by which some guarantee would be afforded the public that audits and such like accountancy work would be well and faithfully executed. This scheme has eventuated in the Incorporated Institute of Accountants of Victoria, of which Mr. William Crellin is the President, and Mr. J.H. Flack the Hon. Secretary; although from neither of these gentlemen did the first propositions emanate. Yet it is due to them and numerous coadjutors that the society has grown to its present position. The third annual meeting was held last week, the proceedings of which are reported on another page.

It will be observed from the report that the Council of the Institute has not been idle. Representations on the subject of municipal audits have been prepared, and although owing to a change in the Cabinet, the Minister communicated with, has not been available to a deputation, there is small likelihood of this serious matter being allowed to drop.

Another most important matter is the recommendations for amendments to the present Companies' Statute, and in this it is quite clear that not only the Council but members of the Institute can lend most valuable aid. They have not only a considerable experience of the difficulties presented and the omissions allowed by the present Act, but they not infrequently have to put up with much hardship and not a few slights in their own labours in connection with certificates and the auditing of accounts. It has been no uncommon occurrence for an auditor to be offered a handsome free provided that he would so word a certificate that the public might believe something very different to what did actually exist. Be it said to their honor that few really professional men have yielded to such temptation, but some have, and therefore there is good work for the Institute to do in getting such weeds disqualified for important work, if not by legislation, by educating the public to look for the professional status of the authority. In a very similar way the balance sheets of some companies are submitted in the most vague terms, essential particulars are withheld, and not infrequently we regret to say inaccuracies are present which it is hoped the auditors will pass—and sometimes some accountants, so called, have "winked at" the proceedings. In connection with this matter there are two reforms which strike us as imperatively necessary. The most important is that of taking care that in any further legislative measures the articles of association of companies are so framed that the auditors should be *defacto* what they are supposed to be—*i.e.* the critics or judges of the financial proceedings of the directors, not left as now, merely tools to be employed as the latter choose under penalty of dismissal. Another matter is, that certificated accountants should decline to be bracketed with laymen, generally mere creatures of the directors put into a good thing by them, and never intended to do any real work in connection with the examination of accounts. By such tactics the professional man is not only insulted, but runs the risk of his fees being unjustly reduced. We are quite aware that much needed reform in these directions cannot altogether be carried out by legislation; but if the Institute be true to itself and its objects, the public mind can be so regulated that its members for whose honour and competency the Council vouches, will alone be accepted as proper persons to be engaged in such work.

In the concluding portion of the record of the year's work, reference is made to the few meetings held, and the absence of any support by members in the matter of reading of papers. As the President very aptly said, if—as is the case—the members of the Bankers and of the Insurance institutes can meet monthly, and assist to educate or entertain each other, surely the Accountants should not be behind. Their literary, technical or social attainments should not be one whit less than those of members of kindred societies. Possibly, however, the difficulty of providing suitable quarters has a deterent effect. Certainly the Institute does not possess any fit room for the holding of periodical meetings in a comfortable manner. This, however, should not deter the Council. The funds are not as yet very large, but they have a steady increasing roll, and a strong effort would doubtless soon double the present number of members. It suggests itself to us that what is being done in this direction by the Institute of Chartered Accountants in England and Wales is to be aimed at. The report of the parent society shows the number of members to be 1,633, and that

10 exclusions had taken place during the year. A hall, with offices, is about to be built in Coleman-street, at a cost of £20,250, of which sum £3,000 is in respect of decorative sculpture. The site of the hall has been leased for a term of 999 years, the net annual rent of which will be for the first twenty years £742, and subsequently £786. The income for the year was £6,210, of which £793 was in respect of interest on investments. The surplus income was £2,322. The funds now amount to £25,589. Of course it is not to be expected that the Victorian Institute can jump all at once into such palatial splendour, or raise its invested funds to £25,000, but much can be done by very little. We would suggest that overtures be made to both the Bankers' and Insurance institutes, and we are hopeful that a scheme could be arranged by which, at no great cost, when distributed *pro rata,* suitable premises could be secured, and other advantages obtained by the members of each and all. Nor indeed is this all. An alliance between bodies whose aims are in many respects identical, who are each desirous of elevating their profession, and inculcating a better tone of commercial morality into every day, would effect. Such a combination would be a power in the land and command respect.

WHAT IS AN ACCOUNTANT?

TO THE EDITOR OF THE
ARGUS

Sir,—This is a question that has been so often discussed recently by aspirants for auditorship and, and for the initials F.I.A.V. of the Incorporated Institute of Accountants of Victoria, that I venture to answer it in one short sentence.

Concisely put, it signifies "skilled bookkeeper," e.g., one versed in the science of bookkeeping—skilled in placing entries in the ledgers so as to produce accurate results in conformity with the science. It is almost superfluous to add that there are figures connected with these entries which involve more or less computation, but it is not his skill in figures, but in bookkeeping, which con-stitutes him accountant. The accountant to a leading trading company, "home or foreign trade," is next to the manager, and chief of the staff, and has usually a cashier and two or more ledger-keepers as assistants, who attend respectively to the cash-book, invoice and sales ledgers, and render customers accounts, while he attends to the skilled or technical portion of the work, which is frequently omitted in the smaller firms through false economy or ignorance. The skilled bookkeeper keeps the books by double entry, strikes the monthly trial balances and half-yearly profit and loss and balance-sheets early for audit. Such experience can only be obtained in the counting-house under such a man. Such a man only is qualified to undertake the business of public accountant, auditor, and trade assignee, in which occupations he will no doubt obtain a more varied experience; only such as he is competent to undertake special audits, adjust complicated accounts, arrange books on double entry basis, compute goodwill and conduct investigations as well in Government departments, banks, insurance companies, building societies, and corporations, as in mercantile firms, and, after reading up the acts relating thereto, he may undertake equity and insolvency business. Only such a skilled public accountant should be appointed audit commissioner, Government, corporation, public company or friendly society's auditor.

From the foregoing statement of the nature of an accountant's duties it should be superfluous to add that astronomers, engineers, actuaries, schoolmasters, or other mathematicians and arithmeticians skilled in figures are not accountants because they are computers, unless they are skilled bookkeepers, which last may be set down as highly problematical. A man may be a doctor or a lawyer, but it would be difficult to be both. Such persons, without a thorough knowledge of bookkeeping, would be utterly incompetent to audit the work of a skilled bookkeeper, or perform any of the numerous duties of a skilled accountant. Notwithstanding this fact, so well known to our long-suffering and patient professional accountants, many actuaries here have the supreme audacity to enter into competition with public accountants for the offices of auditor and assignee, trusting to the magical influence of the initials F.I.A. on a confiding public, who are for ever confusing computation with bookkeeping.

But there is still another class of men in the field as aspirants for mercantile audits, viz.:—Bank accountants, whose entire experience of bookkeeping is confined exclusively to banking business, yet, notwithstanding, have the presumption to compete for mercantile audits with the skilled mercantile accountant, and further seek admittance to the ranks of the Incorporated Institute of Accountants.

After several years' existence, it is surely full time that both the incorporated institutes, viz., the Victorian and English branch here, took steps to introduce a bill into Parliament to protect them-selves as well as the general public.

Only recently a merchant here said he considered that man an accountant, who in a bank could allow him an overdraft of about £10,000; had he served his articles in any leading mercantile house he would have known better.

On another occasion a large shareholder in a public company — a schoolmaster — confidingly told me that there was neither skill nor responsibility required for an audit, "that, like kissing, it went by favour," and solemnly asked me whether I would give him my vote if he stood for auditor. Need I observe I restrained myself, and refrained from a reply.

There should be no difficulty in selecting a first-class man, if not the very best to be had—to have been head bookkeeper, usually termed accountant in leading firms—where books are kept by double-entry, and trial balances are struck and audited monthly (in the inland and also in the foreign trade) whether public company or private concern. He should hold a double first hall-mark of ability, and proof of such should be sufficient testimonial for a similar appointment or that of auditor to any public company. With many apologies for occupying so much place.

Yours, &c,

Aug. 1.   PHILO

ACCOUNTANTS AND ACTUARIES

THE question—What is an accountant? has been raised by a letter which appeared in the Melbourne *Argus* on 5th inst. The writer lays down the proposition that only the skilled double-entry bookkeeper "is qualified to undertake the business of public accountant, auditor, and trade assignee, in which occupations he will no doubt obtain a more varied experience; only such as he is competent to undertake special audits, adjust complicated accounts, arrange books on double entry basis, compute goodwill and conduct investigations as well in Government departments, banks, insurance companies, building societies, and corporations, as in mercantile firms, and, after reading up the Acts relating thereto, he may undertake equity and insolvency business. Only such a skilled public accountant should be appointed Audit Commissioner, Government, corporation, public company, or friendly society's auditor." The writer appears to us altogether to exaggerate the importance of a knowledge of the double-entry system of bookkeeping. That system can be taught to any intelligent boy entering into business in a few lessons, being one of the simplest pieces of mechanism extant. The stereotyped form of the skilled bookkeeper, as we know him, although a personage of the highest value in the particular concern in which he has been trained, is often the least fitted to act as a public accountant. That position demands the possession of qualifications far exceeding the ability to make something Dr. to something else Cr. It is the less advanced members of the public accountants' profession who magnify the importance of a mere technical form of casting accounts. The writer in the *Argus* speaks of "a confiding public, who are for ever confusing computation with bookkeeping." The public are entitled to find in the public accountant the ability to do both. Endued with sagacity and common sense, possessing a wide knowledge of business affairs in general, an adept in calculation and "computation," the really competent public accountant regards the process of bookkeeping by double entry as a very elementary affair. He doubtless prizes the initials F.I.A.V. as some kind of rough "hall mark," but he knows that they may be displayed without their possessor being so highly-gifted as he might be. One object of the correspondence appears to be to warn off actuaries from the profession of the public accountant, and such language as "the supreme audacity" of actuaries in competing for auditorships is employed. As a matter of fact, a qualified actuary (not including the public accountants who strive to raise their status by improperly advertising themselves to a "confiding public" as "actuaries") is immeasurably the superior of the ordinary skilled bookkeeper in education, intellectual training, and sound qualifications. He is a highly-finished product of intellectual forces, whereas the skilled bookkeeper may simply have been drumming away for ten, twenty, or thirty years at the not very exhausting mental work of putting items of accounts into a double-entry shape without much glimmering of anything higher. Given the requisite insight into

affairs, and the possession of business acumen, we would decidedly prefer as an auditor an actuary who has passed through the examinations of the Faculty or the Institute to a bookkeeper by double-entry. While referring to this point, we may mention that the names of the two auditors of a Melbourne bank are advertised in the *Bankers' Almanac* with the initials F.I.A., although they are not fellows of the Institute of Actuaries, but fellows of the Institute of Accountants of Victoria. We do not think for a moment the gentlemen in question have warranted, or are aware of, the improper use of initials we have described; but whoever is responsible evidently thought that to clip off the letter "V" might prove an advantage. In July, 1888, we called attention to the unauthorised use of the word actuary, and quoted from the annual report of the Institute of Actuaries as follows:—

"During the year the Council have exercised a vigilant supervision over the use of the initials of membership confirmed to the Institute by charter; and, both at home and in the colonies, they have taken steps to check the unauthorised employment of these titles."

The president for the year said:—"Our initials have been wrongly used, principally by people in Australia." He could hardly have expected, however, that the names of Australian accountants would be advertised in England with the highly-prized initials F.I.A. attached to them. On the whole question it must be admitted that there is great room for improvement in the calling of the public accountant. But we think that the improvement ought to commence in the ranks of the public accountants themselves. What is really desirable is that the public should learn to discriminate and to encourage the growth of large respectable establishments like the great accountancy firms of London and Liverpool. But if they want the skilled book-keeper to leave his desk to turn public accountant, they can have him by hundreds.

ACCOUNTANTS AND AUDITORS

SIR,—In the August number of your journal you refer to "public accountants who strive to raise their status by improperly advertising themselves to a confiding public as actuaries," and quote in illustration the case of the auditors of a Melbourne bank who are advertised in the "Bankers' Almanac and Directory" (London) with the initials F.I.A., although they are not Fellows of the "Institute of Actuaries," but Fellows of the "Institute of Accountants, Victoria."

This having come under the notice of the council of the Institute, inquiry was made as to the bank referred to, and we now forward you printed copy of the last balance-sheet issued in Melbourne, in which you will note that the initials following the names of the auditors are F.I.A.V., and not F.I.A. as in the London advertisement.—Yours faithfully,

WILLIAM CRELLIN, President.
JOSEPH H. FLACK, Hon. Sec.

INCORPORATED ACCOUNTANTS

In another place we report the proceedings at the annual meeting of the Incorporated Institute of Accountants, Victoria. This is the sixth year, and there is no question but that as the Society grows older so does its sphere of usefulness extend, its necessity become greater, and its power and possibilities for good increase. The past year has brought into strong relief the expediency of some hallmark for gentlemen engaged in accountancy work, more especially that branch of it in which the auditing of the affairs of public companies is in the front rank. From the very nature of things in a young community, it was not to be expected that all persons dealing with such accounts were properly qualified, as we now understand the requirements of the work, and hence it has happened that in many cases through regrettable ignorance or muddling there have been *láches* which have angered the public, and placed the persons concerned in invidious, not to say dangerous, positions. In future, however, there will be little excuse for auditors, the exhaustive examination and the principles taught by the Institute affording evidence that its members are professional gentlemen whose honor and ability may be relied upon. It remains for the Council to keep a close watch upon all matters connected with auditorial and accountancy work, and it is to be hoped that fellows and members will recognise that it is of interest to them to aid in its work and uphold its corporate honor.

The report of the Council is lengthy, and traverses the proceedings of the year in detail, showing that although the work is quietly done, without any ostentatious display or publicity, it is yet of a most thorough and comprehensive character. It is gratifying to note that there has been a considerable addition to the roll of members, the majority after passing the necessary examination. The library has been added to, and is made more use of by fellows and others. This is a branch of the association which should prove invaluable, for text books on finance and allied technical subjects are expensive to the individual, yet no one concerned in accountancy can afford to neglect reading of that character.

It is, however, to be regretted that the attendance at the various meetings for the discussion of matters relating to the work of members has not been larger. It is not necessary to make a "splash" in order to give evidence of life, but it is essential for the well-being of such organisations that everything connected with them should be supported *con amore,* or otherwise there will be a want of interest and a danger of them becoming effete. It is not right that the whole work of the Institute should devolve upon a few enthusiasts whose ardour in the long run is likely to be damped by the neglect of their *confreres.* The Council has been successful in inducing the Government to recognise the Institute in connection with municipal audits, and we notice further that its members are to be accepted as fully qualified for supervising the finances of public companies in the important measure which Mr. Wynne is about to introduce for amending the Companies Act. Nothing else could be expected of trained accountants than that they would view with alarm any legislation calculated to weaken the financial position, and hence it is no surprise to find that the Council of the Institute joins in the protest which has become so general—except from a few land-boomers—against the retention of "The Voluntary Liquidation Act" on the statute book. The finances of the Association are in a flourishing condition, and the statement of the accounts shows clearly how judiciously the funds are expended for the advantage of its members, and due regard paid to obtaining the full benefit of interest on accumulated funds. So far, so good—but it is necessary that members should continue to exert themselves. We do not say, in the words of Hood—

> Work! work! work!
> Till the brain begins to swim;
> Work! work! work!
> Till the eyes are heavy and dim—

Although doubtless in the course of their avocations auditors and accountants are occasionally compelled to experience brain strain to that unfortunate extent, but we do say work hand in hand for the good of the Association, so that each year's record shall stand out as better than that preceding for usefulness and power obtained.

ACCOUNTANTS AND AUDITORS

ACCOUNTANTS AND AUDITORS. At no time, perhaps, in the history of this colony have the methods of preparing and certifying to balance-sheets occupied more public attention. In other words, various defects and flaws have been discovered in bookkeeping and auditorial work. Shareholders, creditors, and the general public, are now scrutinising for themselves figures which hitherto they have taken on trust. It is, however, not to be inferred therefrom that they are much wiser ; probably they are even more likely to form erroneous conclusions, but this new interest gives the opportunity which has long been desired by those who look to elevate the position of professional accountants and auditors. We have frequently dwelt upon the disabilities under which that profession labors : Firstly, from the many incompetent persons employed ; and secondly, owing to the apathy of the general public in such matters, which in the case of some public companies make it extremely difficult for an auditor to maintain his self-respect and do his duty. Now, as we have said, there is an opportunity to alter all this. We venture to predict that if an auditor declines to sign a balance-sheet, or considers the methods employed prejudicial, he will be supported by the shareholders and the public, and not left to the mercy of directors or office autocrats. If a retirement is brought about without explanation, the public will want to know why, and moreover we are quite sure the remuneration will be more adequate for good honest work. It will be understood that it is better to pay a larger annual sum to capable fearless auditors than liquidators' fees and expenses, The annual meeting therefore, of the leading society of accountants in Victoria is opportune, and we are pleased to see not only that the number of members is increasing, but that more interest is being taken in the administrative work of the Institute. The nett increase in the roll is not large, but success lies in the number of candidates offering for examination. If the "passes" are fewer than heretofore we confess we are more pleased than otherwise, for we have no sympathy with any professional body which admits members in a haphazard fashion who are more or less remotely concerned in its immediate work. We want to see all the accountants of Victoria really clever experts in accountancy work, whose signatures will carry conviction to the lay mind that it is not possible for any jugglery to have been practised with documents so attested.   Progress quickly if possible ; but certainly surely.   To that end a perusal of the addresses delivered at the annual meeting of the Institute of Chartered Accountants in England and Wales by men at the top of the profession and other luminaries of the legal and financial world, is a most valuable lesson, and therefore to the report of the proceedings of the local society is added a full account of what took place in London on the occasion referred to.   We notice that recent events have acted as a great stimulus to other representative bodies to take action with a view of rendering our financial and commercial system more complete, and we are glad to see that the accountants have not been idle.   The Institute, however, must not be content, the lance cannot be laid in its rest until the enemy is killed, not scotched.   The opponents we thus figurately describe are well-known to the profession.

INSTITUTE OF ACCOUNTANTS

Institutes of Accountants. WE are asked by a New Zealand correspondent whether there is any precedent for a provision in a scheme promulgated by the Wellington Chamber of Commerce for the establishment of an Institute of Accountants in New Zealand, by which officers of banks, insurance companies, financial institutions, joint-stock companies, wholesale houses, and some departments of the Civil Service are to be "eligible for selection." At its formation the Melbourne Institute of Accountants practically adopted some such procedure. Our correspondent contends that only practising public accountants should be admitted into an association or institute of accountants. We think his contention in the main is right, but where, as in the colonies, the system extensively prevails for audits to be conducted by "outsiders," it is difficult to form a close corporation without provoking the formation of a rival association. But is not the matter a rather small one, for is not too much importance attached to membership in an institute? So far as our experience extends, admission into an Institute of Accountants at its inception is not necessarily a guarantee of ability, or even much knowledge, while outside the ranks there are a great number of able men. Why this should be the case is not difficult to say, for a proportion of the public accountants practising in the colonial centres are such, not because they are the most fit, but because other employments have failed them. At the same time it is only fair to say that the Melbourne Institute is certainly rendering a considerable service to the public by its strenuous endeavours to raise the standard of qualification. Its examining work is very good.

THE STATUS OF ACCOUNTANTS

Elsewhere we reproduce the able address of the President of the Victorian Institute of Accountants, delivered at the annual meeting held on 13th October. The most important part of this address is that which relates to the status of the profession of accountancy. Mr. BRENTNALL referred to the efforts which are being made by the Chartered Institute of Accountants in England and Wales to obtain legal recognition of their status, and discussed at some length the question whether a similar attempt should not be made in Melbourne. He spoke with much moderation, and with a sense of the difficulties which surround the question. The subject is well worth consideration, for it is admitted on all hands that the raising of the status of accountants is desirable. But what is meant by the term *status*? Is it to imply the exclusive privilege of practising as accountants? Or those high qualifications and character which the members of every profession—as being debtors to their profession—should possess? And if a guild of ac-

countants is to be constituted, with pains and penalties upon those rash persons who desire to earn a livelihood by working without the authorisation of the guild, should not the qualifications and character be a *sine quâ non?* First, then, as to the status of the profession of accountants in the sense in which the term can be used in connection with all professions and trades:—Are all the members of the English Chartered Institute and the Victorian Incorporated Institute sufficiently well equipped in knowledge, experience, and conscientious devotion to their work? The answer is obtainable from the practical test of this work supplied in the numerous failures of companies which have occurred in England and Victoria. While the laches of some accountants should not be condemnatory of the profession at large, yet, if the defect is large in its proportions, it should operate against "legal recognition of the status." As regards some of the English chartered accountants, the London *Times* did not hesitate to publish the following trenchant remarks in a leading article which appeared in its columns on 23rd June last:—

Next to the great director swindle, the most cruel trick practised on the poor is the auditor swindle. We have recently had the repeated spectacle of men who call themselves chartered accountants avowing that their pretended audit of accounts is nothing more than a mechanical checking of entries, which does not in the remotest manner touch the question of a company's solvency or honesty. Chartered accountants are persons who hold their heads high. They have an institute, fellowship of which is supposed by the public to be a guarantee for thoroughness in the work of verifying a balance-sheet. But the public cannot too speedily understand that the fellowship conveys no assurance of the kind, and that an auditor's certificate is absolutely worthless for any purpose that an investor need consider. There may be, and probably are, audits which really afford an independent corroboration of the statements in a balance-sheet. But the public have no means of knowing whether an audit means this or merely a clerical comparison of a set of figures with the published copy of them. Indeed so long as auditors are appointed by the persons they are supposed to check, and have no independent power to investigate or disallow improper transactions, it does not seem reasonable to expect their work to be of any real value.

With respect to the quality of the public auditing in Melbourne, we can speak from a lengthened experience in the critical examination of balance-sheets, and we are compelled to come to the conclusion that public audit is so often a mere farce that it would be better if it were altogether abolished, the penalties for publishing inaccurate statements being made more severe against directors and the principal officers. The public have frequently been lulled to sleep by an auditor's certificate, when without it they would have felt the need for inquiry. We admit with great pleasure that some of the members of the Victorian Institute are highly-trained and able professional men. The aims of the Institute directed to the raising of the qualifications of its members are also admirable. But there are conclusive reasons why the Legislature should not step out of its way to give a legal status to gentlemen whose qualifications may be uncertain, and to confer upon them alone the right to check figures. Public accountancy is not an occupation that ought to enjoy the status of a mediæval guild.

CHARTERED ACCOUNTANTS

WE reproduce on another page Chartered the brief report of the London Accountants. *Times* of the proceedings at the annual meeting of the Institute of Chartered Accountants in England and Wales, principally in order to draw attention to the views on the responsibilities of auditors expressed by the president, Mr. EDWIN WATERHOUSE. Those views, we hasten to admit, are quite orthodox within the circle of the accountants and auditors themselves. Outside that charmed circle they are pernicious, although stale enough. To Mr. WATERHOUSE those of the outside public who have been tempted to indulge in a feeling of scorn and indignation at the indifference manifested by some accountants in auditing accounts of public companies to real accuracy of statement are " the critics." "The critics," he said, " forgot that it was no part of an auditor's " duty to draw up a balance-sheet ; it was " his duty simply to examine and report ; " and the Legislature—as it appeared to " him wisely and with intention—had not, " except in a few cases, prescribed any " special form of report to be required from " an auditor." We do not think "the " critics" ever expected auditors to draw up balance-sheets, but what they do expect is that auditors shall see that the form in which balance-sheets are drawn shall at least be honest, so that the form itself shall not become a passive instrument of deception. Let us refer on this point to the statement made on 7th May by Mr. Justice VAUGHAN - WILLIAMS. After enumerating specifically the *laches* of the auditors, he said :—" Having these facts before me, it "seems to me that if the balance-sheet is " really to afford a correct view of the state " of the company's affairs, the auditors ought " to have insisted upon a substantial amount " being written off this credit in respect of "the contingent losses, or ought to have "insisted upon some note appearing on the "face of the balance-sheet to show that "these loans largely consisted of unproduc- "tive capital ; indeed, the auditors them- "selves admitted this. Some sort of justifi- "cation was put forward on the ground that "the colonial accounts were certified by " colonial auditors, but it seems to me that

" this can afford no justification in a case " where the English auditors had before " them this detailed information and pur- "ported to deal with it. If the auditors "intended not to be responsible for a credit " entry like this, certified from the colonies, " they should have expressly said so in their " certificate. As to the entries in the profit "and loss account of sums which were really "not earned at all, being really unpaid " interest and dividends, as to which there " was, to say the least of it, no immediate "prospect of payment, the auditors hardly "attempted to put forward a justification. " Some suggestion was made of a resolution " of the directors in regard to the transfer of " £21,000 from the suspense account ; but " even if there had been such a resolution, " which there was not, the auditors ought " not, with the knowledge they had, to have "acted on such a resolution." In face of these remarks, it is clear enough that if it is "no part of an auditor's duty to " draw up a balance-sheet" it is certainly the principal part of his duty to see that it has been properly drawn up, and to refuse to sanction its publication until the necessary amendments have been made. That Mr. WATERHOUSE is quite aware that auditors shirk matters which might bring them into collision with directors is evident from the following passage :—" The diffi- " culties of an auditor commenced when he " found his views at variance with those who " were responsible for the statement of "accounts—the directors and officers of the "company. Judging from his own ex- "perience, the probability was that, if he " pressed his point so as to bring the question " at issue between the executive and himself " before the shareholders, no due considera- "tion would be given to his objections if "the acceptance of his recommendations " would diminish the dividend proposed by " the board." Then are we to assume that eminent chartered accountants do *not* press their points? If they do not, their certificates are worth nothing, being an affront to the human conscience. One of the chartered accountants at the meeting, however, spoke up manfully. He said that the way in which some of their members had conducted audits

of public companies, had put back by ten
years the position of the Institute in
public esteem, and he would like to know
what steps had been taken, or would be
taken, respecting those members who had
seriously in the minds of many people,
jeopardised the interests of the Institute.
The chairman returned a diplomatic, that is
to say, an evasive reply, and "the critics" will
doubtless be justified in assuming that
nothing will be done. The fact is, bodies
like the Institute of Chartered Accountants
are afraid to put their members under the
mildest kind of professional discipline, if
for one reason only that the majority are,
despite examinations, devoid of real mercantile experience, possess no ability beyond
that which is required for the ticking off of
figures, and have no professional pride,
esteeming fees above all other things. If the
institute has really lost the esteem of the
public so much the better, for it never
fully deserved it.

JOURNAL OF COMMERCE   JULY 17, 1894, pp.5-6

THE ACCOUNTANTS' INSTITUTE

THE ACCOUNTANTS' INSTITUTE.

THE position, obligations and duties of Auditors is a matter now attracting so much attention in English speaking communities that the proceedings of associations supposed to vouch for the ability of their members who are, or should be, professional accountants, are of no little concern not only to the profession as a whole, but to the public at large. For after all it is the public who is most interested in the efficiency and uprightness of auditors, and it is they that require to be satisfied that those who make profession, have actually the necessary qualifications. The space at our command did not permit of our giving as full a report in our last issue as was desirable, of the proceedings at the annual meeting of the Institute of Incorporated Accountants, Victoria, but enough will have been gathered from what did appear to demonstrate that there are important issues, upon which the well being of the Institute depends, at stake, at this juncture. The Council seems to be not only divided against itself, but also is not in accord with the members generally in reference to the revision of the Articles of Association. So that the position as far as it could be gauged by the speeches at the annual meeting may be more fully understood, we give in another place a verbatim report of the discussion which then took place on the important subject mentioned. It is quite apparent to the ordinary reader, and must be very palpable to members of the Institute, that there is a considerable difference of opinion regarding the basis upon which the new Articles should be prepared. And it is equally clear, we regret to say, that a majority of the Council seem determined either in defence of their *amour propre*, or from sheer obstinacy to act in violation of an implied promise given to the members that through a committee appointed by them they should have a consultative voice in the revision of the Articles. The Council in fact insists upon its right to amend the amendments of the Joint Committee, and refer its draft to the members direct without permitting the Joint Committee to be officially heard. This is to be done, despite the fact that a minority of that committee, supported by two of the Council and three of those committeemen nominated by the members to represent them, desires that the committee's amendments should be submitted with the Council's draft to the members as a whole. It is true that the Council intends to submit to a meeting of members, and has in fact already as a preliminary submitted to them individually, a draft set of Articles proposed by the Council, and it may be urged that sufficient opportunity will thereby be given for obtaining members' opinions. But that is not the point. The difficulty is that members are to be asked to submit amendments if they so desire and formulate revised articles practically at a public meeting., Apart from the fact that it is next to impossible to execute so much detail work properly at such a gathering, it is obvious that as the Council has been with the assistance of the Joint Committee over twelve months in preparing the draft to be dealt with by the members, and is not by any means unanimous, there is a physical impossibility in preparing a proper set of Articles in the manner proposed. The chances are that the Council's draft would be accepted despite the fact that it is not approved of by a three fourths majority of that body itself, and is moreover not in conformity with the opinions of the Joint Committee, which it is important to remember, includes representatives nominated by the members themselves. Nor have those dissentient committeemen been heard, and they certainly cannot be properly heard in a general meeting.

This journal has always taken much interest in the proceedings of the Institute of Accountants since its inception, and it may fairly be said has done much to help it forward to its present position. We have done so simply because it is the duty of a public journal to educate public opinion for the weal of the community. Accountants' and auditors' work not many years ago was very perfunctorily performed ; professional men were largely the creation of the times rather than the outcome of technical training and knowledge, while there were shoals of laymen who without the slightest proper qualifications undertook delicate and important work with the utmost *sang froid*. This was a direct menace to the investing and trading public, and we foresaw that the founding of the Accountants Institute was an important step in the proper direction. We cannot say that in the past it has entirely realised our expectations, but possibly we have rather rigid notions as to the duties of such associations and their members. But it has done good work, and it would be a grievous pity indeed, as well as a public loss, if through desire for personal aggrandisment or from other motives, the Council of the Institute proceeding in an unconstitutional manner, creates dissensions amongst members, alienates public sympathy, and wrecks the work of a decade.

AUDITORS AND THEIR ASSOCIATIONS

AUDITORS AND THEIR ASSOOIATIONS. This is a question which has more than once been treated in our columns, as it is also a question of vital importance to the investing public. The protection given to shareholders and creditors by the Joint Stock Companies Acts has been proved, by events of recent years, to be so limited that it is not surprising that a movement with a view to more drastic legislation is current in England as well as here. In Victoria an Amending Act has been before more than one session of Parliament, and although the debates have shown a very clear case for reform, it is singular, to say the least, that none of the various bills have as yet become law. It looks very much like the exertion of a silent but strong opposition, by the very men who in public talk loudest of amendment. That, however, is rather beyond our present point. In England a committee of he Board of Trade is sitting to take into consideration amendments of Company Law. Both in the measure before the Victorian public and under the consideration of the Board of Trade, the question of audit and the responsibilities of auditors has great prominence. In another place we reprint from a leading financial paper, published in London, some most interesting remarks on this important subject, which are well worthy of perusal by the profession and investors   We do not expect the former to agree with all the argument, for unfortunately accountants and auditors here and in Great Britain seem very uncertain themselves as to their duties and their obligations. Indeed it is a matter of keen concern for the general public that the associations of the profession, which should be the most eager to improve the status, enlarge the authority, and safeguard the reputations of their members, do not exhibit a greater willingness to assist the legislatures. It is remarkable that they freely make suggestions as to what should not be in the various measures calculated to impose greater restriction upon auditors, but they, as a rule, show a wonderful want of unanimity in taking decisive action in relation to the qualifications and responsibilities of their members. The principal Victorian institution of accountants has, as our reports have shown, rather sought to enrol a large number of members than to raise the qualification. It certainly has not so far, as the public knows, taken any action in connection with the palpable shortcomings of auditors—

78

except in one or two most glaring cases. In Great Britain the standard is higher, but even there, there is a marked unwillingness to take the initiative in reform on the lines required. Beyond all this, there is the utter want of legal position by such societies. Their status is only determined by their membership, their fees, their examinations, and their age. This defect has been very ably brought into daylight by Mr. A. H. Gibson, who. at the conclusion of an article in the *Bankers' Magazine* (London), last year, made several practical suggestions for the improvement of audits and auditors, of which the following was one :—

" The office of auditor should be filled only by a member of a
" recognised and protected profession. A profession should be
" protected only when it is necessary that the public should have
" some guarantee that those on whose skill they are relying are
" qualified and honest. This is the justification for the restric-
" tions placed on the practice of law and medicine. Looking at
" the enormous capital of the public—totalling thousands of
" millions sterling—which is invested in joint-stock concerns, is
" it not a matter of public interest that the important duties of
" auditors in relation to this mass of public property should be
" undertaken only by men possessing the requisite skill and of
" undoubted integrity? The chartered accountants, endeavored
" to attain this end by constituting, in 1880, an institute under
" a Royal Charter, by making admission therein dependent on
" proof of technical skill and experience, and continuance there-
" in dependent on proper professional conduct. But a man can
" call himself an accountant and auditor, and practise as such,
" without being a member of the institute ; in fact another body
" has been incorporated, composed originally principally of
" practising accountants who could not comply with the con-
" ditions of admission laid down by the institute. Negotiation
" have been carried on with the view of the institute taking ove
" this new body ; but one objection thereto is that, unless
" Parliament will then hedge round the profession, a new body
" would spring up of those who were still outside the pale and
" could not climb over. How is the public to distinguish
" between a ' chartered accountant,' an ' incorporated accoun-
" tant ' and an ' accountant ' unattached ? In the public interest,
" the profession of auditors should be protected in the same way
" as that of solicitors. No one should be allowed to practise
" until he has given proof of the requisite skill ; and when any-
" one is shown to be unworthy of trust, or guilty of unprofessional
" conduct, the judges should be empowered to expel him from

" the profession." Conditions similar to those here outlined, prevail, or may obtain, in Victoria, and we are glad indeed to find so high an authority in perfect accord with the opinion this Journal has enunciated for years. To some extent it is urged in extenuation that action cannot well be taken by accountants' societies to exercise the desired rigid supervision over the actions of their members until the law shall accurately define the duties of auditors. The idea, however, that a hard and fast rule, or set of forms, should be laid down, behind which an auditor might, if he chose, shield himself from responsibility, according to the particular circumstances of the case, is, as a London contemporary has pointed out, wholly unacceptable. We know that there is a great difference of opinion amongst trained accountants as to what the work of auditors should cover, and this is a subject we propose to deal with later, but to put forward such matter of opinion as to details of duties in extenuation of the failure of accountants' societies to take proper steps to ensure the public having perfect confidence in the capacity and integrity of their members, is simply to drag a red herring across the trail. The amending Companies Act Bill before Parliament here, contains some very drastic provisions, we believe, in relation to auditors. Indeed, it is quite possible there may be a tendency to make the auditor the scapegoat for the "indiscretions" of other officials. What action is the principal local association taking in this matter? Has it successfully reached finality in its internal squabbles relating to its new Articles of Association? Has it obtained so many new recruits that it feels it can act with a reasonable chance of success? In fact, having in our opinion greatly impaired its own status, is it doing anything at all to protect its members and the public; —to justify its existence?

INSTITUTES OF ACCOUNTANTS

Institutes of Accountants. WE have received the report of the Council of the Incorporated Institute of Accountants of New Zealand, as presented to the third annual general meeting of the members held at Wellington on 27th August. The membership of the Institute is drawn from every considerable town, and the officers for 1896-97 are so distributed that the president (Mr. WM. BROWN), represents Dunedin, and the vice-president (Mr. A. M. OLIVER), Christchurch, while the members of the council are also the local committees of Auckland, Christchurch, Dunedin, Napier, and Wellington. The membership now numbers 104. In June last examinations were held, and ten candidates were successful, four becoming fellows, five associates, and one a student. From the able address of the president to the annual meeting we learn that in his opinion the articles of the Institute present no feature akin to unionism. He admitted that the Institute does not include in its membership all the able and trustworthy accountants of the colony, and in making the admission he really hit upon one of the serious blots upon institutes of accountants generally. These organisations necessarily partake more or less of the nature of trade, or, let us say professional, unions, tending to restrict employment in accountancy to their members only. But when it is reflected that, for instance, most of the balance-sheets of the bogus and mushroom companies of Melbourne, the administration of which has frequently been marked by the utmost unscrupulousness, have been signed from time to time by Fs.I.A.V., the pretensions of the institutes to a monopoly of accountancy and auditing work ought not to be encouraged. On the other hand there is a great deal to be said against incompetent men being employed, as well as against the hurtful notion that anybody who can keep a set of books, well or otherwise, is qualified to audit a balance-sheet or to investigate accounts. The public accountant and auditor ought unquestionably to be specially trained after acquiring a sound acquaintanceship with business principles. But the fact that he is a member of an institute which, by virtue of the use of a provision in the Companies Statute "incorporates" itself, although it is not incorporated in the sense in which the term is generally understood by the public, does not endue him with the necessary qualifications. The subject is a very difficult one. The public are entitled to the services of competent professional men, but at the same time they are not called upon to encourage the monopolising of a profession by an institute of which some of the members may be both incompetent and untrustworthy. Every effort made by the institutes of accountants to raise the *status* of the profession by the education of their members is laudable, but competent men who are averse to joining these institutes ought not to be regarded by the mercantile world as debarred from receiving employment. Let the best and most capable men, whatever organisation they may belong to, or even if they belong to none, be selected. The president of the New Zealand Institute referred to the gradual cutting-down of the work of the public accountant by Government interposition in various financial concerns, and he strongly protested against the proposal to put the audit of all limited liability companies in the hands of the Auditor-General. This proposal, we regret to say, has become law.

THE SYDNEY INSTITUTE OF PUBLIC ACCOUNTANTS

◆ P A P E R ◆

—ON—

"A Public Accountant's Work and Duties"

READ BY

MR. F.N. YARWOOD,

—ON—

Thursday Evening (9th June, 1898), at 8 p.m.

A PUBLIC ACCOUNTANT'S WORK AND DUTIES.

GENTLEMEN,—

Before applying myself to the particular paper I have the honor to read to you to-night, I should like to say a few words.

As you, probably, are aware, I am one of those who, through the kindness of the members of the Institute, has been put upon the Council. Someone here might think, therefore, that what I have to say to-night is the opinion of my brother Councillors. This is not so, nor have they been, in any way, asked as to how far I should go in the opinions I am about to express. The opinions herein given are my own. Whether Lord Salisbury keeps an equally loose check upon Mr. Joseph Chamberlain as the Council are doing upon me on this occasion will, of course, never be known here; I am certainly not vain enough to suppose that, what I am about to say, is likely to create a similar flutter in the Commercial Dovecot as that astute Birmingham gentleman sometimes does in diplomatic circles at his after-dinner speeches on the other side of the world. I trust there is someone here who will disagree with them so that a discussion may arise.

I was, some time ago, appointed one of the Lecture Committee of the Council of the Sydney Institute of Public Accountants, and, as such, have tried to do my duty by, upon all available opportunities, trying to persuade gentlemen of various positions to give us their views upon subjects, incidental to Accountancy, in this room, but, up to the present, have, I must honestly confess, not been as successful in this direction as I had hoped; partly, I think, in consequence of the fact that a great many in this part of the world look upon Accountants as a species of microbe who fatten upon the misfortune of others, or are simply an invention of the devil, or the Companies Acts, and, therefore, not perhaps deserving of that general attention that, perhaps, any other profession would secure without much trouble. In the American Senate I notice one gentleman describes a Public Accountant as a " Book-keeper out of a job," while, I may here say that it is one of the peculiarities of these parts that, whereas, in England, anyone out of a situation there, with a Commercial experience, starts as a Coal Agent; here the general rule is to start as a Public Accountant. This has not assisted to elevate the status of the profession. When I state that it is reported in one of the recent issues of the " Accountants' " Magazine that some enterprising gentleman has discovered that Auditors were known of in 1543, our ancient lineage is undoubted.

I shall try to-night for the benefit, if possible, of the juniors of the profession, to show that the calling is not such a simple one as the democracy of this country seem to imagine. My remarks are not specially directed in any one direction, but I will, as far as I can, cover the ground which has come under my personal observation during the course of my experience. The Accountant, to my mind, does not fatten upon other people's misfortunes, and, if he used to do so, which I do not admit for one instant, there is an invention in Sydney just at present made, or formed rather, for the express purpose of wiping us all out in this direction. Whether it is going to succeed in this object or not remains to be seen; personally speaking, from what I have heard myself, it seems that, like a child with a new toy, the patrons are about tired of it already—its real existence depends upon exactly what every one of us in this room has got to bear in mind on the ability to give value for money received. No letters after a man's name will ever secure him more than a temporary popularity, and, therefore, connection. There must be the real ability underneath it all to do the best possible in Clients' interests, or the Day of Judgment is not far ahead. I see many faults in the present law as affecting Assignments. I think myself that Assignments should be as absolutely secure for all creditors, and as fair as Bankruptcy, and that, where a debtor has suffered through misfortune only, and not through knavery, it is a fair thing that he should be saved the disgrace and annoyance that applies to all those who are unfortunate enough to get into the clutches of the law in this direction. Granted then that you have an unfortunate, but honest, debtor before you, you have to prepare his Statement and submit to Creditors' Meeting. Trustees are appointed; sometimes the Accountant; sometimes one or more of the creditors. It has always appeared to me that, as a general rule, it saves time and trouble, and therefore, expense, to appoint the Accountant Trustee (with a consulting Committee of Creditors if thought necessary); but you must not expect to be selected for this position unless those, whose interests are at stake, are satisfied that you will deal with the Estate in a common-sense business way; and here we come to another item that I wish to lay before you. To know what to do with an Assigned Estate, in order to get the best out of it, you must understand your business. *Your business is to understand every business*—not to run to lawyers over every little hitch that occurs, but to avoid complications as far as possible—and law, as you would the devil. You can only get this experience by a good training in an office where businesses of a varied nature are dealt with—and Study. To be a good Accountant necessitates your being thoroughly conversant with the requirements, if possible, of any and every business; to be able to show a man, if needs be, where he can do better than he is doing; how he can save money; how he can make it. This is the true sphere of the Accountant—not that of a semi-commercial policeman seeking whom he may devour by prying into this or that. You have to study the weak points, and there are some in every business. You have also to bear in mind that, if you spend too much time on the business, either your rate of charges must come down, or the Client will begin to think he is paying too much for his whistle.

One of our oldest Official Assignees here once said to me, what every business man knows to be the truth, that three-quarters of the Bankruptcies that take place are due to inefficient, or the absence of, book-keeping in the first instance. Speaking personally, I have derived a great deal more satisfaction and money from saving a man from himself and his creditors than ever I have from any "Assigned Estate" business. To do this you must thoroughly learn the art of financing; not as our Colonial Treasurers, do, gentlemen, although they do occasionally show surpluses, but in such a way as to show the owner of the business whether he is over-trading or not. I know of nothing harder than this—but the Accountant, who is worth his salt, has got to do it. There are more commercial wrecks through carrying too much sail in this direction, than through any other cause I know of. You generally hear it explained in the phrase—"Oh, the Bank shut down on me." The great scope there is for Accountants in this city is in this direction. Hundreds of businesses are controlled by men who thoroughly understand the goods they have to handle, and how to sell them, etc., but they will tell you they are not good at finance. Our Bankers in the past have not, to my mind, in their own interests I am speaking now, sufficiently applied the brake in this direction. I suppose competition in Banking circles is the excuse they would give, but, in England, things are different. Bankers there, I should think, are assailed with quite as much competition, and yet I know of lots of instances in which, before granting or continuing accommodation, Bankers there have insisted upon customers having their affairs gone into by a duly qualified Accountant. If, gentlemen, you fit yourselves for similar confidence upon the part of our Banking Kings in these parts, *and you can do this by close attention and study,* for which this Institute gives you all facilities, you will have given the only return to the Founders of the Institute which they can ever get or expect.

The Library here has now in it a large number of Books dealing with the intricacies and salient points of a good many businesses. It is our intention to add more and more to it as Funds will allow, and, by the time all of you have read all there is there now, it will be time, like Oliver Twist, to ask for more—but the Council will not wait until you have done that even. We have already a fresh lot on the way out. These include Books, where procurable, showing the nature and ruling of the Books for as many businesses as possible, and it behoves all and especially would-be Accountants to closely study these, so that, when called upon to advise a client, he has confidence enough in his own ability aud knowledge to be able to recommend any alternatives that will simplify matters without sacrificing clearness in expression with regard to any of the details in the working of a business. Remember the object of trade is to make money for the worker ; not book-keeping for a staff of clerks ; or work for the Accountant. Therefore, always throw your influence on the side of economy in Book-keeping as well as everything else, even, although it may be, you reduce your personal importance apparently thereby. My own personal experience is that, in large offices, as a rule, you can often save more than your own fees by alterations tending to economy in the Book-keeping; in small offices, as a rule, memory is more often relied on—Single Entry, and what not, which generally result in such looseness in method as resolves itself into losses later on. The happy medium is what is wanted, and this the Accountant ought to be able to supply.

The first thing to find out is exactly what information it is necessary to supply in order to satisfactorily conduct the business, and then get at this by such a method as will give the result with the minimum of labour. It is not always easy to do this, but, with care, thought and experience, it is to be done. While, on this point, I may add that the most valuable hints I ever got in my life in this direction, have been obtained from the staff who have had the Book-keeping to do, but who often do not get their own way with the books they have to work because their chief is wedded to the old system which has been in vogue in his office for so many previous years. There is no detail hardly that is not worth listening to from the average book-keeper in an office who has, what I call, lived and slept with the books for years past perhaps with which you have to deal. And here a word of caution. Never try to alter an existing system until you are absolutely satisfied that the one suggested by you is an improvement. The old motto of " Better the devil you know than one you don't " is always present in the mind of the average business man.

Now a word as to Balance Sheets. Private people will often get you to sign a Balance Sheet for them after you have gone through it. You are satisfied as to the general honesty of the whole thing perhaps, but there may be certain allowances for depreciation, etc., that you would have insisted on in the case of a

Company, which have not been made, as it is the man's own Balance Sheet made out for himself, and, therefore, you do not see any necessity to insist on it.   In these cases, I would advise you to put some comment on the foot of the Balance Sheet so that, in the event of any third person (about to take an interest, say) being shown the figures, he will have only himself to blame if he does not obtain permission from the principal concerned to see you respecting.

If F.S.I A. and A.S.I.A. are to be made of any value in this City, they can only be so by faithful, steady work, and I think, in this direction, we should be more than careful that no carelessness on our part should be answerable for reducing the value of this Hall Mark, as we are going to try and make it, I hope, in the Commercial World.   Some people might argue that "You are not to blame, etc."; those individuals are your worst enemies in ninety-nine cases out of a hundred, because they put you off your guard, or have a tendency that way.   The Public should look upon an Accountant's Certificate, not like a legal document, etc., say in which it may be material where the commas and stops come in, but as a Guarantee which he, who runs may read that, in his judgment, which is a skilled unbiassed one, the statement is a full and fair one; and while, therefore, it might be argued that you had signed the Balance Sheet of your private friend mentioned above, in all good faith, you may have innocently assisted him to take an advantage of someone by omitting to add certain words showing how the values, etc., were got at.   While on this part of my subject, I might, perhaps, with advantage, add a few words on the subject of tact—ending this paper with a few very short directions on the subject of Audits, Company and otherwise.

One thing an Accountant must have is tact.   You may remember the three great virtues mentioned in Holy Scripture, as necessary for a successful apostle, were "Faith, Hope, and Charity, but the greatest of these is Charity."   I do not often quote Scripture, gentlemen, but it seemed to me in this case fitting to say that, to be a good Accountant, you must have also three virtues at least—"Patience, Energy, and Tact," but the greatest of these is "Tact."   It shows itself always in the way men go about things.   Some, I hear, go into their sphere of action like a whirlwind and come out generally with the average luck of the man who tries to boss everybody he comes in contact with.   I do not mean to say that I have heard of this gentry in Sydney, but I have heard of such things, and I have never yet heard of anyone achieving phenomenal success by such a process.

Some people think that all the duty of an Auditor consists of is to sign a Balance Sheet and draw his fees, and go home and be happy, considering himself about the best paid man in the whole concern. My New South Wales experience is that our profession is, for the risks we regularly run, one of the worst paid—not the best. If the Balance Sheets could speak, gentlemen, they would and could very often tell a very different tale. I remember one instance, some years ago, in which I was paid three guineas for auditing a Balance Sheet. It was said when the appointment was made it might take me an hour. It would not have taken that if the gentleman, who drew it up, had understood his business. He did not. I had to square it for him. I did so on three different occasions, and then, as I had begun to get tired of educating him, or trying to, I applied for an increased fee in consideration of the work involved. I did not take much trouble about the business, as I had explained matters to the principal man concerned, but you may judge of my astonishment when I received a letter to say that my services had been dispensed with. They evidently mistook mê for a sort of Benevolent Asylum or Hospital for crippled Balance Sheets. They got some one else, of course ; that was easy enough, but it is some consolation to me to remember, without being spiteful, that they only lasted eighteen months after they made the change ; not that I pretend that I could have averted the close up, but I simply give this as an illustration of one of the things that impressed me with the necessity for tact in this business. If I had had tact I should have been exactly another year on that three-guinea job, and then have had sense enough to leave it to someone else to finish up with. Auditing is a profession, as known in this country, which is open to all-comers. It is a sort of a " Go as you please " business, and here, again, I am reminded of a story of a bit of personal experience. A gentleman having a vote for one of the large Audits here, which is put up to popular vote, asked me if I was going up. I said " No." He said : " Thought you were. If you were I would have voted for you." I proceeded to discuss the different candidates, and tried to explain their various qualifications, but my friend said : " Oh, so and so is a friend of yours, is he ? " I replied I had that honor. He said, " All right, I'll vote for him ; I don't care a ——— for his qualifications." Gentlemen, " Of such is the election of Auditors here."

Municipal Government in New South Wales has, take it all round, been almost an absolute failure. It has, I venture to think, been more extravagant than any Commission could have been, and, except in the erection of Town Halls, seldom, if ever, wanted, and certainly never justified, and the accumulation of debts, involving Interest Charges, absorbing, in many cases, best part of the Rates, has signally failed to carry out the object of all Municipal Expenditure, which should be to afford the inhabitants, etc., of a town the maximum of comfort and sanitary arrangements with the minimum of expense. This we can partly trace, I think, to the class of individual generally selected for the position of Alderman, and, when this is so, is it at all surprising that these gentlemen should pick Auditors, or arrange for their election, whose chief qualification is their utter ignorance of the work they ought to do, or that they ought to insist upon being done. I may say here in order to remove any wrong impression, that these remarks of mine in no way apply to the Sydney Council, the Auditors of which are two of the Members of our Institute, but, even in their case, judging as far as one can from the published evidence that was given at the enquiry recently held, it seems to me that any recommendations that were made need not have been, and, as a matter of fact, were not paid any considerable amount of attention to. The gentleman who seems to have stirred up the Council in this respect, more even than that mercurial gentleman of unlimited language who figures largely there now, was the late Treasurer, but his process of "stirring" is too expensive to allow of repetition.

Since I wrote the foregoing a Report from the Sub-committee of the Council has been published.

This report, gentlemen, would carry more weight in my mind had it been the verdict of an outside impartial authority; it, at any rate, carries self-condemnation in every line of it as far as the Aldermen are concerned, and, for one, I should be very glad to see legal proceedings arise out of the notorious " No. 2 Account," so that we could rely on getting a really impartial and judicial ópinion as to who was and was not to blame. Laying blame on an Auditor for not discovering what, they agree, might have been disclosed by accident, does not seem to me exactly fair play. It means that an Auditor's success must depend not so much on his ability, but his luck, and the handling of the evidence alone in this case, to say the least of it, has, from a public point of view, been unsatisfactory. I do not think, however, at this stage it would be fair to go deeply into the matter, as even, in the Council itself, the report is still *sub judice*.

At this particular point it is not out of place, I think, to read you a letter which appeared in the Press some little time back, written by our friends, Messrs. Starkey and Starkey, on the subject of Municipal Auditors :—

Empire-chambers, 93 York-street, Sydney, August 23.—Sir,—In connection with the paragraph recently calling attention to the qualifications of Municipal Auditors, it may be of interest to note that the 22 Auditors of Suburban Municipalities whose names appear in this year's Directory comprise one of each of the following occupations :—One carpenter, one Custom-house agent, one accountant, one poultry farmer, one potter, one surgeon, one bookbinder, one draper, and one bank manager, and that the occupation of the remaining 13 is not disclosed.

Yours faithfully, STARKEY and STARKEY.

Need I say, after all this, that I have never been as yet honored by the appointment as Auditor to any Municipality in this Colony. I think not, but one thing I can honestly add, and that is, that I hope I shall never be while there is any risk of having as a co-Auditor some well-meaning gentleman whose qualifications to divide fees are undoubted, but whose knowledge of " simple book-keeping even " is confined to the making out of Weekly Bills against his customers from books kept upon very " Single Entry " principles. I may here mention, however, just to relieve the monotony, that the race is not always with the swift, or the battle with the strong. My wife tells a story of a wonderful baker who would persist, until she went elsewhere, and, therefore, ceased to take any further interest in his methods, used regularly to charge her with two loaves a week more than we ever had. I can quite understand that a gentleman of this class would be a great acquisition to some of the Councils if they could rely upon him only exercising his peculiar talent in their favor always and in all directions. The danger would be when he got out of bounds, as we used to say at school. In any case, however, I doubt very much whether he would want me as a co-Auditor even if I were disposed to occupy the position. There is such a thing, gentlemen, as being too keen an observer—and too keenly observed—and I am rather afraid his previous experience of my family would be more than sufficient to satisfy even this gentleman's cravings in this particular direction. However, we can let these possibilities pass.

I have little to say on the subject of Life Insurance Audits, beyond what I said some time back in a paper I had the honor of reading before you on the subject of the Victorian Companies' Act. These Audits should be severe, well paid, and above suspicion, *and I have no sympathy whatever with the ruling craze for appointment of Auditors by Public Vote.*

There are too many individuals in this world like my good friend, whom I previously mentioned, who are quite prepared to " dam a man's qualifications." The common sense of the situation should be that the qualifications be everything, and, if this system is to continue, really I am strongly in sympathy with those who advocate a State Audit for these Institutions—much as I dislike any State interference, because of its liability to tout for political popularity in its appointments. I cannot picture a greater disaster to a community than that any important Life Insurance Society should get into difficulties. In one case recently I was only too glad to see that some of the Members of our Institute had, I think we might almost call it, patriotism enough to face the ordeal, but the result has almost made me wish that the time was ripe for the Members of this Institute to stand aloof from the thing altogether till the method of appointment was made on a par with that of the Directors, or altered in such a way as to bring into play more of the common sense of the Policy Holders. Perhaps the mildest reform, and, therefore, the best to advocate would be to give the Directors the right to appoint one of the auditors. Whether a Certificated Auditor, or not, I have confidence enough in the Board to think that, for their own sakes, they would select *the best man available in their opinion,* and the constant change amongst themselves would prevent any fear of the thing becoming too much of a family party business.

I now pass to Company Audits. I do not propose to more than skim the subject. It is too deep, too varied, to be treated by me this evening in any more than a brief manner, and I hope no one here will blame me, therefore, for omitting many points that must occur to most of us as of importance to our profession.

In a Company's Audit the Auditor is appointed to see that :

1st. The Balance Sheet is correct.

2nd. That it states the position as clearly as possible.

3rd. That the Directors, etc., have carried out their duties in a *bona-fide* manner to the Shareholders, and with due regard to the objects and intentions of the Company.

And the special peculiarity about the business is that often his fee is fixed upon a similar basis to that of an ordinary laborer, while he is supposed to bring to bear on the subject the brain of a know-all and be-all.

The first and second duties, mentioned above, call for little or no comment, except that in the first instance, as a rule, it is necessary to remember that various matters affecting the Balance Sheet at the inception of a Company arise that considerably increase the responsibilities and work of the Auditor, and, as a general rule, although you can return the Balance Sheet for amendment as often as you like, it being no part of an Auditor's duty to draft the Balance Sheet, still, in the end, I believe in most cases you will find that, ultimately, it is shorter and easier to set matters right yourself.

With regard to the third clause, dealing with the Directors, there are many here who might argue that I had enlarged the duties of the Auditor. I may have done so, but, from what I have seen, as a rule, when people lose money they throw the blame on to any one but themselves, and my own conviction is that, if you cannot get your views attended to, and paid attention to, so as to right the ship if you can, if you see that the Management is running her on to the rocks in spite of all protests, even although it may not strictly be your duty to actively try and stop it, you had better get out, for if the crash does come later on, whatever you may have done, some indignant individual will arise who will point out that you have left undone something you ought to have done. Every man does something of this nature every week if the experience of the compilers of the Book of Common Prayer goes for anything, and I do not for one instant contend that the average Accountant is a being who cannot and will not make mistakes.

In the foregoing paragraph, I may state, in order to avoid any chance of misconception, that I am, of course, *only here referring to cases where, not fraud, but errors of judgment, to a more or less degree*, in your opinion, are present. In cases of distinct fraud, of course, it is your duty to acquaint those interested without hesitation.

Some few years ago, you will remember, some Building Societies went smash. The majority of these deserved no better fate. A Corporation that carries on business on the lines they did could expect nothing else. Well, if ever I am called upon to audit such as these in future, I hope 1 shall have sense enough to try and bring the Company on to a common-sense basis first if I can, or there is a possibility, and, if not, then that my name will disappear from its Balance Sheet.

Perhaps some gentleman here might say "Rats," but if there be one who says or thinks so, permit me to point out that the Auditor's position is something like that of a Doctor giving a clean bill of health to a patient; he may fence the question as much as he likes, but, if the patient is wrong in any serious respect, the Doctor is expected to say so. Gentlemen, as Auditors, so are you, if the operations of the concern you are going into fail to meet with your ideas. If a Doctor recommends a patient a certain course, and the patient does not take it, what does the Doctor do? Throw up the case of course, and so can you, and so ought you in my humble opinion. Tact will come in there as to how to do it. No man has a right to wreck a concern; remember that; never be too cocksure that your own opinion is the right one, and it is in complicated cases that may occur to you in your professional career, that you may find the Council of the Accountant's Institute will be of service. It is impossible to lay down general rules. There can be no rules except the one "do what is right"; but, when you get into a difficulty, if ever you do, you can lay the case before the Council. You need not mention names, although you may rely upon the absolute secrecy of the Members of the Council in any case even if you did, and then, if you want it, you will get their support and assistance. Gentlemen, we are all here to help one another—not like a lot of savage beasts that, after consuming their prey, will turn and rend one another. No, the field at present is wide enough to ensure indemnity from that. Companies' Audits are curious things. Some Secretaries and Managers think that the Audit ought to be as they think fit; that is, they, and not you, should say what ought to be gone through. In these cases, I strongly recommend you to go through what is offered first, and take what you want further afterwards. Never be put off anything material. If you are seriously blocked at any stage, or thwarted in any way, look out; and, while on this subject, I may add that there are difficulties often in Auditing that you cannot get all the books you want at once, and sometimes they are not ruled off, and there are all the risks of you checking an item, and its being afterwards added to or altered. Tick things as far as you can in these cases, so that you can, if possible, recognize your own ticks. Take matters at random in all directions ; if you can get a separate room to yourself and your assistant, and, in these cases, more particularly, watch the conduct of those who have had to do with the books. If they show the slightest anxiety about your movements, look out for squalls. In these cases, where cookery has been, or is being resorted to, by a clever scoundrel, you will want all your wits about you. I heard of a case once in Melbourne, where the Auditors passed half the securities before lunch on more than one occasion, and the balance after lunch. The Secretary, in this case, had pledged the second half, but used to get the first lot passed ; redeem the second with the first while the Auditors were away, and thus be enabled to produce the necessary quantity every time without exciting suspicion. Well, I am not going to suggest you go without your meals—nothing so awful—, but see that these tricks are not played on you. Never, I may add, show that you are suspicious of anyone ; let them think you are a silly old fool if they like, but, under it all, let your scent be as keen as a fox. Lull them into a false idea of security in case where you "have your doubts," and, probably, you will see through the whole scheme before your very innocent friend thinks you have the slightest suspicion. I may here add that I have never seen a case yet where fraud was present and a careful, thorough audit would not have discovered it. I, perhaps, am inclined to be a bit old fashioned, but I like always to go through all entries where a business is not too large, and where it is large you have all the security of the necessity for there to be collusion before anything can be cooked for your inspection and the cook's profit. In large concerns, and small ones too, study the habits of those whose work you have to deal with and try, if you can, to persuade the people owning the business to give all their staff every year at least a week's holiday, if possible, more, and at uncertain dates. A gentleman who has anything to be afraid of, generally, you will find, is the last one that was suspected—and such a good man, too, never neglected his work, probably attended church regularly, and would not go for a holiday even. I do not mean, for one moment, to say that you need be suspicious of anyone, but your duty and mission is to find flaws in the conduct of the business, and, if the Managing man be any good, he will be only too happy to accept any suggestions you may make to him in the direction of keeping his officers from falling into the very serious blunder of thinking they are not being supervised. No honest man ever wishes to be insulted, but I never saw one yet who was not almost anxious for the Auditor to go through his work. As a professional Accountant, and, therefore, at any time, likely to be called upon to Audit a Company's affairs, *never hold any shares*. Should qualification be necessary under the Articles, take the minimum quantity and do not sell because you afterwards have doubts. Better make a loss than get a reputation for having saved your own skin at other's expense.

In Company Audits you have many things to bear in mind. Whether dividends ought to be declared ; whether writings off are adequate, and so on—and any fault there may be in this direction may be, with the best of us, an error of judgment ; but there is one thing, when in doubt, see that the whole situation is shewn clearly to every Shareholder on the Balance Sheet, and then, I think, you may say roughly that you are on the right side. Never let the question of whether you will lose an audit or not affect you in your decision for one moment. Do your duty whatever the consequence, and, in the end, I am satisfied you will agree with the writer of that famous proverb—" Honesty is the best policy." Gentlemen, *it is the only policy*, and we have not the same excuse for allowing circumstances to carry us away as ordinary Directors have. You have probably often noticed the average mother thinks her baby is the best in the world. You would undoubtedly be quite on the right side to tell them so, is my experience, at any rate. Well, please remember that those involved in a business always think better of it (not worse) than they might fairly be expected to. I have often said, and I believe it, that no traveller was ever worth his salt who did not think (whether rightly or wrongly) that the goods he was dealing in were the best; that the firm he is travelling for merit the same adjective, and that he, like the American Nation in their own estimation, is the " best " also. I believe the proper adjective is "top loftiest." I will and can safely, I think, say the same of the average man of any go and push who has to manage a business. Well, be careful not to damp his ardour, but do not be carried away by it. You can listen to all he says, but, in the words of that song which was so ably rendered recently in one of the theatres, " Don't jump at your conclusions." In all cases, where you can, check gross profits made in any business. It is often a steady and good guide as to whether the result is what it should be, and, although no man can expect you to discover *everything, whether appearing in the books or not,* you should remember always that it is *your duty to be the maximum of assistance to your Client,* whoever he may be, *at a fair rate of remuneration ;* and, while on this question of remuneration, let me say that if you cannot get a fair fee for work done, tell your Client the position in lieu of slumming your work and leaving him in a false state of fancied security on account of your supervision. In ninety-nine cases out of a hundred you will find men reasonable on this subject.

I have recently come across the "Accountant " for 2nd April, 1898, in which Mr. Whinney's Examination before the House of Lords Select Committee is reported. With your permission, I propose to read therefrom a paragraph which appears to me to have a most important bearing on my subject to-night—

" THE WHOLE DUTY OF AN AUDITOR."

" The Bill cast upon Auditors—the duty of checking the
" Balance Sheet, including the amount of debts due to the
" Company after making a proper deduction for debts con-
" sidered to be bad or doubtful. It would be impossible for
" the Auditors to do that in the case of large Companies
" where the debtors numbered, say 1,000. In the case of
" Banks, for instance, where the number of debtors was very
" large, it was found necessary to keep an aggregate account
" of debtors, showing the total amount due to the Company
" by its debtors. The Auditors would have to take that
" Account, and schedules would be prepared, and, if
" necessary, would be tested afterwards. The duty should
" not be thrown upon Auditors of checking every
" balance. In one case he might mention the debtors
" numbered 750,000. (Laughter). It should be sufficient

" if they gave a certificate to the effect that they had used
" all reasonable care and diligence in ascertaining that the
" Balance Sheet was true."

" LORD DAVEY : I should like to ask whether you conceive it
" to be the proper duty of an Auditor to say not only
" whether the books are properly kept, but to go into
" questions behind the books, and say whether the assets are
" properly valued ? I do not know that I can give a better
" definition of the duties of the Auditor than that laid down
" by Lord Justice Lindley. He said that it was the duty
" of an Auditor to be honest, to exercise all reasonable care
" and skill to ascertain that that which he certifies is true,
" and to exercise all reasonable care and skill in ascertaining
" the truth."

" LORD FARRER : That is all very well ; but what is the truth
" which he is to ascertain ? LORD DAVEY : Yes, that is it.
" Can he, for instance, when the properties are valued at a
" certain sum in the books, and on the face of the books are
" properly valued, can it be his duty, not being a valuer, to
" go into the question of value and say that the Directors
" have put too high a value on the real estate ? No, I do
" not think so. It would be giving the Auditor a different
" position from that which it was contemplated he should
" have—namely, that he should examine the accounts of
" the Directors and see whether they are correct. Anything
" calculated to arouse his suspicion, he ought, of course,
" to look into."

" LORD FARRER : After all, the responsibility lies with the
" Directors ? Not altogether with the Directors. There
" are the Managers of the Company."

" LORD FARRER : Do you wish to place the Auditor in the
" position of an Administrator, who is to check the
" Directors in their management of the Company ? Certainly
" not."

" LORD DAVEY : Is not the sounder principle this—that the
" Auditor is bound to know everything the books tell him,
" to have all the suspicions that the books suggest, and to
" make all the inferences to what he finds in the books
" would lead him ? I think that would cover the whole of
" his duty. I think it is his duty not to certify a Balance
" Sheet until he believes it to be true, and he has taken all
" reasonable care that it is so. He is bound to see that
" the Balance Sheet is brought before the Shareholders in
" such a form that they themselves can exercise their
" judgment upon it."

"PAINS AND PENALITES OF AUDITORS."

" The next suggestion that he had to make was that the
" pains and penalties of Auditors should be modified. At
" present the Auditor was supposed to be responsible if
" dividends were paid out of capital. LORD DAVEY : Is
" he ? I never knew it. THE LORD CHANCELLOR : Put-
" ting aside fraudulent connivance, what do you suppose
" to be the responsibility of an Auditor ? THE WITNESS :
" That if dividends have been paid out of capital,
" assuming, of course, that the Company is wound up, the
" Directors and Auditors are responsible for the amount of
" the dividends so paid, subject to the statutory limitations
" in favor of the Auditors. LORD DAVEY : Where do you
" find that ? THE LORD CHANCELLOR : I am not aware of
" any such law. I am not aware of any case in which the
" innocent mistake of a Director has been held to be the
" subject for an action. THE WITNESS : There was a case
" before Mr. Justice Stirling. LORD DAVEY : There there
" was fraudulent connivance. THE WITNESS : I think there
" was not connivance, but that the Auditor himself was
" ignorant. THE LORD CHANCELLOR : To me it is a
" startling suggestion that for an innocent mistake an
" Auditor should be liable."

" After the usual interval for lunch, Mr. Whinney produced
" certain books in which a case was reported, which, he
" maintained, had a bearing upon the statement which he
" had just made. The Lord Chancellor examined the
" volume, and, while expressing no absolute opinion, he
" indicated that, in his view, the witness had misunder-
" stood the existing state of the law."

"LIABILITY OF AUDITORS."

" On Clause 34, which provides that if any Director or
" Auditor of a Company knowingly violates any of the
" provisions of this Act with regard to accounts and
" audit, he shall be guilty of a misfeasance within the
" meaning of Section 10 of the Companies Winding-up
" Act, the witness said that he did not see that a clause of
" this sort was needed. Lord Davey said that he, too, was
" disposed to think the clause was unnecessary. Mr.
" Whinney said that the effect of the whole of the
" suggestions he had made in this connection was that, if
" an Auditor was to be punished, he should be fined, not

" by being made liable for the whole of the amount of the
" dividends paid out of capital, but that the fine should be
" limited to a certain number of times the annual fee he
" received. An Auditor, he pointed out, had no interest
" whatever in the payment of dividends out of capital,
" and it was quite possible that such payment might be
" made by mistake. It was impossible for an Auditor to
" overlook the whole of the work done by his clerks, and
" therefore he thought the justice of the case would be met
" by limiting, as he had suggested, the penalty to a certain
" number of times the Auditor's fee."

" LORD DAVEY : I think you said you thought it was the
" duty of an Auditor, if he knew that a debt was over-
" valued, and ought to be put down as depreciated, to call
" attention to that fact. Do you think that if he failed
" to do that he ought to be liable to the Shareholders? It
" is a question of degree. Supposing it were a very
" important debt I think he ought to be liable. I can
" give you an instance illustrative of this question of
" degree, which arose in the case of a bad bank failure.
" The bank had included in its assets a debt due by a firm
" which, in the books of the Company, was divided into
" two parts—one part was a live debt and the other was a
" dead debt. I do not think that the Balance Sheets of
" the Company were audited ; but, if they had been, it
" would have been the duty of the Auditors to object to
" such a course, to tell the Directors in the first instance,
" and, if that failed, to make the matter known to
" the Shareholders. Do you think that if the Auditor
" had failed to report this matter he ought to have been
" liable ? Yes ; I think he should have been made liable
" for negligence. I take it that, if a man accepts the
" position of Auditor, he is bound to exercise that position
" with reasonable care and skill, and if he fails to do so
" he ought in some way to be punished."

In conclusion I may add that, if you find any man's affairs
in such a state that he is undoubtedly insolvent, it is your duty to
impress upon him the absolute necessity under our Bankruptcy
Laws of not going on incurring other liabilities. He may, of
course, carry on with the consent of his then creditors as
long as he does not run up new debts and let one of the " in the
know " creditors take advantage of someone not equally posted
as to the position ; but it is very seldom, if ever, wise under these
circumstances, I think.

You will often, perhaps, be asked to look after what I might call "Proprietary Companies," generally consisting of one creditor and the required number of single shareholders in order to meet the requirements of the Act. Some such invention is necessary to meet special cases. There can be no objection to these Corporations as long as they do not take large or prolonged credit. The Registrar regularly receives particulars, and anyone intending to give credit can always easily obtain the particulars of the special position. If you are acting as Director it is, of course, always safer to pay cash for everything, but not always feasible for many reasons; but, in these cases, always be open, and you may rely upon the Trade Protection people informing the general public fully—in some cases, perhaps, a little more than fully. It seems to me a very good provision, and not one that can be objected to, seeing the convenience the restricted liability of the Limited Liability Act is to the trading community, that it should be imperative that every Company should be compelled to exhibit a copy of their Balance Sheet—not necessarily the Profit and Loss Account—in some public place on the premises where the business is carried on.

Now, a word with regard to the Examinations in order to fit yourselves for the Institute. My advice is "Don't be frightened of them," and do not neglect to take advantage of the status the passing of it will always give you in any part of the world, no matter where your lot may be cast or what you may take in hand. There was a saying a few years ago : "Always learn a trade." My advice is : "Get your Certificate as a qualified Accountant." It may come in handy when you least expect it, and is always a mark of an earnest desire to be at the top. Things in these Colonies, some people say, are "overdone." I remember reading once a story of an American gentleman, who remarked to his son who had made that self-same remark : "They always are, my boy, but there is plenty of room on the top." To you all here, I can safely say : "There is room on the top" in our profession still, and I sincerely hope you will all try and fit yourselves for the box-seats. Some, of course, will have to go inside, but, if you persistently bear in mind that the other fellow must do that, not you, and, if you remember that sheer merit is the only way to get on the box-seat, you will not be last in the race unless I am very much mistaken. After this you will not expect me to give you a hint as regards how, in my opinion, you can make the Examinations easier, or increase your chances of getting through, but I will try to all the same. When you get your paper bear in mind that the time is limited in which you have to answer the different questions. Read carefully through it first, mark off those you can answer without any difficulty, and do these first ; then take those you have the least doubts about, and so on. This will ensure you getting the benefit of all you know, and avoids what often happens—that candidates tackle some of the harder conundrums first, and then have not sufficient time left to do justice to themselves in some of the questions they thoroughly understand. There may be some questions which you must answer, but these will be always specially referred to as such in the papers. In reading through the books on the various subjects you have to go through, take notes of points you may see therein of importance that you did not know before, and write them out yourself so as to impress them on your memory, and, before you go up for the Examination, read through these points carefully. Here, perhaps, it is fitting to tell you that in making your notes it is not necessary to imitate the small boy who on going into an office to make a start in life was given a slate on which to put down anything of importance which he must not forget. His master, on going round the office the first day he was there, was somewhat surprised to find that the only note made for a start was "leave at six." I think it is better if you get some one to read with you ; a few minutes' conversation on a particular point will impress the facts upon your memory. Do not go up for the examination before you feel that you are ready, and if at first you don't succeed try again—and, if necessary, again. It is a thousand to one that he, who passes first go off will, in the end, not know as much of the particular points pertaining to our profession as he who has the pleasure, I will call it, of reading for several examinations, so do not let failure cause you to lose your pluck.

Perhaps it is as well for me to mention that very great stress is paid to the " Practical Book-keeping " paper. It must be obvious to you, gentlemen, that no man can be an Accountant, or ought to be passed as such, who does not thoroughly understand practical book-keeping in all its varied phases. " The blind cannot lead the blind." How, therefore, can it be expected that the Institute can overlook any weakness in this respect ? If the Examiners were disposed to do so they would weaken the value of your Certificate when you did get it, and thus be doing you an injury. Well, what I have to say on this subject is that, if your particular daily work only brings a limited variety of accounts under your particular notice, I strongly recommend you to study the books that have been written on Advanced Book-keeping, or get a coach who has had more varied experience than yourself. You may rely upon me when I say you cannot know too much in this direction.

At this point, gentlemen, perhaps you will allow me to relate a bit of personal history. I remember distinctly, my father, after punishing me for something I had done, said I had a lot to learn. I thought so with him at the time—it occurred to me even then it would take a lot of very careful thought to discover a way of sitting down without pain, but I never said so. Perhaps, after what I have said to-night, some here may think they have a lot to learn before they can hope to be full-fledged Accountants. If some have discovered that this is so, and they take the best steps to remedy their want of knowledge by some cheaper process than paying for their experience (by which I mean studying other people's in the various works affecting our profession that have been written from time to time). I am more than satisfied, and if there be any here who, after hearing this, are inclined to despair and think they can never acquire the necessary knowledge, I will add, in spite of the risk of being accused of egotism, that I still agree with my father as I did in days of old, only for a different reason. I have still lots to learn, and suppose it will ever be so right on to the end. This feeling, I may add, need never engender despair ; it will rather make us all tolerant and anxious to hear the opinions of others, and it is with a view to eliciting these on any of the matters contained herein, that I ventured to hope no gentleman here present will hesitate to ask any question, or venture any criticism he thinks fit.

In finally closing I should like to say a few words in answer to the very natural query that may arise in some of your minds, and that is—Why should you bother about joining the Institute when you have heard that "ability" and not letters after a man's name is the necessary element to make a good Accountant？ My reply is that passing the Examination is a proof that you have that ability, and, if you like to take a jump into the deep waters of commercial competition without using the spring-board, then you don't know enough, as some put it, to be able to decide when to come in out of the rain. The work the Council of this Institute has to get through in the next few years is the very large one of impressing on the mind of the Government and Public here in all directions the absolute advisability of—on all " Audits "—having one professional Auditor who has been tried and not found wanting in a knowledge of his work. That duty the Council will not shirk. It is one the Accountants of England, etc., have, as you know, with great success been engaged on through their Institute for years past, but it is very hard here and takes time, to avoid giving the impression that we are grinding our own axes only, and you, gentlemen, who have not yet arrived at that stage which involves sitting on the Council will, when you do—and I wish every one of you that luck—realise what I mean when I say we have " a hard row to hoe," but you can support us, and I hope you will, by proving that in you yourselves there is that *extra ability* for Auditing and other Accountancy work which we are contending the Professional has over the Amateur.

THE INCORPORATED INSTITUTE OF ACCOUNTANTS, VICTORIA

The more general portions of the annual report for 1897 of the Incorporated Institute of Accountants, Victoria, are presented on another page. As a society for the promotion of interchange of views and of joint action on great questions affecting accountancy, the *raison d'être* of the Institute is perfect. But as an attempt to establish an exclusive right to a profession, we have never admired it, and have always hoped that Parliament will never be induced to recognise any claim to such exclusiveness. Public accountancy is not a profession to be hedged by legislative prescriptions and exclusiveness. That there are many able public accountants and auditors in Melbourne is beyond all doubt, and it has been a matter for surprise to us that they have expended effort on plans which could only have the result of "watering" the profession at their own cost. The Institute has necessarily, and we quite believe in a *con amore* spirit, found itself obliged to establish an excellent system of examinations, which if it were universal in Victoria would certainly tend to raise the status of the profession. The encouragement thus given to aspirants to swell the ranks has militated against the interests of some of the older members of the Institute, and to that extent any desire to monopolise has been frustrated. Moreover, the Institute when it was established did not, and as a matter of fact could not, include all practising accountants and auditors, and many of those who could not, and those who would not be admitted, became members of other institutions, one or two of which do not stand particularly high. When the new Companies Bill was passed it was deemed necessary in the provisions for audit to recognise not only the several institutions but also outsiders—it may be said "rank outsiders," who could satisfy a board appointed by Government that they possessed, not necessarily sufficient ability, but sufficient qualification. The results are very unsatisfactory, and

Victorian Government, in its professed desire to provide that auditors of public companies shall be qualified, has distinctly lowered the profession of the public auditor. Companies can, of course, select their auditors, but the pretensions of a candidate must be enhanced, especially in the eyes of ignorant directors (a numerous class), by his possession of a Government certificate. A distinct blow has thus been administered by the Parliament of Victoria to efficiency in an important manner. It was not wonderful, therefore, that the council of the Incorporated Institute of Accountants "views with great alarm the inevitable lowering of the standard and status of future entrants into the profession," and that it expects that the number of applicants for admission to the Institute by examination will be affected by the ease with which the Government license can be obtained. Under all the circumstances, it appears to us unwise for the Institute to prepare a bill for the recognition of practising accountants as a profession for submission to Parliament. The council would discharge a more important service to the members, as well as to the public, if it could prevail upon Parliament to ex-punge from the Companies Act of 1896 the provisions made for the recognition and licensing of companies' auditors.

BANKERS' MAGAZINE OF AUSTRALASIA

[NOVEMBER 15, 1898, pp.242-7]

INTERESTING ADDRESS TO YOUNG ACCOUNTANTS

By the President of the Incorporated Accountants Students' Society (Victoria)

ᴥ ᴥ ᴥ

THE inaugural address delivered to the members of the above society, was delivered by Mr. Thomas Brentnall, F.I.A.V., President, on Wednesday, 12th October, 1898. He said: Gentlemen, it becomes my first duty to thank the members of the Incorporated Accountants Students' Society, Victoria, for the honour they have conferred upon me by electing me as their first President. I, of course, recognise that this distinction has been bestowed upon me by virtue of my position as President of the Institute for this year, but I can assure you that, whether in my official or private capacity as a member of the body of accountants, I shall always watch with great interest the progress of your society, and shall, at all times, be glad to render you any help which lies in my power.

My next duty is to recognise the invaluable assistance which has been rendered by Mr. Walker, who, I am pleased to see, has been appointed one of your Vice-Presidents. To him mainly is due the credit for the inception of this society, and if I may venture to give you, at this early stage, a little friendly advice, it is to retain him as one of your co-adjutors and advisers as long as you can.

The necessity and wisdom of the institution of such a society as yours go without saying. As an adjunct to the work connected with your preparation for the examinations of the Institute, its value cannot be overestimated—and even after that stage has been successfully passed, its utility is not lessened, but, in my opinion, increased. It is to be feared that the same ideas which prevail amongst students at school, and which lead parents and scholars alike to imagine that when matriculation has been passed, the be-all and end-all of education has been achieved, so there is a grave danger to be apprehended that as soon as a student in accountancy has safety steered through the straits of the Associates' examination, he imagines that he has then arrived at the port of his desires. But rather let me impress upon you that he has only then reached the wide expanse of waters which open up illimitable scope for further voyages

104

into the thousand and one bays of knowledge which are worth exploring on every side. After all, these primary excursions are mainly useful in giving experience for the more daring and difficult passages which have to be navigated as soon as we feel sufficiently confident in our own powers to take command of the vessel ourselves, instead of having a captain over us to give directions as to the steering, and upon whom necessarily devolves all the responsibility of mapping out the course to be followed.

I apprehend that those of you who are listening to me are fully seized of all the advantages to be gained by associating with your fellow members and exchanging ideas upon topics of practical interest; and, in this direction, I foresee the immense possibilities which attach to a society like this. I know of no more useful method of attaining knowledge, outside of practical experience, than the plan which I understand you intend to adopt.

First of all, it is assumed that every member will be an active helper in the work of the society, and that the work will be so allotted that there will be no undue pressure upon anyone. If the burden of responsibility be well distributed, the task of carrying it becomes an easy one, and the danger of "growing weary by the way" is proportionally reduced. You will, I am sure, not lay yourselves open—any of you—to a charge of selfishness, by quietly sitting still and watching others toil for your benefit. There must be no drones in this hive; and then you will realise, practically, that "many hands make light work."

As I understand the scheme of operations, it is that the members shall be divided into sections, each section taking up some specific subject, and collating as much information thereupon as can be obtained from the study of the literature of that particular branch. Then at your periodical meetings the convenor or spokesman of these divisions will give the members the benefit of this sectional work either by a spoken address or by a written paper, to be followed, of course, by discussion. In this way, a vast amount of helpful work can be achieved at a minimum of personal labour, although, of course, you do not need to be reminded that no *good*, solid work can be done without serious and steady efforts, and it is useless to expect that a vicarious sacrifice will be of lasting benefit to any except the man who "does and suffers." The law of compensation properly bestows the greatest advantages upon the man who bears the burden. It is as unwise for you to rely upon the zeal and industry of your fellows in intellectual pursuits, as it is to expect to reap the advantage of physical exercise by watching others take it.

One of the main benefits, in my opinion, of such a plan as sketched above is that of the habit of systematisation which is essential to all effective study. The trend of habit nowadays is too much in the direction of generalisation. Our outside reading partakes too much of the same fault. What with newspapers and monthly periodicals, we become a sort of Whiteley's—or Mutual Store—no one department of knowledge fully furnished, but with a limited assortment and smattering of an infinite number of subjects. We must, most of us, confess to this weakness. It is so easy and pleasant to have serious and abstruse subjects prepared for us in tasty and attractive form; but these dainty dishes are very apt to spoil our appetites for wholesome, solid food. Cultivate the habit, therefore, of concentration, not only in your professional but also your general reading, and you will find that instead of your work being irksome and wearying, it will become easy and pleasant. I may here say that the student of the present day enjoys immense advantages over those of five and twenty or thirty years ago. He certainly has infinitely more aids to the acquirement of knowledge in every branch of professional work, in the form of text books and treatises, and to this extent he is advantaged; but, on the other hand, these helps may really prove to be hindrances to the thorough acquaintance with a subject which personal research, and often only practical experience, afforded us in our student days. It is the case of the scholar who patiently puzzles out his translation for himself as compared with the perfunctory knowledge gained from his "crib."

You have, therefore, decided wisely to apportion your work, so that every division may be well and thoroughly done. Of course, I do not mean to convey that these sections shall be confined absolutely to one department of professional study only, but that in rotation all the subjects embraced in our Institute syllabus shall be dealt with, and, by this means, every member ought, if he be diligent, to be fully equipped for his examinations when his time comes.

These Students' Societies have become at home a very successful and important adjunct to the work of the Accountants' Societies; and the leaders of the profession there gladly acknowledge the valuable help which they have afforded to the work of their articled clerks. There is no reason why the same result should not be achieved here. Depend upon it, in these days of severe competition in every branch of professional life, the men who will come to the front are those who are best furnished, first of all, with the technical knowledge of their work, and who, consequently, will be most apt in assimilating and adapting the knowledge which comes only of experience and practice. I need hardly say that the scope of usefulness of Students' Societies is by no means confined to the preparation of subjects upon which you have to be examined. There are numerous other directions which will suggest themselves to your minds, and which, if followed, will lead to beneficial results. I am hopeful that, as an outcome of this society's work, more interest will be taken in the business meetings of the institute (which title, by the way, I have always regarded as an unfortunate and misleading designation of our gatherings for the reading and discussion of papers on subjects relating to accountancy). These ought to be resuscitated—although our experience of late years has not been such as to afford much encouragement to a lecturer to devote several evenings to the preparation of a paper, and find that not more than perhaps twenty have thought it worth while to give up an evening to listen to the result of one's labours. More than once, I think I am right in saying, our visitors have exceeded in number our own members.

All the papers which I have had the pleasure of listening to have been worthy of better audiences, and some have been of exceptional merit and interest. In justice to our students I am fain to admit that they have always formed by far the larger proportion of the audience; the fault lies markedly with the senior members, and it is a grave reproach to their interest in the work of the institute.

Then, again, the practice of concise thinking and speaking will be of immense advantage to you, and I know of no better school for the development of these faculties than such a society as this. You have all experienced the feeling of impatience which is engendered when listening to the diffuse wanderings of a speaker who meanders all round his subject, and who, therefore, never grips his audience. As a matter of fact, you feel that if courtesy permitted, you would like to drive home and clinch his arguments for him in half a dozen short sentences. This gift of crisp and ready speech is simply invaluable, and it is worth all the pains taken in its acquirement. Its possessor wields a weapon of immense power, and enjoys an advantage which only those who have had occasion to cross swords with him know how to appreciate.

BANKERS' MAGAZINE OF AUSTRALASIA

[NOVEMBER 15, 1898, pp.242-7]

I apprehend that it is not intended to confine the literary work of your society purely to accountancy matters; at any rate, I hope not. I hardly know any profession in which the man of the world—and by this term I mean the man who is well furnished mentally and who has tact in dealing with his fellow-men—stands at such an advantage as in ours. Indeed, one might almost go so far as to say that without these qualities, an accountant becomes simply a book-keeper. To this end, I hope to see your governing body suggesting subjects for lectures and discussion which, though not strictly a part of accountancy, yet should form an important part of the equipment of a business man. Questions relating to political economy in its various branches, taxation, currency, notation, etc., ought to be included in your syllabus of topics for study. You do not need to be reminded that the course of reading necessary to enable you to write a short essay on any of these subjects is simply invaluable, and even though you only had the scriptural "gathering together of two or three" to listen to your effort, you would never regret the time spent in its preparation. Opportunities are, by this means, afforded to those who perhaps hesitate to take part in debates, and who are almost afraid to hear their own voices—of giving the benefit of their labours to their fellow members—and the confidence begotten of a careful acquaintance with a subject is a most important factor in allaying the nervous dread of rising to discuss it in the presence of your fellows.

In this connection, I strongly incline to the wisdom of the conduct of your ordinary meetings for discussion being left as much as possible to yourselves. Occasionally I have no doubt some of the seniors in the profession would be glad to give you help, but I would like you to avoid taxing their time and energies as far as possible, as that can only be done at the expense of the institute as a whole. Then let me advise you to strive after conciseness in the preparation of your papers, avoid diffuseness in your written as well as in your spoken efforts. A paper of fifteen or twenty minutes, well prepared, is quite as instructive, and more easily grasped than one of double the length. The physical labour of writing out, say, thirty sheets of foolscap is a serious deterrent, even though you may have sufficient subject matter to work upon. Better by far divide it into two papers, both for yourself and your audience.

Will you allow me now to invite your attention to a few of the more salient qualifications which every accountant should possess in addition to his expert knowledge of accounts? Perhaps one of the most important is that of tact and discretion. It is inevitable that, occasionally, you will be called upon to deal with difficult questions, and, what is worse, difficult clients. It goes without saying that amongst this class the self-sufficient man is by far the most difficult. If you attempt to coerce his opinions, you will soon find that he is as adamant and unimpressionable as marble. You have, therefore, to impress him with your views very carefully and insinuatingly, and whilst giving him full credit for his opinions, gradually enforce your own by practical illustrations. A simple example from every day experience will carry conviction, when an hour's theoretical discussion will fail to move him a hair's breadth from this position. Always strive to simplify your argument so as to bring it within the scope of his mental grasp. A familiar instance occurs to me which has doubtless also come within the experience of most of you. To some people, it is simply incomprehensible that a balance of loss should appear on the assets side, and a balance of profit on the liabilities side of a balance sheet. You may expound the scientific theory of book-keeping *ad nauseam*, and your sceptical friend will remain unconvinced; but when you explain in simple language that the balance of profit simply represents a liability to the shareholders which the company has to discharge by dividing or otherwise disposing of it, then it begins to dawn upon them that there is some "method in your apparent madness." In like manner, when you show them that the balance of loss is an amount which has to be recovered from some source, either from the capital of the company or from future profits, then they realise that it can only be set out on the assets side of the balance sheet. In like manner, many apparently knotty questions of accounts can be simplified, and made plain to the meanest understanding.

Then you must cultivate the habit of treating courteously those who may differ from you. It is sometimes a severe trial of patience to be condemned to listen to arguments which one knows are radically unsound, but impatient contradiction and controversy will only aggravate the difference, and probably lose you a valuable client. Besides being discourteous, it is impolitic. Of course, stick to your guns when your cause is just and right, but don't fire shot and shell when blank cartridges will answer every purpose. And again, let me impress upon you the virtue of *punctuality*, not only in your personal attendance, but in the performance of your promises. How often one hears the perverted though, unfortunately, too true adage—"punctuality is the thief of time." It is simply another form of breaking one's promise, and whilst, in the verbal case, it is properly regarded as a serious and unpardonable offence, the non-appearance at the appointed hour is looked upon as a very venial transgression. There ought to be no such distinction, except under unavoidable circumstances. The habit is easily acquired, and, when acquired, not easily thrown off, and you will save much heart burning on the part of your friends. It is simply another form of slovenliness, against which let me earnestly warn you. Be methodical and orderly in your work, and guard against the too prevalent fault of a careless, slip-shod style. In my experience as an examiner of our institute, I have almost invariably found that the candidate who indulges in a slovenly style of writing his papers is equally slovenly in the matter and arrangement of his answers. The same characteristic will also run through his every-day work, and if he could at the end of the year reckon up the time lost in consequence of his untidy habits, he would simply be appalled. Not only does the tidy man as a rule do better work, but he does a great deal more of it, and, reduced to concrete fact, it pays to be orderly in one's business habits.

By this time most of my audience have no doubt realised that no great success is to be achieved in any department of life without steady application and patient work, and, in accountancy, these qualities are specially valuable. Indeed, if these graces do not form part of your adornment, I am afraid you have missed your proper vocation. The demand for the exercise of these qualities comes so frequently in our work that it is imperative we should possess them, and, in addition, we ought also to be fired with a large measure of enthusiasm. How often one hears people say, "Don't you grow weary of constantly toiling at figures?" Weary! No! The work is interesting, and, in many aspects, fascinating; but unless the spark of earnest eagerness and keen pleasure in your work is burning within you, I fear that you have a monotonous and somewhat dreary path to travel.

[We regret pressure on space compels us to hold over the remainder of this address until next issue.—ED.]

(To be Continued.)

BANKERS' MAGAZINE OF AUSTRALASIA

[DECEMBER 15, 1898, pp.328-31]

INTERESTING ADDRESS TO YOUNG ACCOUNTANTS

By the President of the Incorporated Accountants Students' Society (Victoria)

❧ ❧ ❧

One other essential I would like to mention, and that is the wisdom of cultivating a good style of caligraphy. You may not know how all-important this is, but I can assure you, in my own experience, I have been compelled to pass over dozens of young men who have come to me seeking billets, simply on account of their shocking hand-writing. One of the first questions invariably asked of an applicant is, Can you write a good hand? In this connection, too, let me also strongly urge you to commence the practice of short-hand writing. It is becoming every year more and more an indispensable part of a clerk's education, and from a pound, shillings and pence point of view, it pays. A larger salary can always be commanded by an applicant who has acquired this qualification. Besides, its utility in taking notes of lectures, interviews, and meetings is incalculable. But let me remind you that in this, as in everything else, you must take pains to learn it thoroughly and to write it carefully, or you will find that when you come to transcribe your notes, you yourself will probably be unable to decipher your own stenography.

It may probably be known to some of you that it is in contemplation to institute uniform examinations for the various colonies, and a conference is to be held during this week comprising, in the first instance, representatives from Sydney, Adelaide, and Melbourne, to make the necessary arrangements. This, it may be expected, will be but a prelude to even closer communion with kindred societies, and if Australian federation be brought about, this will be a practicable and feasible possibility. One difficulty, which is a serious one at present, is that of the differing laws of the colonies, but it may reasonably be anticipated that it will not be long before company, insolvency, and mercantile legislation will be brought into line. There is also, for the time being, a wide divergence in the conditions of membership, particularly as regards New South Wales and the other colonies. With the former, no one can be admitted as a

member who is not practising as an accountant, and they do not recognise our two distinctions of Associate and Fellow. Of course, they are
horrified at the absurdly simple qualifications which are required under
our Companies Act, 1896, and until this is altered they will not be likely
to accept the Victorian legal definition of a Licensed Auditor as sufficient for admission to their more conservative organisation. I have so
often had occasion to express my views on this subject, that I do not like
to weary you by the reiteration of my opinion that company legislation in
1896 set back the clock of our progress by at least *ten* years. Just as we
were beginning to see the good effects of the wise policy which was initiated by this Institute ten years ago, and steadily pursued ever since, the
Legislature in its wisdom thought fit to throw open the door so widely
that a "wayfaring man, though a fool," could enter in without difficulty,
and we now see the anomaly of all sorts and conditions of men legalised
as Licensed Auditors, whose only qualification may be the fact that they
have audited the accounts of a small mining company. In my own experience, I have been called upon to audit the accounts of a mining company with a colleague who absolutely did not understand the difference
between the "Dr." and "Cr." side of a ledger. Of course, the shareholders
are themselves to blame, but these matters are often left to the tender
mercies of half a dozen directors who hold a controlling interest in the
company, and of whom the auditor is probably a personal friend.

It is satisfactory to know, however, that care is generally exercised in
the selection of men for responsible audits, and I venture to think that our
own Institute deservedly holds a high position in the estimation of investors and commercial men. We have the satisfactory consciousness at
any rate, that the Incorporated Institute of Accountants, Victoria, has
always set a high standard of attainment before its members, and I trust
that, whatever happens, nothing will be done to lower that standard of
efficiency.

By request of the members, the council is moving in the matter of
obtaining legal recognition of the accountancy profession. This will, of
course, necessitate the admission of *all* who are at present recognised as
accountants in the widest interpretation of the word, and I need hardly
tell you what this means. The result, in my opinion, will simply be appalling, and I frankly confess that, personally, I am not enamoured of the

proposal. At the same time, I am fain to admit that fifteen or twenty years hence, the good effects of such a law would begin to be beneficially felt, as, after the first batch of admissions, no one would be allowed to append the title of Public Accountant (or whatever designation might be adopted) to his name except he has passed an examination. Under any circumstances I am strongly of opinion that it would be better to wait until we see whether federation is likely to become an accomplished fact, after which any step of this kind might be taken by the federated colonies as a whole.

One aspect of this question of federation is of importance to us, as there will doubtless hereafter be much greater community of interest as between the colonies, and we may expect naturally that business houses will be represented in each of them to a larger extent than now exists. This will lead inevitably to a more frequent interchange of staffs, and accountants will have to be prepared to take up work with equal readiness, either in New South Wales, South Australia, Queensland, or Victoria, and this will afford valuable experience, and must tend to make good all-round men.

Now, my allotted time has nearly expired, or I shall be tempted to wander afield, and discuss some of the anomalies and inconsistencies of both the recent Companies and Insolvency Acts as they affect accountants. So far as the Companies Bill is concerned, I would only say that the flaws are mainly due to imperfect drafting, a result which is almost inevitable from the hasty manner in which the last and mostly vital amendments were rushed through the two Chambers.

The consequence is seen in clauses placed under different sections of the Act which relate to the same subject, and a glaring instance is that of the provision as to the registration of Proprietary Companies which necessitates all the formulae in regard to an ordinary Limited Liability Company to be first of all gone through, to be followed immediately afterwards by the procedure governing the change to a Proprietary Company. This involves needless cost, and is absolutely useless.

Then as to the auditors' duties, we have to look to, at least, four different sections, in different parts of the Act, to find out what we must certify.

I have a very vivid recollection of the sense of responsibility which rested upon me in framing the first certificate which had to be attached under the new Act to a bank balance sheet, lest, by any chance, I had omitted to cover all the different requirements of the Act.

Then, again, some of the conditions attaching to the formation of companies, such as the two-monthly statement, and accompanying affidavits, do not in any wise give effect to the intention of the framers of the Act. But, on the whole, the Act is a marked advance upon previous legislation except as to the definition of a qualified auditor. That is a distinctly retrograde step, and could only have been put on our Statute Books in a community where provincialism is to a very large extent the key note of legislation.

Then, again, the Insolvency Act teems with useless and restrictive procedure, which, whilst affording no further material protection to creditors beyond what they enjoyed under the old Act, increases the cost of administration by at least 30 per cent. The cumbrous and needless provisions as to rendering accounts, is simply an intolerable nuisance to trustees and no additional safeguard against dishonesty.

One cannot help but wish that instead of rushing into experimental legislation, our law-makers would be content to keep abreast of English legislation. There, for every single practical illustration which we can furnish, they can point to a thousand, and as the wisdom of experience teaches them, they give effect to rational, but never hysterical, changes.

An example of the care which characterises commercial legislation at home has been furnished during the past week, and which, if followed here, would have prevented the striking difference in the decisions of the Chief Justice and Mr. Justice Hood on the important question of the rights of holders of promissory notes. The anomaly of the position as disclosed in the case of the Union Bank v. J.B. Dean, tried before Mr. Justice Hood, is that an action having been commenced by a writ under the Instruments Act, and the defendant having got leave to defend, an application had been made for final judgment under Order 14 of the rules of summary procedure, the effect of which was to deprive the defendant of the advantage he had got in his first action.

The Chief Justice had ruled that the summary procedure was not available to a plaintiff when the defendant had got leave to defend (vide

Sargood v. Britten), but Mr. Justice Hood did not follow this decision, and gave an exactly opposite ruling, and the whole question is now in that indeterminate condition. This difficulty was foreseen in England some time ago, and the law relating to procedure under the Instruments Act was repealed.

But I must now draw these discursive remarks to a close. I should have liked to have been able to put my thoughts on paper more at my leisure, but as you were naturally anxious to get your session commenced as early as possible, I have had to steal sundry sleeping hours from a very busy fortnight in order to carry out my promise to address you to-night.

However, I was so sensible of the honour and responsibility of the position which, by your grace, I occupy, that I regarded it as a pleasure to obey the mandate of your committee, and felt that it was due to you that, instead of availing myself of the opportunity of simply inaugurating your first session by an extempore address from the chair, I should, with some amount of care, commit my ideas to writing, and this suggests to me my parting word of advice to you, "Whatever is worth doing, is worth doing as well as you can." It is comparatively easy to gloss over work which may be perhaps physically irksome, but the gain which accrues from careful preparation is incalculable. It maintains the elasticity of the mind; and I can assure you, as one who has enjoyed a more than ordinarily busy life, that the sense of pleasure and enjoyment in your work in-creases with the practical experience of it. Our profession is interesting by reason of its diversity, and if I had to make my choice again, I do not think that I should hesitate for a moment to enter upon accountancy. I am glad to have been permitted to assist at the birth of this society, and I trust that as the years go on, it will attain great strength, and be the means of helping its members to occupy honourable and useful positions both as accountants and citizens in this vigorous community.

BANKERS' MAGAZINE OF AUSTRALASIA

[OCTOBER 31, 1899, pp.179-81]

REGULATING THE PROFESSION OF PUBLIC ACCOUNTANTS

A Bill for this purpose has been brought in by Mr. Theo. Fink and Mr. Watt, M.P's., in the Victorian Parliament, and read for the first time on August 23, and the second time on October 18. As the matter is of public interest, the clauses of the bill dealing with its principles may be of interest to our readers:—Whereas it is expedient to provide for the registration of persons practising as accountants and auditors in Victoria so as to distinguish qualified from unqualified persons and otherwise to amend the law as to persons so practising: Be it therefore enacted by the Queen's Most Excellent Majesty by and with the advice and consent of the Legislative Council and the Legislative Assembly of Victoria in this present Parliament assembled and by the authority of the same as follows (that is to say):—

1. This Act may be cited as the *Public Accountants Act* 1899.

2. In the construction and for the purposes of this Act the following terms shall if not inconsistent with the context or subject-matter have the respective meanings hereby assigned to them:—

> "Board" shall mean the Board of Accountants of Victoria.
>
> "Institutes" shall mean and include all the following bodies (that is to say):—The Incorporated Institute of Accountants Victoria, the Victorian Division of the Society of Accountants and Auditors Incorporated (England), the Federal Institute of Accountants Incorporated, and the Australian Institute of Incorporated Accountants; and "Institute" shall mean any one of such bodies unless there are words to restrict the meaning to one in particular thereof.

3. For the purpose of carrying this Act into execution there shall be a Board and the said Board shall be a body corporate under the name of "The Board of Accountants of Victoria" and by that name shall have perpetual succession and may adopt and use a common seal and may sue and be sued and shall have power to purchase take hold sell lease ex-

change or dispose of land and all other property for the purposes of this Act.

4. All Courts Judges and persons acting judicially shall take judicial notice of the incorporation and also of the common seal of "The Board of Accountants of Victoria" affixed to any deed instrument or writing, and shall presume that such seal was properly affixed thereto, and such deed instrument or writing when sealed whether such instrument or writing required to be sealed or not shall be admissible in evidence for and against the said Board on the mere production thereof without any other or further proof of the making of such deed instrument or writing or of the due incorporation of the said Board.

5. The members of the Board for the first year after the passing of this Act shall be the persons appointed in the manner following within two months after the passing of this Act and their successors (that is to say):—Three Fellows of the Incorporated Institute of Accountants Victoria, two Fellows of the Victorian Division of the Society of Accountants and Auditors Incorporated (England), two Fellows of the Federal Institute of Accountants Incorporated, and two Fellows of the Australian Institute of Incorporated Accountants to be respectively appointed by the Institutes and Victorian Division to which they are by this section assigned, and one Accountant practising in Victoria to be appointed by the Governor in Council. Provided that notwithstanding failure to appoint any member or members as aforesaid the members who may be appointed within the said two months not being less than seven in number shall constitute the Board.

27. Subject to the provisions of this Act any of the following persons who must be of full age shall be entitled to a certificate from the Board that he is duly qualified for registration under this Act.

(a) All persons being members at the passing of this Act of any of the respective institutes but not including student members;

(b) Any person who proves to the satisfaction of the Board within twelve months after the commencement of this Act that during the three years next preceding such commencement he had been continuously and *bonâ fide* practising for one year as a public accountant in Victoria;

(c)   Any person who shall have passed the examinations prescribed by the Board in pursuance of this Act and paid the prescribed fees; but the Board may dispense with examination in the case of any person who proves to the satisfaction of the Board that he is a member of some institute society or association of accountants outside Victoria of which the qualifications for membership are in the opinion of the Board equal to those required for the time being in respect of the prescribed examinations and who pays the prescribed fees.

No person shall be registered under this Act unless he produces to the registrar a certificate given to him by the Board under the provisions of this section.

28. The Board shall by regulation prescribe examinations to be passed by persons who desire to obtain a certificate from the Board under subsection *(c)* of the next preceding section, and may by regulation vary the subjects and conditions of such examinations whenever it may think fit.

29. The Board shall appoint a Board of Examiners consisting of the president and two members of the Board of Accountants of Victoria and one member of each of the institutes of whom not less than four shall be a quorum, and such Board of Examiners shall in the absence of any regulation to the contrary act as Examiners in respect of the examinations held in pursuance of the last preceding section. Provided that the Board may make regulations for the appointment of special Examiners by the Board or by the Board of Examiners or by each of the said institutes and for the remuneration of all Examiners whether members of the Board of Examiners or not.

30. The Board may refuse to grant a certificate that he is duly qualified for registration under this Act to—

(a)   Any person who has been excluded from membership of any of the institutes;

(b)   Any person who has been suspended from membership of any of the said institutes so long as such suspension continues;

(c) Any person who is proved to the satisfaction of the Board—

(1) To have been convicted of felony or misdemeanour or to have been declared by any court of competent jurisdiction to have committed any fraud.

(2) To have been guilty of fraudulent dishonest or discreditable conduct in the practice of his profession as an accountant.

35. No person who is not a public accountant shall recover in any court of law any fee or other remuneration for services rendered in the capacity of a public or professional accountant or auditor. Provided that this section shall not apply to any accountant employed exclusively at a salary on accounts and not carrying on business on his own account so as to prevent him from recovering such salary nor to any person employed at the passing of this Act as a licensed auditor under the Companies Act or as a certificated auditor under the Local Government Acts so as to prevent him from recovering his remuneration as such licensed auditor or certificated auditor.

36. Whenever it is provided by any Act of Parliament or Rules of Court that any duties thereunder shall be performed by a public or professional accountant (whether under any special description or of any particular class or otherwise) such accountant shall unless otherwise expressly provided be deemed to mean a person registered under this Act and any such duties may be performed by a person so registered.

37. The Board shall in the month of January in each year cause to be printed published and sold a correct register of the names of all public accountants, and in such registers respectively the names shall be in alphabetical order according to the surnames with the respective residences or places of business of such accountants and such printed register shall be called "The Accountants Register of Victoria for 1899" and for every succeeding year.

BANKERS' MAGAZINE OF AUSTRALASIA

[DECEMBER 29, 1899, pp.291-300]

HOW TO BECOME A SKILLED ACCOUNTANT

॥ ॥ ॥

By R.T. Oehr, A.I.A.V. Bank Officers' Students' Society

ALECTURE was delivered before the Bankers' Institute of Australasia on the 20th inst., by Mr. R.J. Oehr, A.I.A.V. Mr. Emery, President, in the chair.

It is with diffidence that I venture to appear before you this evening to say something regarding the title of this paper. In the first place, I would like to point out that I was much concerned about the choice of a subject suitable for delivery before those engaged in banking business. The Secretary desired a paper on some phase of Accountancy, and the first intimation to me of what the subject was to be was the notification of it in the last Annual Report of the Bankers' Institute.

In order to adhere as closely as possible to the title of the paper I will give you a brief sketch of the accountancy profession during the latter half of this century, and will indicate to you the matter necessary to be studied by those who desire to become Incorporated Accountants.

"The vast development in manufactures and trade during the present century, the enormous increase in personal property which has resulted from that development, and the high degree in which it has been found necessary to apply the principles of the division of labour have entirely altered the economic conditions and practices of the nation, and there has been called into existence a multitude of new businesses and professions to meet the demands of the most gigantic fabric of trade and commerce which the world has ever seen. Not the least useful or notable of the occupations which have in this way had their origin or development is that of a public Accountant." The desirability of forming a Society of Accountants was advocated by "The Times," London on January 9, 1868, in the following paragraph:—"It has been one of the leading evils of recent times that an occupation like this, which requires the highest qualifications of commercial experience, and a degree of integrity capable of resisting the most constant and insidious temptation, should have been left

120

without any means being provided by which the most respectable members of the body might earn a definite position, calculated to exclude the herd of disreputable persons, who act merely as the tools of delinquent directors and officials, or of the lowest class of attorneys, and whose knowledge of their calling has generally been derived from personal experience of failure in every other pursuit they have tried."

In Scotland, societies had already been in existence. The Society of Accountants in Edinburgh, was incorporated by Royal Charter, on October 23, 1854, while the Institute of Accountants and Actuaries in Glasgow was likewise incorporated on March 15, 1855.

In England the first step to establish a society was taken in Liverpool, in 1870. During the same year the Institute of Accountants was formed in London, and two years later another society in the same city styled the Society of Accountants. In 1871, a Society of Accountants was established in Manchester, and in 1877, one in Sheffield.

A few years after 1870 it was thought advisable in England to take steps to amalgamate the various societies and to obtain a charter. The petition embodied in the charter states, amongst other things, "that the profession is a numerous one, and their functions are of great and increasing importance in respect of their employment in the capacities of liquidators in the winding up of companies, and of receivers under decrees, and of trustees in bankruptcies or arrangements with creditors and in various positions of trust under courts of justice, as also in the auditing of accounts of public companies, and of partnership and otherwise."

The charter was signed on May 11, 1880, and the societies became amalgamated and formed the Institute of Chartered Accountants in England and Wales.

Other societies have since sprung up, one of which, The Society of Accountants and Auditors, is represented in this city. "There can be no doubt whatever," says Mr. Worthington in his work on "Professional Accountants," that in Scotland, accountancy has developed a degree of importance, and that Scotch accountants rank higher than in any other part of the world. The gentlemen at the head of the profession are thoroughly accomplished and possess very extensive acquirements and experience."

In February, 1893, a federated arrangement between the following three Scottish Societies, viz.:—The Society of Accountants in Edinburgh, the Institute of Accountants and Actuaries in Glasgow, and the Society of Accountants in Aberdeen, was agreed to, "providing for uniform rules for an admission to membership of their respective corporate bodies, and for the establishment of a general board for the examination of apprentices, etc.," in order that "the object contemplated by the said respective Royal Charters would be further promoted."

According to this agreement no person who is under seventeen years is eligible to be taken as an apprentice by a member of any of the societies. His period of service is to be four years.

Every apprentice has to undergo a preliminary examination before commencing his apprenticeship, or within six months thereafter, in the following subjects, viz:—

(1) Writing to Dictation, English Grammar, and Composition.
     NOTE.—Special marks will be awarded for handwriting.
(2) Arithmetic (Elementary), including Vulgar and Decimal Fractions, Practice, Proportion, and Interest.
(3) Algebra, Simple Rules, Factors, H.C.F., L.C.M., Fractions, Equations (and Problems) of the first degree with one unknown.

And three of the six following subjects, each candidate having the right to select the three he may prefer:—

(1) British History.
(2) Geography of the world, with special reference to the geography of Great Britain, its colonies, and the Continent of Europe.
(3) Geometry, Euclid, Book 1., with deductions.
(4) Shorthand, dictation and transcription of notes.
(5) Latin, including Grammar and short translations.
(6) French or German, including Grammar and short translations.

(Exemptions from this examination: Any candidate who has taken a University Degree, or has obtained the Government School-Leaving Certificate (Lower Grade), or has passed junior or senior local examinations conducted by any of the universities, in all cases including three subjects, one of which shall be Mathematics and one English.)

After the commencement of his second year, the apprentice has to undergo an immediate examination in the following subjects, viz:—

(1) *Mathematics:—*

  (A) *Arithmetic* (advanced)—
  Including Vulgar and Decimal Fractions, Practice, Proportion, Simple and Compound Interest and Discount.

  (B) *Algebra:—*
  Including Quadratic Equations, Arithmetical and Geometrical Progressions, and the nature and use of Logarithms.

(2) *Professional Knowledge:—*

  (Special attention to be given to neatness of handwriting and style.)

  (A) Bookkeeping, including the framing of Balance Sheets, and Profit and Loss Accounts.

  (B) Framing Accounts, Interest States, etc.

  (C) Correspondence.

The apprentice has also, before he can become eligible to be admitted as a member to any of the societies, to attend the class of Scots' Law in any of the Scottish Universities for one complete session, or such Extra-Mural Classes on Scots' Law as the examining board has approved of, together with such other lectures as the society to which he is seeking admission may in general meeting prescribe. When the term of apprenticeship has expired, and his indenture has been discharged, the apprentice is entitled, upon giving notice of his intention so to do, and producing certificates that he has attended the necessary law and other classes, to come forward for the final examination, the subjects for which are:—

(1) *The Law of Scotland:—*

  (A) Insolvency and Bankruptcy, including Trust Deeds for Creditors.

  (B) The Companies Acts.

    (C)   Judicial Factories.

    (D)   Partnership.

    (E)   References and Arbitrations.

    (F)   Bills, Cheques, and Deposit Receipts.

    (G)   Sale, Insurance, and Cautionary Obligations.

    (H)   Fee and Liferent.

(2) *Actuarial Science:—*

    (A)   Compound Interest and Annuities Certain.

    (B)   Elementary Principles of Life Annuities, Assurances, and Reversions.

(3) *Political Economy:—*

The Examination will involve an elementary knowledge of Economic principles, and more special knowledge of one or more of the following topics, to vary from time to time:—Statistics, Rate of Interest and Investments, Currency, Banking, Credit, Commercial Crises, National and Municipal Debts, Taxation.

Apprentices whose Indentures were executed, or who, in the case of the Glasgow Society, had entered their term of Service with a Member of that Institute, prior to the adoption of the agreement in question, may, in lieu of Political Economy, take a second and more advanced Actuarial paper, covering:—

    (A)   Probabilities.

    (B)   Mortality Tables.

    (C)   Life Contingencies.

(4) *General Business of an Accountant:—*

    (A)   The Theory and Practice of Book-keeping, including the preparation of Balance Sheets, Profit and Loss Accounts, and Partners' Accounts; also Joint Adventure and Consignment Accounts.

124

(B) The procedure and requisites in the Audit of Accounts and Books, including those of Public Bodies, Companies, Firms, and Trust Estates.

(C) The Management of Bankrupt Estates, Private Trusts, Heritable Estates, Curatorial and Judicial Factories, etc.; and the framing of the necessary Accounts of Intromissions, Schemes of Division, Interest States, etc.

(D) The Formation, Administration, Reconstruction, and Liquidation of Public Companies.

(E) The procedure under Judicial and Private References, Remits, and Proofs.

It will thus be seen that the standard of qualification necessary for becoming a Chartered Accountant is a very high one indeed.

In the colonies a high estimation has been put upon the profession, and societies have been formed with objects, such as the Memorandum of Association of one of the Societies recites:—

(A) To aim at the elevation of the profession of Accountants by the dissemination of professional knowledge and the inculcation of sound practice.

(B) To increase the confidence of the banking, mercantile, and general community in the employment of recognised Accountants and Auditors by admitting to the Institute such persons only as shall in future pass satisfactory examinations in the theory and practice of the work, and by the prevention of illegal and dishonourable practices.

(C) To afford means of reference for the amicable settlement of professional differences, and to decide upon questions of professional usage and etiquette.

(D) To promote good feeling and friendly intercourse amongst the members.

(E) To watch over and promote the interests of the profession generally.

In Melbourne there are two societies, exclusive of the London one represented here, as before mentioned. These are the Incorporated Institute of Accountants, Victoria, founded on April 12, 1886, and incorporated on March 1, 1887, and the Federal Institute of Accountants, a society of a more recent date. To illustrate to you that a high qualification is likewise required in Australasia, I will indicate to you directly the subjects one must pass in to become a member of either of the principal institutes in each of the colonies, between whom an agreement has lately been entered into for holding examinations on a common platform.

The societies in question are:—

The Incorporated Institute of Accountants, Victoria.
The Sydney Institute of Public Accountants.
The Institute of Accountants in South Australia (Incorporated).
The Queensland Institute of Accountants (Incorporated).
The Tasmanian Institute of Accountants, and
The Incorporated Institute of Accountants of New Zealand.

The range of practice in the profession of an accountant has been summed up in the following words:—

"The business open to an accountant in Edinburgh is varied and extensive, embracing not merely all matters of account, but requiring for its proper execution a knowledge of actuarial science, and a thorough acquaintance with the general principles of law, particularly of the law of Scotland, and more especially with those branches of it which affect mercantile relationships, insolvency, bankruptcy, and all rights connected with property."

Although this is written of Scotland, a somewhat similar definition, to a certain degree, could be given of the profession here, and a high state of excellence is sought to be reached, so in order to raise the status of the profession, the three local societies already named, together with the Ballarat one, have lately acted in concert, for the purpose of endeavouring to get a bill passed in Parliament to recognise the profession of public accountants, as it is deemed "expedient to provide for the registration of persons practising as accountants and auditors in Victoria, so as to distinguish qualified from unqualified persons, and otherwise to amend the law as to persons so practising." The consummation of this resolve has been hastened on by the absurdly simple qualifications of the Victorian Companies Act of 1896, which almost permits the "man about town" to become a "licensed auditor."

Having briefly sketched you a somewhat imperfect history of the accountancy profession at home and locally for the past fifty years or so, permit me now to touch upon what is indicated by the title of the paper, viz.—"How to Become a Skilled Accountant."

Let us take for our illustration a young man starting. In the first place, it would be necessary for him to seek to become a member of one of the institutes, according to the rules of the particular one he selects. There are three examinations held by the Incorporated Institute of Accountants, Victoria, of which I have the honour to be a member, viz.:

Preliminary Examination.—This is just a test of the general education of the applicant. This examination can be dispensed with in the case of a student who has passed a matriculation, public or Civil Service examination, in any of the colonies, or in the United Kingdom, or whose experience and attainments entitle him, in the opinion of the Council, to proceed at once to the intermediate examination.

Intermediate Examination.—This is to test the progress the student has made in professional knowledge, and the following are the subjects:—

(1) Bookkeeping, including Partnership and Executorship Accounts.

(2) Auditing.

(3) The Rights and Duties of Trustees, Liquidators, and Receivers.

Final Examination:—The subjects for this are:—

(1) Bookkeeping, including Partnership and Executorship Accounts.

(2) Auditing.

(3) The Rights and Duties of Trustees and Receivers, and the Law of Arbitration and Awards.

(4) Principles and Practice of the Law of Insolvency.

(5) The Principles and Practice of the Law relating to Joint Stock Companies.

127

(6)   Mercantile law.

Upon passing this examination, the examinee can be admitted as an Associate to the Institute, the advance to the degree of Fellow, which is the highest, being followed in due course upon the fulfilment of certain conditions as to age, practice, etc.

It is of course recognised by you that one cannot do more in a short paper than state the subjects, and name the text books.

In addition to the Acts of Parliament relating to those subjects for which laws have been framed, the following text books are recommended, and although those on legal matters deal with English law, our statutes are modelled to a great extent upon home laws; but there are differences, notably in the Companies and Insolvency Acts, which render it compulsory that the necessary Victorian statutes should likewise be studied. The text books are:—

Bookkeeping:—

Jone's English System of Bookkeeping by Single and Double Entry.

A manual of Bookkeeping for Students (Thornton)

Works by Pixley and Wilson, and Van der Linde.

Auditing:—

"Auditors, their Duties and Responsibilities," seventh edition (Pixley).

"Auditing," third edition (Dicksee).

Company Law:—

"The Law and Practice under the Companies Acts, 1862-90 (Buckley).

"Lindley on Partnership and Companies."

"Palmer's Company Precedents."

Arbitrations and Awards:—

"Redress by Arbitration" (Lynch).

"Russell on Arbitrations."

"A Manual for Arbitrators" (Salaman).

Mercantile Law:-

"Smith's Mercantile Law."

Insolvency:—

Up till the recent Insolvency Act (1897), Duffy and McHugh's work on Insolvency was the recognised local text book, but the amendments have been so many that that book will now be useless. However, Mr. P.D. Phillips, the well-known authority on Insolvency Law, is preparing a work, which will be published shortly, and which will replace Duffy and McHugh's.

Bills of Exchange:—

"Chitty on Bills of Exchange" (Russell).

"Byles on Bills."

Partnership:—

"Lindley on Partnership and Companies."

Trustees and Executors:—

"Walker's Compendium on the Law of Executors."

"The Law of Executors and Administrators" (Williams).

This is a nice little library for one to digest, but it must not be supposed that, when a student has passed his final examination, he has become an expert accountant. Far from it. As one has put it, "he has only then reached the wide expanse of waters, which open up illimitable scope for further voyages into the thousand and one bays of knowledge, which are worth exploring on every side."

An accountant can be very serviceable in the conduct of the business of a commercial man, and he should accordingly be more often utilised than he is.

In the beginning, in his capacity of book-keeper, to open his books in a proper manner. At different periods in his capacity of auditor to see that they are being kept correctly. If the business requires a partner, the Accountant is then necessary for his advice, as he is also, if it be desired to form the business into a company, on account of his knowledge of the necessary law. If there be any disputes then, in his capacity as arbitrator, the Accountant should be called in. Again, if the business man goes insolvent, or the company into liquidation, it is the Accountant in his capacity of Trustee or Liquidator who is best qualified to wind up the estate or company. And lastly, in case of death, the knowledge of executorship accounts that an accountant should have, should be the inducement for the executor, to whom figures are unintelligible, to engage him to open and keep proper books of accounts.

To banks, too, the Accountant is necessary, for it is in his capacity of auditor that he is relied upon to safeguard the shareholders' interests by periodical inspection of the books, securities, etc. He might be made additionally useful to them if, in cases of large accounts when any financial statements were necessary, either in connection with new business, or for purposes of ascertaining progress, or where a customer's affairs became involved, an accountant were requisitioned to prepare them, for with his superior knowledge of accounts he would be able to draw them up in a clear and more lucid manner than might otherwise be the case if the customer had to do it himself. The banks might even go further, and require firms to whom accommodation is granted to have their books periodically audited. An authority, Mr. F.W. Pixley, F.C.A., in a lecture delivered to the Chartered Accountants' Students' Society of London, in 1885, said: "It may be safely predicted that the time is not far distant when every person engaged in a profession or trade will have his books periodically audited. ... There can be no doubt many frauds are prevented through a knowledge that the books of an employer are subject to a periodical scrutiny by experts, and the probability of detection is too great to be risked."

A general idea of commercial transactions is extremely useful, as such a knowledge will always be of assistance to an Accountant who may be called in to examine very varied classes of accounts.

A knowledge of shorthand will also be found very handy.

The Accountant should be a person of strict integrity.

> "This above all,—to thine own self be true.
> And it must follow, as the night the day,
> Thou canst not then be false to any man."

A person therefore can only be termed a "skilled accountant" who has had, combined with the theoretical knowledge, much practical experience. This latter is recognised by the home societies, hence the term of apprenticeship.

Mr. Pixley sums up his lecture aforesaid with the following advice: "Theoretical knowledge is not sufficient. A student who takes every opportunity of becoming acquainted with the details of as many matters of business in his principal's office as he can, will find his zeal well repaid in his future career. The initial work may be monotonous, but no duties fall to the lot of members of any profession which can be more varied or interesting than those of a chartered accountant."

I have to thank you, gentlemen, for your patient hearing. No doubt you have been wondering what practical benefit you will derive from what has been said.

Possibly there might be among you those who desire to extend their range of knowledge, and with that aim, to study those subjects which give a man a better grasp of commercial matters, or those who have intention, either now or at some future time, to change their calling and qualify themselves for the accountancy profession.

The choice of a suitable subject gave me much concern, so that I thought of altering it, but the time (the original date of February 22, 1900, being altered to to-night's date) was too limited in which to prepare a paper on any banking subject that I would feel justified in delivering before an audience more critical than one would expect from a Students' Society, therefore, I have kept closely to the subject selected by your secretary.

In conclusion, I would like to mention that a Students' society was formed last year in connection with the Incorporated Institute of Accountants, Victoria. Meetings are held monthly at which papers are read on subjects cognate to the profession, followed by discussions.

A popular night with us is "Question Night," that is, the evening on which some of the questions set for the examinations of the Institute are discussed. Such a night is of great practical benefit to students, and those meetings are conducted in a free and conversational manner without any stiffness of "school" about them, so that young fellows are not awed from taking a part.

In his inaugural address, the President of this Society remarked: "These Students' Societies have become at home a very successful and important adjunct to the work of the Accountants' Societies; the leaders of the profession there, gladly acknowledge the valuable help which they have afforded to the work of their articled clerks."

There should be no reason why a similar result should not be achieved by the Bank Officers' Students' Society. I trust that it may be so, and I wish you every success; likewise a merry Christmas and a happy New Year.

BANKERS' MAGAZINE OF AUSTRALASIA

[AUGUST 29, 1900, pp.14-19]

THE LEGALISING OF THE PROFESSION OF ACCOUNTANTS

ﺀ ﺀ ﺀ

By J. McA. HOWDEN, F.I.A.V.

HE "Bankers' Magazine" (London) has a masterly article by Mr. Charles Woolley on this subject in its issue for July. After showing how the legal profession has only come into existence since 1825, it goes on to indicate the necessity for action by the profession of accountancy. I quote the whole of the latter portion of the article below with acknowledgment of its wisdom and application to the profession in Australia. As I am one of the Laws Committee of the Incorporated Institute of Accountants, Victoria, and one of its representatives on the Conference of Institutes appointed to deal with the framing of the proposed Bill, I am pleased to accede to the request of the editor of the BANKERS' MAGAZINE OF AUSTRALASIA to give some of the reasons why the measure has been brought forward here, and what has been done in the matter.

In Scotland the first Institutes of Accountants were established, and, subsequently, the English accountants established various associations of which the Institute of Chartered Accountants of England and Wales is a splendid example of what may be done, both professionally and financially.

In Victoria, in 1886, the Incorporated Institute of Accountants, Victoria, was founded, and about the same time the Society of Accountants and Auditors (London) established a branch here ; later there was formed the Federal Institute of Accountants, and, lastly, at Ballarat, the Australian Institute.

Admission to these Institutes is now by examination upon the subjects of Book-keeping, including partnership and executorship accounts, Auditing, Rights and Duties of Trustees and Receivers, the Law of Arbitration and Awards, Mercantile Law, Company Law, and Insolvency Law. Successful candidates become associates, fellowship requiring, in addition, practice as a public practising accountant for a certain number of years.

It was hoped that after a few years the public would recognise the advantages of having properly qualified accountants, and the efforts of the Institutes have been directed towards this, and the Institute to which I have the honour to belong has been particularly active in encouraging its students by establishing a Students' Society, which has the use of an extensive library containing all standard works of reference, and has regular courses of lectures upon technical subjects, at which full discussion and inquiry is encouraged.

133

When the Amending Companies Act of 1896 was passed, the qualifications for an auditor were defined, and though not quite so stringent as could be wished, was still a step in the right direction. It provided for the granting of Certificates of Competency by the Licensed Auditors' Board to (1) Those holding certificates from the Municipal Auditors' Board ; (2) the members of the existing Institutes, or any other approved institute ; (3) any person who had for three years, prior to the passing of the Act, practised in Victoria ; and (4) to any person passing an examination to be set by the Board. These were fairly liberal conditions, but as the Licensed Auditors' Board very strictly construed the Act, the three years' practice qualification was subsequently reduced to one year. Political representations were subsequently made by those who had not the qualifications, or could not pass the prescribed examinations, and in September, 1897, an Act to "remove certain doubts" was passed, whereby it was declared that any person, who, in order to aid or help him in earning his livelihood, was, on his own behalf, paid as an auditor of any company was to be deemed to have practised as an auditor.

This had the effect of enabling a large number of persons to obtain certificates as Licensed Auditors who otherwise would not have been qualified.

The title of Licensed Auditor vouched for by an imposing certificate bearing the Royal Arms and an impressive seal apparently carried with it all the qualifications necessary for an accountant.

Further complications arose through the varied methods of appointing auditors for companies in liquidation by the Supreme Court, the only qualification being that of Licensed auditor, no matter how large and complicated the liquidation, or what the real qualifications of the Licensed Auditors were.

Although considerable difference of opinion existed as to the advisability of some action being taken to formally fix the qualifications of all persons professing to be "accountants," it was generally recognised by the Institutes that in view of the enormous and continually increasing interests, which it was really their duty to protect, something should be done to establish a standard. The local Institutes, including the branch of the London Society, met in conference, and after much discussion by the delegates, their conclusions and recommendations were remitted to their various Councils. After further consideration and discussion the Institutes unanimously resolved to promote "a Bill to regulate the profession of public accountants," which has been introduced into Parliament, and is set down for its second reading.

134

In considering the position, the Conference of Institutes had before it all the Bills which have of recent years been introduced in Great Britain, as well as all other available information.

In framing the Bill the promoters had necessarily to take into consideration the whole of the local conditions, and the fact that all vested interests must be provided for. While by doing so it was more than probable many not possessing the full qualifications might register and become entitled to practise, yet the benefit to be gained by the public generally, ultimately, if not at present, more than compensated for any loss of prestige that might immediately result to the members of the Institutes from the passing of such an Act.

Consequently the Bill provided (section 27) that those entitled to be registered as public accountants were (1) The members of the Institutes; (2) any person who during three years prior to the commencement of the Act had been practising in Victoria for one year as a public accountant; (3) any person who passed the prescribed examinations ; (4) any person who proved he was a member of any Institute outside of Victoria possessing qualifications of membership equal to that required by the Board. It further provided that the existing rights of those registered under the Local Government Acts, and as Licensed Auditors under the Companies Acts, should be preserved. The Bill also contains a provision for appeal to the Supreme Court of any aggrieved person should the Board refuse to register.

The Bill provides for two Boards, one to act for the first year for registration purposes, which comprises representatives of the Institutes and nominees of the Government, and the subsequent, permanent Board consisting of representatives of the Institutes, members appointed by Governor in Council, and four members elected by, and from, the persons whose names are on the register.

These are the main provisions of the Bill, the remainder (the Bill comprises 44 clauses) being machinery clauses in connection with the administration of the Act.

As Institutes, we do not say the Bill is perfect, but it is an honest endeavour to definitely fix the legal status of accountants without in any way touching upon vested interests. Any amendments that may be suggested in good faith will have every consideration, and will be given effect to, so long as they do not abrogate the main idea, and that is, of ultimately only having thoroughly qualified persons to deal with the many important interests with which accountants have to deal, and are supposed to protect interests even now involving many millions, and which are continually increasing.

In the protection of the investing public, and generally where accountants' services are required, it is of paramount importance in view of the increasingly complicated character of modern legislation that when persons offer themselves as experts there should be some efficient standard, and while, doubtless, individual ability will always assert itself, yet so long as the minimum standard is sufficiently high, the general interests will be protected and confidence assured, and this is the aim and object of the " Bill to regulate the profession of accountants."

SOCIETIES AND INSTITUTES:

THE VALUE OF THEIR EFFECTIVE SUPERVISION AND CONTROL TO THE PUBLIC AND TO THE CRAFTS REPRESENTED.

Mr. Woolley, after speaking of solicitors, who only became a profession in 1825, and describing various "institutes," "guilds," and "crafts," goes on to say, speaking of auditors: " If, therefore, this form of presentment for the creation of power is acceptable to the nation, free to choose its form of government upon recognised constitutional lines, what argument can usefully be framed for its rejection by a fraternity or community, where fraternity and community of interest are alone desired, and where a homogeneous whole must surely be preferable to fragmentary parts, having unexpressed or possibly wayward interests, inducing a waste of power by contending for issues which are probably identical in the main, or could without difficulty be made so. It is no secret that these remarks apply to the profession of accountancy, and that its ranks are not yet welded into that condition of organised representative power identified with other professions, and for which lack no substantial reason has yet been forthcoming. None can dispute that it is a learned profession—that it is a necessary profession—that it is recognised in both cases as such, and, moreover, that increased recognition is necessary and desirable to it, and to the public, which it seeks to serve, and does serve. The evidence of these facts are patent, and potent when a flaw is discovered.

"While the 'wheels go round' in the world of auditing and accountancy with their accustomed and seemingly automatic precision all is well, and the auditor and the accountant is left apparently to his own devices, and his statement passes current as though such a thing as base metal or inaccuracy, or again, inefficiency, were an idea wholly to be eschewed. Such an acceptance and such an ideal is, doubtless, very flattering. But there is a reverse side to the picture, and the howl of execration which follows upon default should bring conviction to the minds of all true friends of auditors and accountants; that, be they who they may, they are dwellers upon the threatening surface of fields of thin ice, and that its easily puncturable surface may reveal a gulf of waters whose depth is not yet an established ascertained quantity. It is probably well known that in the new Company Bill, which has for some time past been under consideration and critical review from all those bodies and persons presumed to be interested and versed in company procedure, professional auditors and accountants are seeking for increased recognition and power. That they will achieve this laudable desire is the fervent hope of all interested in the welfare of the profession, whose usefulness cannot be ignored or denied. But while a certain proportion of the profession considers that a monopoly is preserved to it, and that that monopoly can be sustained in the face of facts openly disclosing that, while there are good men and true in the ranks of these supposed monopolists, there are equally good without their ranks, and whose appraisement is that by which they also live, viz., the public voice; they refuse to set the house of the learned profession of accountancy in order in the eyes of the world, and allow it to be rent by disunion; and, further, allow it to be ruled by the indefensible fears and the discordant cries of its young men who 'dream dreams, and see visions.'

" If it be, as it is alleged, the desire of all parties to secure enhanced status for the profession generally of which they are all accepted members, whether under a particular brand or not, the value of the retention of this particular brand matters very little as compared with the interests of the profession generally, and if such professions as law and medicine have seen in this a protective guarantee, not only to the professions themselves, but to those by whom the members live, is it asking too much upon these grounds that the individual interest in accountancy wherever it may clash may, for the time being, be allowed to disappear in order that the greater interest may be attained?

" It has been well said that the closing of a profession upon proper lines cannot increase its efficiency by the mere act of closing it, and none can well reason against this statement if the matter were to rest there.

" But whereas now it is practically open to anyone, young or old, to dub himself an accountant, and to practice under that title without let or hindrance wherever he may find trusting friends, by the closing of the profession means could be found for excluding inexperience and practically inefficiency by the standardising result of admission only within the ranks at the onset of proved experience, and the continuation of the submission to qualifying tests on the part of aspirants.

" It has also been stated that Parliament might hesitate to legislate for the suppression of the supposed interests of any part of the industrial or seeking professional members of the community by interfering in this particular branch of work with the liberty of the subject to choose for himself a vocation, and to follow that presumably only according to the dictates of his own sweet will and pleasure. The fallacy of this form of objection is proved by the lines regulating inclusion and admission to other learned professions, which have all had a starting point, and have been drawn down thence to their present position possibly by only the same conciliation compromise and subsequent recognition which is alone sought now with reference to accountancy.

" And, moreover, it is well known that, in spite of any fears that may have been entertained in this direction, Bills for submission to Parliament have from time to time been drawn by properly representative bodies, seeking powers to close the profession, and in one instance a particular Bill was conferred upon by delegates from these bodies, and the terms agreed upon by these delegates.

" It is not, therefore, conceivable that the responsible members who attended this representative conference could have doubted their power to do that ultimately which they then sought to do, and it must further be borne in mind that they were supported in their efforts by Members of Parliament of admittedly good judgment and experience, and were further fortified by valued and experienced legal advice, countenance, and support. This particular form of agreed upon Bill was submitted in general meeting to the members of these bodies, who in one instance broke wildly away from it for reasons of a purely personal nature. It can, therefore, truly be stated that caprice has been allowed to outweigh judgment, and that the case upon its merits stands still where it has done for many a long day past, in a position satisfactory to no one. Until the ordeal can be faced with an entire suppression of personal prejudice cowering under a flimsy measure of protection, the principle involved will remain untested, unsought, and ungained.

"For those who are loyal to their cause, whose love for their profession and its advancement in public esteem outweighs all other considerations of mere personal advancement, which may in no sense be interfered with, and may possibly be materially enhanced, the opportunity should be vigorously sought until the end and aim is accomplished of placing accountancy in its proper place as a close profession, identical with others, and recognised as such, instead of being, as it is now, an undisciplined army, self-recruited; and it is practically due from all its members to give this added guarantee to the public, which the present moment seems an admittedly good opportunity for doing."

AUDIT

A DEFINITION OF BANK AUDIT

A DEFINITION OF BANK AUDIT.

(*Australasian Insurance and Banking Record*, 8th May, 1880.)

IN the anxious and alarming period which was inaugurated for bank shareholders, by the collapse of the City of Glasgow Bank, and intensified by subsequent disasters in England and her colonies, a large section of the Press vehemently took up the cry against the inefficiency of audit, and the perfunctory manner in which even its imperfect requirements were carried out. The *Economist, Bankers' Magazine*, the *Insurance Review* (London), and various other organs of financial importance have, during the past year, put forward proposals for continuous and exhaustive audit of joint stock companies' accounts, ranging, we deferentially submit, from the cumbrously impracticable to the simply useless. But the agitation was not confined to the Press. A large number of the banks in England voluntarily adopted a much more verbose form of certificate for their auditors to sign, indicating in detail the nature and extent of these examinations, and many of them published a more amplified form of balance-sheet, without necessarily affording much new light to the uninitiated. It was, however, a deference to popular opinion, and at some of the bank meetings held in the early part of last year the chairman, in his address, dwelt at unusual length on the means adopted to verify the correctness of the published statements of accounts. A cursory examination of the reports of these meetings exhibits the wide diversity of opinion that prevails as to the nature and value of the safeguards to the shareholders' interests which are found in an outsider's examination of these transactions. While some of the younger banks seized the opportunity to dilate upon the efficiency of these periodical verifications, and paraded the names of eminent firms of accountants as specially called in to bear witness to their soundness, many of the older and more conservative institutions reprobated the idea of the introduction of professional auditors as an element of false security, the operations of which could never, within reasonable limits of time and expense, compare favourably with the elaborately organised system of which experience had demonstrated the sufficiency.

The chairman of the Union Bank of Australia, at the meeting in London on 13th January, 1879, said :—

" At present the audit was conducted by the chairman, the manager, and the accountant, and by two directors,

who were chosen for the purpose by routine, and he should like to know what they wanted better than men who were so deeply interested. [A voice : Men who were disinterested.] He did not really know where they were to find men who would go over the colonies to investigate the affairs of all the branches. To ask for such a thing would be to ask for an impossibility."

The chairman of the Bank of Australasia, at its meeting on 17th March following, said :—

"Then it was said there should be an independent audit of the accounts. He did not suppose anyone would recommend that the auditors should report on the value of the securities. In their case that would be impossible. But many were in favour of an audit of verification, and possibly such an audit might have sooner brought to light the state of the City of Glasgow Bank. But, depend upon it, if the directors of a bank were determined to deceive, they would work their way through any audit. With regard to this bank, every branch was visited at least once a-year by one of the inspectors, who had nothing at all to do with the actual conduct of the business, and whose duty it was to report on every account and every security. By means of these reports the superintendent controlled the whole business of the bank, and there was no need of an independent audit in the colonies. . . . . . ."

The tone of the foregoing remarks was also that of some of the largest and wealthiest of the London banks, and it was specially dwelt upon at more than one meeting that auditing was not management, and that it was the directors whom the shareholders called to account if anything went wrong with their property.

It may be fairly assumed that the banking bills introduced into the House of Commons last year were not framed without the fullest consideration, and the advice and approval of practical financiers of the highest standing. An examination of the clause relating to audit, in each of these measures, shows that the auditors are strictly to confine themselves to the verification of the accounts ; that the published balance-sheet is a correct epitome of the books used in the conduct of the bank's business is all that they are required to certify.

The clauses in the bill introduced by Mr James Barclay, M.P., run thus:—

"14. The duty of the auditors shall be to certify to the accuracy of the statements on the balance-sheet and accounts to be submitted to the partners, and they shall have full and complete access to the books, vouchers, accounts, and securities necessary to enable them to certify as aforesaid, but the auditors shall not value or appraise any debts, liabilities, assets, or securities of the company, or offer any opinion thereon.

"15. The balance-sheet of every banking company shall be signed by at least five directors, and by the responsible officials of the company, and if a balance-sheet so signed shall be fraudulent, the directors and officials who have signed such balance-sheet shall be guilty of a misdemeanour, and, being convicted thereof, shall be liable, at the discretion of the judge, to be imprisoned or kept in penal servitude for a period not exceeding five years."

The corresponding clauses in the bill introduced by the Chancellor of the Exchequer are:—

"Once at least in every year the accounts of every banking company, registered after the passing of this Act as a limited company', shall be examined by an auditor or auditors, who shall be elected annually by the company in general meeting.

"Every auditor shall have a list delivered to him of all books kept by the company, and shall at all reasonable times have access to the books and accounts of the company, and any auditor may, in relation to such books and accounts, examine the directors or any other officer of the company.

"The auditor or auditors shall make a report to the members on the accounts examined by him or them, and on every balance-sheet laid before the company in general meeting during his or their tenure of office; and in every such report shall state whether, in his or their opinion, the balance-sheet referred to in the report is a full and fair balance-sheet properly drawn up, so as to exhibit a true and correct view of the state of the company's affairs, as shown by the books of the company; and such report shall be read before the company in general meeting."

It might be assumed from the wording of the third clause in the latter extract, that the Government bill contemplated unlimited powers of comment and criticism on the part of the author; but Sir Stafford Northcote, on moving for leave to introduce the bill, said :—

" . . . . All we propose is that in every bank there should be a provision made for the appointment of an auditor or auditors, independent of the directors, who shall audit the accounts, and publish the report which they will be called upon to make; and in making the examination, and drawing up the report, what we call upon the auditors to do is, to certify whether the accounts give correctly and disclose truly the state of the company as shown by its books. It is impossible for an auditor to go into the books and say whether this is a good bill or security. That is not only impossible to effect but almost to attempt. We keep free from that. What we propose in the bill is that a proper examination shall take place of the books, and that the auditors shall declare, assuming their correctness, if the statement of accounts properly put together does give a full and fair description of the state of the bank."

The views enumerated by such eminent authorities received further confirmation, if it were needed, by the remarks of His Honour Chief Justice Stawell, at the trial of the directors of the Provincial and Suburban Bank, and it may be safely concluded that, from a legislative and judicial standpoint, the auditor is not regarded as being called upon to act as a valuator of his bank's securities. Nor, when the subject is dispassionately considered, is it possible to take any other view of the matter. It has been neatly said, that banks do not fail from bad book-keeping, but from bad securities; hence it may be asked, what is the value of an audit that concentrates its force on the former and ignores the latter? The answer is, that an audit may be thoroughly efficient and amply protect the shareholders' interest, without any opinion being expressed as to the value of a single debt. If the auditors, as the result of their examination, are able unreservedly to certify that the system of accounts is perfect in conception and accurate in its working; that the checks between the various departments (especially the accountant's and the cashier's) are sufficient, and regularly tested; that the inspections are frequent and thorough; that the

several books submitted for their examination are kept by the properly appointed officers, having an intelligent knowledge of the nature of the entries they pass ; *that no manipulation of the advances could be worked even by the manager without the knowledge and concurrence of at least one senior officer ; and that the cash, bills, and securities are under such custody as would render any single-handed dealing with them all but impossible—then, plus the customary verifications, they have fully discharged their duty,* and the shareholders have good grounds for believing themselves free from danger by "fraud." Had there been auditors to the City of Glasgow Bank (as many of the press writers erroneously suppose there were), they could not have failed to detect the course of deception that was being practised for years, even though they had never cast a doubt upon any of the advances. Books were kept by the manager, from which accounts were compiled, the bases of which were unknown in the office, and books kept in the office were ruthlessly altered in the board-room in a manner that could never have been explained to an auditor's satisfaction.

It must be admitted that while deliberate frauds could never be carried on under a proper system of accounts without the complicity of some of the senior officers, a manager prone to take very sanguine views of the value of his securities, might, without any evil intention, be storing up for his bank a crop of bad debts for which no provision was being made. But here the function of the director comes in, and it is to the election of the most suitable and experienced representatives at the board that the shareholders should devote their greatest energy and exercise their soundest judgment. If auditors were required to examine advances with a view to reporting on their safety, to value mercantile names, as well as properties and chattel securities, they must not only be men of a different stamp to those now selected, but they must be prepared to devote to an audit as many weeks as they now do hours, and they would still be unable to compass their object. Even in our local institutions it would require two or three months of close application for the auditors to master the details and valuations of all the branch advances, and then they must necessarily mainly rest for their decision on the opinion of the local manager, or the branch inspector. Such being the case on the spot, where the generality of bank auditors are men well informed of the mercantile standing of their fellow-colonists, and with general ideas of the value of properties, it follows, as the Chairman of the Bank of Australasia said, that a valuation audit is "impossible" in the case of the Anglo-Australian banks, where the investigation is held in London, except in so far as it is based on the reports of the local officers whose opinions can be far better gauged by their own directors.

It would be difficult to find a more apposite illustration of the inutility of valuations made by professional auditors even under circumstances where their suspicions were aroused and their thoroughness challenged, than in the case of the late Australian and European Bank. The regular auditors, reinforced by three admittedly able and practical business men, made "a careful and patient investigation of every advance at the head office, and of the securities connected therewith," and assured the shareholders that the loss would be less than one-third of what it was actually proved to be a few months later. It will be universally admitted that these gentlemen had no desire to mislead. Though, unfortunately for themselves, shareholders, they sincerely desired to get to the bottom of the difficulty and to know the worst. But, being unfamiliar with the workings of the various accounts, their opinions were moulded by the manner in which things were presented to them. On the other hand, take the result of the prior investigation by a committee of bank managers—men whose lives are passed in gauging a man's capacity to pay up. They sought no explanations, asked few questions, but in less than twelve hours they assessed the losses at within £10,000 of the ultimate outturn of £114,000 loss.

Unfortunately, bank managers, when they are efficient, have got a habit of sticking to their posts until they die in harness or are superannuated in old age. If they would only occasionally resign, and want temporary employment, what a magnificent corps of auditors might be inaugurated, doubtless at a largely increased rate of remuneration.

It must be admitted, however, that, leaving out the question of valuations, there are many cases of lamentable shortcomings on the part of auditors even in matters of accounts. The revelations connected with the Provincial and Suburban Bank evidence the most flagrant neglect in passing accounts, manipulated in violation alike of banking practice and Statute law.

To sum up, it may be said that, in addition to what has been already indicated as the proper sphere of the auditor's examination, he should make it his duty to see that none of the business transacted is at variance with the articles of association, or act of incorporation under which the bank works; that every line in the balance-sheet is *bonâ fide*; and especially that the capital is really paid-up, and not represented by paper promises.

It is only in extreme cases that auditors need venture outside these lines and act the part of general censors. *If, in their opinion, insufficient provision was made for admittedly bad debts, or an item was included in the balance-sheet which they could not accept as an asset, they should clear themselves by so reporting to the shareholders; but on questions of policy they would be justified, we consider, in addressing the directors, but not in commenting in their report.*

Further, auditors should make it their business to know that the balance-books and returns submitted to them are in regular course laid before the directors, and that their manager does not use their certificate as a means of staving off the continuous investigations of his board, without which the best of officials will in time relax the vigilance of his control.

Further, over-reliance upon audit is, we repeat, a latent danger to shareholders. Depending upon it as a check upon the board, has a tendency to diminish care in selection of the very best directors. It cannot be too strongly impressed upon the public, that this is the point to which earnest attention should be directed. Between the two stools of divided responsibility, proprietors run the risk of coming to the ground. It is far better that the limited functions of audit should be clearly defined and understood than that there should be mistaken dependence upon any false safeguard. It is of the utmost consequence that directors should feel that the full responsibility for their acts attaches to themselves solely—that their accounts being passed by the auditors neither condones nor exculpates—and that it be, on all hands, understood, that the true concretion in the balance-sheet of *res gestæ* is the proper function of the auditor, and defines the limit of his responsibility.

Second Class Audit

Second-Class Audit.

At the last meeting of the shareholders of the National Bank of Australasia, some discussion took place as to the desirability of the bank's auditors refraining from performing like duties for other banking institutions. The chairman of the bank (R. Murray Smith, Esq., M.P.), who was probably unprepared for such a question being suddenly raised, expressed an off-hand opinion that "considering the im- " portant duties which the auditors had to " perform he was personally in favour of " their not being connected with rival " establishments." Now we are disposed to believe that if Mr. Smith gave this subject the intelligent consideration of which he is so very capable, he would probably arrive at a directly opposite conclusion.

In our last issue we furnished a definition of the proper functions of audit, of the duties of auditors, and their limitations of duty, showing that the design of Imperial legislation upon this matter was, that auditors should decide whether the accounts submitted exhibited a true and fair view of the state of a company's affairs as shown in its books, and "not that the auditor should," in the words of Sir Stafford Northcote, the late Chancellor of the Exchequer, "go into the books and say, this is a good bill or security." If this view be the correct one as to the duty of an auditor, as we confidently maintain it is, what possible objection can there be to the same expert filling the office in more than one banking institution? If, indeed, it were the auditors' duty to value the advances, and supplant the directors in *their* duties—to estimate the worth of the bills discounted, instead of merely identifying their current existence, and that they count up what is represented in the balance-sheet placed before them—then indeed, there might be some excuse for each bank having its own special auditor.

We are, however, under any circumstances, ready to repudiate on behalf of the leading professional auditors of this city the implication that they would turn to improper use in one institution, the information acquired in another. It is indeed possible, that the general knowledge obtained by an auditor extensively, instead of exclusively, employed, might be most valuable to all who had the advantage of his services. It is within the bounds of possibility that excessive engagements of one firm in several banks (each one of such banks being perhaps in ignorance of liabilities elsewhere) might induce a word of caution to the different managements which would be of the greatest value. This might certainly be disadvantageous to the expansive customer, but could only be for the benefit of the shareholders. And it would not in such circumstances be for the latter to take exception to the general knowledge of the generally employed auditor.

Re-asserting our opinion, that the simple duty of the auditor is to satisfy himself that the accounts are in conformity with the books, then there is every ground for maintaining the present system in its integrity. The very fact of an auditor being engaged for the work of audit for a number of banks or companies, in itself proves that he is recognised as capable and expert, and the frequent exercise of his trained acuteness tends to develop his skill in dissection and discovery to the highest point of usefulness. Thus the more generally his services are availed of, the greater will be his competence for his work and the advantage of his employers.

The proposal of an exclusive or special auditor means probably the election of some estimable shareholder, who may be a sound man of business, but with no sharply trained instinct of detection. Or, it may lead to the choice of a second or third-rate accountant, who would be very willing to desert the ranks of the unemployed for an exclusive auditorship. If, however, instead of either of these contingencies, a large salary were attached to the office, so as to secure the best possible auditor, that would simply mean the undertaking of a wholly unnecessary expenditure for an article which was readily available at a lower market price.

In connection with the proposal of an auditor " earmarked" for each institution, it was suggested that he would be "independent." We submit that this is diametrically opposed to the probability. An auditor of recognised ability, with an extensive business, is practically independent of any one client. An auditor who is the auditor of one institution only would, in all human probability, drift into subservience to the management. It is well known that no new candidate need seek a seat at the board without the board proxies. It would be just the same with the auditor. And why indeed should the shareholders trouble themselves with an exclusive auditor, when it would be a simple and easy course to delegate the duty to one of the bank's officers, which the auditor-exclusive would practically be?

There should, we think, be some respect in banking affairs, if not in political, for British precedent. Who ever heard an objection raised at a bank meeting to Messrs. TURQUAND AND Co., or Messrs. QUILTER, BALL AND Co., of London, that they were auditors of other banks? Why, the certificate of skilled men is at home regarded as worth a large remuneration. And why should the precedent be lost upon Melbourne? We can count up many a public failure here, where the amateur and exclusive auditor has approved the accounts (keeping very quiet subsequently); but we cannot recall a single instance where creditors have suffered through the failure of a company whose accounts have been audited by men who are easily recognisable as in the first class, inclusive, we may say without invidiousness, of the present auditors of the National Bank of Australasia.

CONTINUOUS AUDIT

Continuous Audit.*

A PAMPHLET on the continuous audit of public accounts, by the late ANTHONY DILLON, originally published a few years ago, has just been re-issued in London, with an introduction by Mr. MALCOLM DILLON, the son of the author, and has been favourably noticed by some of the financial papers in the United Kingdom.

It might have been thought that the miserable apology for a check, which commonly goes by the name of "audit," in connection with nine-tenths of our public companies, had been pretty thoroughly exposed; that the perfunctory character of its operation, and the paltry scale of its remuneration, were in keeping with its utter uselessness, and the contempt with which men of business capacity regarded its fraudulent pretensions.

When a national calamity like the crash of the City of Glasgow Bank overtakes us, the country is flooded with suggestions for preventing the bare possibility of such an evil, and schemes of check and counter-check, special audits, intermittent and unexpected audits, continuous and exhaustive audits, are preached in turn as the only true solution of the difficulty and safeguard of the past.

The pages of the *Banker's Magazine*, and kindred journals, are gay with endless varieties of new forms of balance-sheets; and freshly-devised attestations of accuracy are canvassed logically, literally, and legally. Here and there a new form of return, or a new practice of check, is adopted, and with that the excitement dies away, and the old indifference returns. The remark recently made by Mr. GLADSTONE, that the wealth of Great Britain was increasing at the rate of £100,000,000 a year, and that a very large proportion of this must find an outlet through the operations of joint-stock companies, has naturally set men thinking how best to hedge round these stupendous and ever increasing investments, with such safeguards as shall not only keep away the MONTAGUE TIGGS, but shall protect shareholders from that mal-administration of their funds, which comes of fatuous incapacity or daring hazard, rather than from absolute dishonesty. The writer of the pamphlet under notice is undoubtedly an extremist, and while we heartily concur in his condemnation of the existing methods of so-called audit as ineffective and misleading, we very much doubt the possibility of applying his principles of inspection to the affairs of banks without a radical change in the present system of management.

He defines the duties of an auditor thus:—

1. To examine every individual receipt and payment.
2. Frequently, and at irregular periods, to verify cash balances, and banker's pass-books.
3. To see that securities for investments are in hand.
4. To see that all payments are authorised by minutes of his board.
5. To see that proper vouchers are produced for all such payments.
6. To report on the assets, *giving an independent valuation of these*, and generally,
7. To act as a check upon the company's accounts.
8. To report the number of boards held, the number and nature of the committees (if any), the names of the directors attending, and the number of their attendances respectively at each board and committee.

Now, the veriest tyro in banking will know that no man, devoting his whole

---

* SUGGESTIONS FOR THE CONTINUOUS AUDIT OF PUBLIC ACCOUNTS, by the late ANTHONY DILLON, J.P., &c., with introductory preface. London: William Brown and Co., Old Broad Street; 1880.

time to the duties, could cover all this ground single-handed. He would not only require to possess special abilities to comply with the sixth clause, which would eminently fit him for management, and would readily command the emoluments pertaining to such qualifications; but he must also have an efficient staff of experts, at least, equal to the complement of an ordinary bank inspector's office. A large portion of his work would be merely a duplication of the ordinary routine of the bank, the only practical difference being that he would submit his information direct to the shareholders, while that of the management would be filtered through the board.

Irrespective of the serious consideration of its costliness, the establishment of such an *imperium in imperio* would be fraught with innumerable difficulties in the conduct of the business, and lead to much heartburning and dissatisfaction, while it would certainly tend to deteriorate the status of the class of men whom most banks would desire to secure as directors. It would undermine the self-respect and self-reliance of the manager, unduly deprive him of the credit of success, and offer him an easy excuse to escape the consequences of failure.

Of course, by multiplying the number of responsible officers in any public company, the danger of fraudulent collusion to conceal disaster, until it can be surmounted, is lessened; but it is doubtful whether a highly-paid and practically-permanent official is as likely to make a bold stand against the sophistries of his colleagues as a director, whose financial interest in his position is as nothing in comparison to his reputation. We have already pointed out at some length (see *ante* p. 143 *ut supra*) the legitimate aim and the proper limits of an auditor's duties, as applied to banks, and we venture to reiterate the conclusions then expressed, that over-reliance on audit, which would almost certainly result from the proposed increased status of the auditor, is fraught with great danger to shareholders. Let them take as much interest, and, if necessary, spend as much money, in securing the services of the best possible board of directors, as in establishing a check on them; and, having secured them, let no opportunity be lost, even at the risk of wearisome iteration, of making them understand the full measure of their responsibility, which they cannot lessen by blaming incompetent officers or too credulous auditors. We venture to predict that the results will be far more satisfactory in the end, and that they will be attained with less friction, and the avoidance of injury to the business of the bank.

THE AUDITOR-GENERAL OF QUEENSLAND ON BANKING RETURNS

The Auditor-General of Queensland on Banking Returns.

THE seventh annual report of the Auditor-General of Queensland (Mr. W. L. G. DREW) is a valuable and complete public document. It discusses questions of interest and of moment outside the limits of the colony in which it is issued.

The point which has especially attracted our notice is a paragraph in which Mr. DREW directs attention to the meagreness of the information afforded by the periodical statements of banking liabilities and assets. Mr. DREW has very definite opinions, and he does not hesitate to set them forth plainly and with decision. Some of the objections raised by him have been frequently indicated in our columns, and strongly press for reform. In other respects we think Mr. DREW demands more than prudence requires, and his compulsory schedule we regard as inquisitorial in its character, unnecessarily exposing a bank's transactions, without any countervailing advantage to the public. Mr. DREW sets out with the undeniable proposition that the present time, when the mercantile, banking, and leading industries of the colony are unusually prosperous, and suggestions are consequently unlikely to be misunderstood or misapplied, appears a fitting opportunity to invite attention to the unsatisfactory nature of the statements of banking liabilities and assets provided for and published under the provisions of " *The Banking Companies Act of* 1840," and to recommend that such alterations may be made in the form of those statements as will give to the public the fullest general information which can be embraced in such returns. There have been periods of financial pressure and political excitement when such proposals as Mr. DREW makes would have been seized upon by some popular orator as implying official distrust of banking institutions, and lead to some hasty and perhaps absurd legislation. Mr. DREW has thus shown tact and prudence in bringing forward his objections at a time when the financial atmosphere is calm and when prosperity prevails. It is admitted, he asserts, by all whose business leads them to consult and endeavour to utilise the periodical banking statements, that in consequence of the meagre information contained in the form in which they at present appear, they are of little practical use save as crude statistical records, and that for the purpose for which the Legislature directed their publication, viz., " for " the information and better security of " the public," they are almost valueless.

We are unable to go so far as the Queensland Auditor-General. It is hardly justifiable to say that returns which show the precise note circulation, deposits, coin held, advances, with assets and liabilities of the whole of the banks, are " almost " valueless" for information or security. We are prepared to go further and say that in the aggregate results, the banking statistics of the Australasian colonies (including Queensland) are the most complete with which we are acquainted.

When the London *Economist* essays to furnish a summary of the affairs of British banks, it is obliged to preface such with the caution that they are only approximate. They cannot obtain the returns of all banks. In setting forth the banking accounts to 31st December, 1881, at a date so late as 20th May, 1882 (Australian banking accounts being available each quarter within six weeks or so), the

Economist says:— "We have to repeat "that since all the banks in England, "Wales and Ireland do not publish their "accounts, this statement is necessarily "incomplete, so far as showing the total "banking resources of the country is "concerned." Our Australasian banking statistics are better, because they are compulsory, complete (as it is obligatory on every bank to furnish them), and they are promptly published.

Mr. DREW is not the man to make complaint without proposing a remedy, and he has submitted a form of return which he submits "would better suit the present "requirements of Queensland, and more "serve the interests of shareholders and "the public, than those prescribed in the "existing Act." Mr. DREW's suggested schedule in many respects reminds us of forms of balance-sheets suggested by some British banking authorities at the time that discussion was rife regarding the extension of the Limited Liability system, after the failure of the City of Glasgow Bank. This is his model form :—

RETURN OF THE ACCOUNT OF LIABILITIES AND
ASSETS OF THE   BANK, ON THE
        DAY OF   , 18   .

LIABILITIES. £

Notes in circulation .. ..
Bills in circulation ... ...
Government deposits at call... ... ...
Other deposits at call ... ...
Government deposits payable after notice bearing interest ... ...
Government deposits fixed bearing interest
Other deposits fixed bearing interest ...
Due to other banks in the colony ... ...
Due to other banks out of the colony ...
Liabilities other than the foregoing ...

        Total liabilities   ...   £

ASSETS. £

Coined gold and other coined metals ...
Gold and silver bullion ... ...
Notes of, and bills and cheques on, other banks ... ...
Balances due from other banks in the colony
Balances due from other banks out of the colony ... ...
Government securities ... ...
Advances to the Government ... ...
Government drafts negotiated ... ...

Advances to Corporations or other local bodies ... ...
Bills discounted and current payable within the colony ... ...
All other bills discounted and current, exclusive of those drawn against shipments of produce ... ...
Bills discounted and overdue, and not specially secured ... ...
Advances unsecured ... ...
Advances secured by mortgage or lien on real estate, or by deposit of scrip, bond warrants, bills for collection, &c. ...
Advances secured by mortgage or lien on sugar and other agricultural lands, and by lien on crops ... ...
Advances secured by mortgage on stock and on station properties, or by lien on wool, &c. ... ...
Advances on shipment of station and other produce drawn against or otherwise ...
Real estate, the property of the bank (other than bank premises), and mortgages on real estate sold by the bank ... ...
Bank premises ... ...
Assets other than the foregoing ... ...

        Total assets   ...   .
                                  £

Amount of capital stock paid up on the 18 ... ...
Rate of last dividend declared to shareholders ... ...
Amount of the last dividend ... ...
Amount of the reserved profits at the time of declaring such dividend ... ...

Taking up the suggested schedule of liabilities, there can be no doubt that it is an obvious improvement. We are weary of asking that the deposits made by the public should be distinguished from those of the Government. The disturbance of the current of banking finance by so frequently recurring an event as a Government loan, the proceeds being deposited with the banks, or the running down of the Government balance, can at present only be guessed, and facts or consequences cannot be logically demonstrated. Again, the distinction drawn in Mr. DREW's model sheet between liabilities to banks out of or within each colony respectively, would lead to a better apprehension of the banking status.

Coming to the assets, the comment just made has a like application in respect of balances due from banks by banks, within or without each colony. We further approve that separately distinguished should be Government securities and advances to Government. But we think Mr. DREW goes too far when he would call upon a bank to distinguish liens on wool from liens on sugar! The differentiating the assets in the microscopic manner demanded by him, might be very prejudicial to a bank in disclosing to rivals the nature of its business, and (as we have already said) without compensating advantage to the public or to statistical science. We are not prepared to deny that it would be an improvement to distinguish the manner in which a bank's money is lent in some manner more instructive than the stereotyped "All debts due to "the bank, including notes, bills of "exchange, and all stock and funded debts "of every description," &c., &c. With regard to advances, the New Zealand returns hit the happy medium of usefulness, without being indistreetly communicative. The lent money is divided into the following heads :—Notes and bills discounted ; Government securities ; other funded securities ; debts due to the bank, exclusive of debts abandoned as bad; securities not included under other heads. This classification, we think, fairly meets public requirements.

Mr. DREW looks forward with confidence to a period when " some system of general " Government supervision or control over " the banking institutions of the colony, " such as exists elsewhere, as well as peri- " odical effective independent audit of their " accounts, will be by law established." With his aspiration for Government super-

vision or control of the banks, we have no sympathy. We shall, however, be glad to hear from him what he really means by this, especially in connection with the system which he alleges "exists elsewhere." If by " periodical effective "independent audit" of banking accounts Mr. DREW means Government audit, we must again part company with the Auditor-General. The perpetual reliance on Government interposition is sapping Australian manhood, and almost justifies the sarcasm of Mr. ARCHIBALD FORBES, "that in this country a man will shortly "ask for Government help to scratch him- "self." In the history of our banks as a whole, there is nothing to justify any sweeping change in this practice of audit, and we have strong views upon the undesirability of relieving directors and managers of their just responsibility by overdoing the audit system.

Mr. DREW advocates monthly, instead of quarterly returns. Of course, the more frequently the real condition of the money-market can be clearly ascertained the quicker the remedy for over-stringency or undue liberality. We confess that there is as yet no very urgent need for this requirement. We cannot conclude without complimenting the Auditor-General of Queensland as a Government officer who takes sufficient interest in his country to emancipate himself from the bonds of red-tape, and throwing aside the straps and buckles of Government harness, to display an intelligent interest in a subject which he has the capacity to understand and the power to elucidate.

THE AUSTRALASIAN INSURANCE AND BANKING RECORD

[MARCH 15, 1886, pp.117-8]

BANK AUDIT

Bank Audit.

UPON the occurrence of any banking disaster the inevitable first suggestion is that there has been a perfunctory and useless audit, and then follow proposals that Government should interfere, that auditors should be invested with larger powers, that they should make valuations of the securities held, and not content themselves with simply identifying them as existing, in accordance with the books of account. Of course some untoward event such as that which has just occurred in South Australia gives a certain emphasis and force to suggestions suited to a hysterical condition of the public mind. But a calm consideration of the practical operation of some of these heroic remedies deprives them of much of their value. It is hardly necessary to propound as novelties proposals that auditors should be men of good qualification as accountants, of unblemished character, and that they should possess the courage to express their opinions fearlessly if the occasion arose for so doing. No qualification could, indeed, be too high for this important office—whether it be membership of a London guild of experts or that of some local institution requiring from those who established it, or joined it, evidence of highest competency. And whilst on this point we may suggest that the best men for bank auditors would be retired bank managers or bank accountants, who, from their knowledge of the internal workings of a bank, would be quick to detect the slightest deviation from the best administrative practice, and to probe such to the utmost extent.

The real point at issue is to determine the limit of the duty of auditors. It is upon this that the entire question hinges. It is put forward as the best remedy against banking frauds or failures that the

auditors should not only identify securities, but should make valuations of them, and report thereon. Against this view we join issue. In the first place we should like to have it explained, in the case of an Australian bank with a head office in London, and with branches throughout our colonies, what would be the worth of the valuation of its securities by two London auditors, no matter to what society or guild they belonged? Or even take the case of one of our local banks, with its head office in Sydney or Melbourne— what would be the value of the head office auditors' opinions of the worth of each individual bill discounted through the length and breadth of Queensland, New Zealand, and Tasmania? It is beyond denial that any attempt to make such a valuation would absolutely be worthless, misleading, and inferior to the system now in existence. The duty which it is proposed to put upon the auditors is performed far better by the inspector's department, which exists in most institutions—the branch inspectors keeping themselves always informed as to the details of what is being done by the branch managers.

But it may be said that this need not prevent the auditors checking the values of bills and securities held at the head office. To this the objection is that it would create a divided responsibility. If Messrs. A. and B., the auditors, are to be clothed with the right of making valuations, and of thus practically determining what the business of the bank is to be, then why not simplify matters by placing Messrs. A. and B. on the board of direction? It is in this quarter that shareholders must seek for protection from disaster— not absolute immunity from loss (for that is impossible), but the best available defence. The election of directors is the point to which proprietors should carefully address themselves. It ought not alone to suffice that a candidate held a large interest, or was a respectable citizen, but they should endeavour to place upon the board, men of keen, shrewd business intelligence, who might be a match for even a fraudulent manager.

The question of audit has been repeatedly discussed in the *Record*, and we do not think we can do better than reproduce " A Definition of Audit" from our own columns published in May, 1880. In this reprint we have italicised two suggestions (both within existing powers), which, if acted upon by the auditors of the Commercial Bank of South Australia, would have brought to light the shameful abuse of the trust reposed by the directors in their manager. We also publish for information the sections of the Imperial Act which refer to banking audit.

There remain two points which may be touched upon. The one is that there is an idea that the Legislature might enact a measure authorising the appointment of Government auditors, upon whom it would be compulsory to inspect and vouch for banking and trading companies accounts. This would be a fatal mistake. It would, in fact, transfer the responsibility of management to a Government department which, logically and morally, ought to be liable for any malfeasance if such occurred (as it would) in spite of the State audit. The other point is that, considering the vast volume of banking business, the losses which arise from banking failures or from frauds are an infinitesimal percentage of the whole.

Of course when a disaster, such as has lately occurred, is close at hand, it looms large. But even in that case creditors are not likely to suffer anything more serious than delay. As in the Oriental Bank, or the Australian and European Bank, it will be the shareholders only who will suffer. And, deep as is our sympathy with them, their losses do not concern the community in the same way as would losses by depositors, note holders, or other creditors. The proprietors voluntarily entered into a partnership which has resulted unfortunately, but their acts were their own, their officers of their own choosing, and their mishap does not call for special legislative interposition to protect men against themselves. For fraud there is the ordinary criminal penalty.

THE NEW BANKING AND TRADING COMPANIES' BILL

The New Banking and Trading Companies' Bill.

A MEASURE proposing to amend the law with respect to the liabilities of shareholders in trading and other companies at present engages the attention of the Legislature. It is doubtful whether any more useful subject could occupy the consideration of Parliament, and it is some guarantee that the design is not crude nor reckless that its sponsor in the Legislative Council is the Honourable JAMES LORIMER, a merchant of mature experience, proverbial for his prudence, and constitutionally cautious. In the category of trading companies, banking institutions are, of course, included, and it is in this aspect that the bill possesses especial interest for our readers. If it were necessary to further bespeak Parliamentary countenance of Mr. LORIMER'S bill, such may be done on the ground that it is in its main provisions an almost exact counterpart of a measure which became the law of Great Britain in 1879, and which has favourably stood the test of the time that has since elapsed. One of its main purposes is to enable companies previously unlimited, to come under the prudent provisions of limited liability. This broad statement, taken by itself, might perhaps suggest that companies could, by taking advantage of the provisions of this measure, attempt to evade or determine their just responsibilities. But this is carefully guarded against in the 3rd section, by which it is provided that the regulations of a limited company, registered under its provisions, shall not affect or prejudice any debts, liabilities, *contracts* or *obligations* incurred or entered into by, to, with, or on behalf of such company prior to registration. (It may be noted that the words italicised

are in addition to those of the corresponding section of the Imperial Act.) The section proceeds to provide that all liabilities, as enumerated above, shall be recoverable in the manner prescribed in the Act of 1864, which was the first legislative enactment in Victoria recognising the principle of limited liability. The effect of this is, that if a banking or other company registered itself under the measure now proposed, " the limit " could only apply to transactions subsequent to registration. All prior obligations would, until fully liquidated, continue in force just as if advantage had not been taken of the provisions of the new bill.

Is it the intention of this bill that banking companies now trading under special Acts of Incorporation may register under it? Section 3 apparently opens the door for companies already registered as " unlimited." Section 9, with marginal note, reads thus :—

Privileges of Act available notwithstanding constitution of company. 42 and 43 Vict. c. 76, s. 10. – A company authorised to register under this Act may register thereunder and avail itself of the privileges conferred by this Act notwithstanding any provisions contained in any Act of Parliament Royal charter deed of settlement contract of copartnery letters patent or other instrument constituting or regulating the company.

Now section 3 seems to *authorise* the admission of only two classes of companies to the privileges of the new bill, viz., companies registered as unlimited, or those already registered as limited. Can incorporated or chartered companies come in under sections 3 and 9?

The fourth section of the bill provides specifically for the creation of what is known as " reserve liability." The principle of this is that—beyond the power of directors to make calls in a going concern —there will be a further defined calling power, which liquidators can exercise for

155

the benefit of creditors in the case of failure and winding-up.

It may be here convenient to point out that the Imperial prototype of this bill came into existence through the attention drawn to banking concerns by the failure of the City of Glasgow Bank. There then existed fifteen different constitutions of banks in Great Britain and Ireland. Sir STAFFORD NORTHCOTE grappled the subject with great ability and determination, and on 15th August, 1879, his bill became law. Of its merits there can be no better test than the experience that a large majority of the home banks have come under its provisions. Amongst the earliest were such powerful institutions as the London and Westminster Bank, and the Union Bank of Australia. We look back with satisfaction to the fact that the adoption of a like measure in the Australasian colonies, was earnestly advocated in our columns in December, 1879 (when we re-published the English Act), and again in March, 1880. After seven years' delay there is now a serious legislative effort to follow the good example of the British Parliament.

A very important branch of the subject relates to the placing of the note issues in a position of exceptional strength. We have for a long time advocated that notes issued by a bank should be legally made a first charge upon its assets, and we are inclined to think that this simple remedy would accomplish all that is needed. We are, however, aware that this view does not receive universal acceptance amongst bankers, and some believe that it might not be workable in practice. The new bill proposes the repeal of section 119 of the Companies Statute 1864, in order to strengthen the preference which it is intended that holders of notes should enjoy. This is the text of section 5 :—

5. Section one hundred and fifty-nine of "The Companies Statute 1864" is hereby repealed, and in place thereof it is enacted as follows :—[No banking company that issues notes in Victoria (unless the contrary be provided by an Act of Parliament or by Royal charter establishing or regulating the same) shall] be entitled to limited liability in respect of its notes, but the members thereof shall continue liable in respect of its notes in the same manner as if it had been registered as an unlimited company ; but in case the general assets of the company are in the event of the company being wound up insufficient to satisfy the claims of both the noteholders and the general creditors, then the members after satisfying the remaining demands of the noteholders shall be liable to contribute towards dayment of the debts of the general creditors a sum equal to the amount received by the noteholders out of the general assets of the company.

For the purposes of this section the expression "the general assets of the company" means the funds available for payment of the general creditor as well as the note-holder.

It shall be lawful for any banking company that issues notes registered as a limited company to make a statement on its notes to the effect that the limited liability does not extend to its notes and that the members of the company continue liable in respect of its notes in the same manner as if it had been registered as an unlimited company.

In the English Act (the Companies' Act 1879) the operation of the provisions concerning liabilities for notes appears to be confined to those banks which register under it. The proposal in the Victorian bill seems to widen the scope of this section and to apply it to all banks whether registered under the new bill or not.

The wording of the latter portion of the first paragraph is, we submit, obscure. It is a literal transcript of the English Act, and despite so good a precedent, we have heard it described as vague and almost unintelligible. Some experts incline to the belief that every shareholder might be made liable for the whole circulation, over and above his liability on his shares; and that this liability must be defrayed by the shareholders, not out of the ordinary assets, which are pledged to the general creditors. This matter we commend to the consideration of the introducer of the bill.

In whatever shape the proposed bill becomes law, it will probably have the effect of reassuring the public mind and possibly, for ever, put a stop to the senseless doubts about bank notes which now and again agitate the minds of ignorant and timid persons. Even under existing systems, in at least thirty years the Australasian public has lost nothing by unpaid bank notes, except in the case of the farcical Provincial and Suburban Bank, and then the loss was under £5000.

An important part of the bill relates to bank audit. The terms of the section are precisely those which we approvingly quoted from the Imperial Act in March of this year (p. 125), and previously in December, 1879 (p. 378). As we reprint the bill now before Parliament elsewhere, we need not repeat the section here. It is a good point that the balance-sheets must be signed, not only by the manager, secretary, and auditors, but by the directors, or by at least three of them. This will tend to keep up a lively sense of their serious responsibility amongst the members of the board.

We submit with great respect that it might be possible to enact a form of audit certificate, or, if that were going too far, to furnish a form of audit voucher in a schedule to the bill — which form it might be optional for a banking or other company to adopt or not, at the will of its shareholders. As a practical contribution to this part of the subject, we furnish in another column a reprint of the varied forms of audit certificates appended to the balance-sheets of most of the Australasian banks and those of some important British banking institutions. The inharmonious variety in itself suggests the desirability of something like uniformity. Where a common end is to be attained there should be a common method of expression.

And whilst on this point it might be possible to schedule a desirable form of balance-sheet for adoption by choice of shareholders. In a " Trading Companies " Bill," this, admittedly, would be difficult. But what is thus termed is mainly a Banking Companies Bill, and for banks a form of balance-sheet for voluntary adoption might be scheduled. In the original bill introduced by Sir STAFFORD NORTHCOTE on 21st April, 1879, a form of balance-sheet was enjoined, but the proposal was abandoned, and Dr. CAMERON made an effort in a similar direction in the House of Commons at the same time. Both these forms of accounts will be found in our July issue of 1879 (p. 200). We think that a convention of Victorian bankers might be able to suggest a form of accounts which would produce a uniformity useful for comparison and instruction both to shareholders and creditors. Our Life Assurance Act prescribes a Victorian form of balance-sheet which all life companies trading here may adopt, and there is no reason why all banks should not have a like opportunity to display in fuller detail than they now do, their meritorious condition.

We trust, and we believe, that so useful a measure as that under the care of the Minister of Defence will not fail in a prosperous Parliamentary career.

EXAMPLES OF AUDITORS' CERTIFICATES

EXAMPLES OF AUDITORS' CERTIFICATES.

I.—AUSTRALASIAN BANKS.

AUSTRALIAN JOINT-STOCK BANK.

We have examined the annexed balance-sheet, made up to 31st December, 1885, and report that we find the several items therein stated to conform to the balances in the general ledger, and the balance-sheets of the respective branches and agencies of the bank collectively. We have counted the cash balance, and examined the bills and other securities held by the bank at the head office in Sydney, on the 31st December last, and hereby certify that we have found them correct. The cash, bills, and other securities held at the branch banks and agencies in London, New South Wales, and Queensland, on the respective dates of balancing, have been certified to as being correct by the usual documents.

CHAS. H. MYLES, } Auditors.
LOUIS PHILLIPS, }

BANK OF ADELAIDE.

We hereby certify that we have counted the cash, checked the bills and abstract of advances and deposits of the Bank of Adelaide, and compared the returns of its branches with the above balance-sheets, and found the same to be correct.

J. FORD QUILL, } Auditors.
HENRY STODART, }

BANK OF AUSTRALASIA.

(Signed) PRIDEAUX SELBY, Secretary.
R. W. JEANS, Accountant.

BANK OF NEW SOUTH WALES.

Audited 29th April, 1885.
R. C. CLOSE, } Auditors.
SYDNEY BURDEKIN, }

AUDITORS' REPORT.

We have examined the annexed balance-sheet, made up to 31st March, 1886, and report that we find the several items therein stated to conform to the balances in the general ledger, and the balance-sheets of the respective branches and agencies of the bank collectively. We have counted the cash balance, and examined the bills and other securities held by the bank at the head office, in Sydney, on the 31st March last, and hereby certify that we have found them correct. The cash, bills, and other securities held at the branch banks and agencies in New South Wales, Victoria, and South Australia, on the 31st March, in Western Australia and New Zealand on the 1st March, and in Queensland on the customary dates, have been certified to as being correct by the usual documents.

SYDNEY BURDEKIN, } Auditors.
29th April, 1886. GEORGE M. MERIVALE, }

BANK OF NEW ZEALAND.

We hereby certify that we have examined the accounts of the Bank of New Zealand for the half-year ended 31st March, 1885, and that we have counted the cash balances and examined the bills and other securities held at the head office, and compared the returns of the branches with the statements in the foregoing balance-sheet, and have found the same to be correct.

(Signed) J. L. WILSON, } Auditors.
A. K. TAYLOR, }

BANK OF SOUTH AUSTRALIA.

We have audited the books and examined the securities at the head office and have compared the certified returns from the colonial branches with the foregoing statements, and find the above results are correct,

JOHN O. SURTEES, } Auditors.
W. E. BAGSHAW, F.C.A., }

We approve of the above accounts.
W. RICHARDSON, }
JAMES GILCHRIST, } Directors.
JOHN BALFOUR, }

By order of the court,
WM. G. CUTHBERTSON, General Manager.

BANK OF VAN DIEMEN'S LAND.

C. SPOTSWOOD, Jun., Manager.

BANK OF VICTORIA.

We hereby certify that we have examined the accounts of the Bank of Victoria for the half-year ending 31st December, 1885, and that we have counted the cash balance, and examined the bills and other securities held at the head office, and compared the returns of the branches with the above balance-sheet, and found the same to be correct.

J. CHATFIELD TYLER, } Auditors.
W. H. HULL, }

Certified before me at Melbourne this 23rd day of January, 1886. W. H. TUCKETT, J.P.

BALLARAT BANKING COMPANY.

We have counted the cash, and examined the books, documents, and vouchers relating hereto, together with securities, and find the above to be a true and faithful record of the position of the bank at the date hereof,

DUNCAN CAMERON, } Auditors.
FREDK. C. DOWNES, }
I. J. JONES, Manager.

Ballarat, 11th January, 1886.

CITY OF MELBOURNE BANK.

We hereby certify that we have examined the books and accounts of the City of Melbourne Bank, Limited, and that the above balance-sheet is correct.

ANDREW BURNS, } Auditors.
H. W. LOWRY, }

Certified before me this 9th day of April, 1885.
JAS. FERGUSSON, J.P.

CITY BANK, SYDNEY.

WILL. NEILL, Manager.

We hereby certify that we have examined the securities, compared the balances, and counted the cash in The City Bank, at head office, and examined the returns from the branches as at 31st December, 1885, and found the same as specified above.

HALEY C. D'ARDIER, } Auditors.
ALEX. DEAN, }

Certified before me this 14th day of January, A.D. 1886.
HENRY PRINCE, J.P.

COLONIAL BANK OF AUSTRALASIA.

W. GREENLAW, General Manager.
W. BOULLY, Accountant.

We hereby certify that we have examined into the position of the accounts and affairs of the Colonial Bank of Australasia as on the 31st March, 1886 ; that we have counted the cash balance, and carefully examined the bills and other securities held at the head office, and compared the returns of the several branches with the above balance-sheet, and found the same to be correct.

THOS. RUSSELL,　⎱ Auditors.
J. J. SMART,　⎰

Certified before me this 16th day of April, 1886.

R. BALDERSON, J.P.

COLONIAL BANK OF NEW ZEALAND.

GEO. M'LEAN, Chairman.

We have examined the cash and bills on hand at head office, and compared the abstracts of balances from the various branches, and certify the foregoing statement to be in accordance therewith and correct.

A. G. FENWICK,　⎱ Auditors.
A. BARTLEMAN,　⎰

Dunedin, 11th January, 1886.

COMMERCIAL BANK OF AUSTRALASIA.

We certify that the above is, in our opinion, a true and correct statement of the affairs of the bank on the 31st day of December, 1884.

W. H. TUCKETT,　⎱ Auditors.
W. G. SPRIGG,　⎰

Certified before me this 13th day of January, 1885.

W. BOWEN, J.P.

COMMERCIAL BANKING COMPANY OF SYDNEY.

T. A. DIBBS, General Manager.

We hereby certify that we have examined the securities, compared the balances, and counted the coin in the Commercial Bank, as on the 31st December, 1885, and that we have found the same as specified in this balance-sheet.

E. M. STEPHEN,　⎱ Auditors.
J. R. STREET,　⎰

Sydney, 12th January, 1886.

COMMERCIAL BANK OF SOUTH AUSTRALIA.

Last auditors' certificate prior to suspension as follows :
—" We hereby certify that we have counted the cash and checked the bills, and abstract of the advances and deposits of the Commercial Bank of South Australia, and compared the results of the branches with the within balance-sheet, and found the same to be correct,"

H. STODART,　⎱ Auditors.
W. J. OLDHAM,　⎰

ENGLISH, SCOTTISH, AND AUSTRALIAN CHARTERED BANK.

Examined, compared with the books and vouchers, and, together with the securities, found correct, 16th January, 1885.

(Signed)　J. H. STEINMETZ,　⎱ Auditors.
HENRY R. SPERLING,　⎰

LONDON CHARTERED BANK OF AUSTRALIA.

T. DYER EDWARDS,　⎫
C. D. ROSS,　　　　⎬ Directors.
JAMES F. GARRICK,　⎪
ROBERT T. WATSON,　⎭

We have examined the cash balances, bills and securities for investments at the London office, and find them in order, and have compared the above balance-sheet with the books in London and with the certified returns from the branches, and find the same to exhibit a true statement of the bank's affairs.

WILLIAM BOTLY,　⎱ Auditors.
EDWIN WATERHOUSE,　⎰

6th May, 1885.

MERCANTILE BANK OF SYDNEY.

F. A. A. WILSON, General Manager.
HECTOR ALLEN, Secretary.

Examined and found correct.

JAMES SCROGGIE,　⎱ Auditors.
H. E. COHEN,　　　⎰

Declared before me, this 12th day of January, 1886.

FRANK SENIOR, J.P.

NATIONAL BANK OF AUSTRALASIA.

JOHN SALMON, Acting Chief Manager.

We hereby certify that we have examined the accounts of the National Bank of Australasia for the half-year ending 31st March, 1886, that we have counted the cash and examined the other securities held by the bank at its head office (the assets and liabilities at the branches are taken on the certificates of the managers and accountants), and that to the best of our knowledge and belief the above balance-sheet is correct.

W. H. TUCKETT,　⎱ Auditors.
ANDREW BURNS,　⎰

Certified before me, at Melbourne, this 22nd day of April, 1886.

SAMUEL MULLEN, J.P.

NATIONAL BANK OF NEW ZEALAND.

Audited and found correct according to the books and vouchers at the head office, and to the certified balance-books received from the several branches.

QUILTER,　⎫
HALL,　　⎪
CROSBIE,　⎬ Auditors.
GLEGG,　　⎪
WELTON,　⎭

3rd July, 1885.

QUEENSLAND NATIONAL BANK.

We hereby certify that the above is a true and correct statement of the affairs of the Queensland National Bank Limited, on 31st December, 1884.

TH. UNMACK,　⎱ Auditors.
WM. WEBSTER,　⎰

TOWN AND COUNTRY BANK.

We hereby certify that we have counted the cash and checked the bills and abstract of advances and deposits of the Town and Country Bank, and compared the returns of the branches with the above balance-sheet, and have found the same to be correct, and are further satisfied that the whole of the advances have the knowledge and sanction of the directors.

WM. J. OLDHAM,　⎱ Auditors.
H. D. O'HALLORAN,　⎰

Adelaide, 16th April, 1886.

UNION BANK OF AUSTRALIA, LIMITED.

ARTHUR FLOWER,　　⎫
J. R. BULLEN-SMITH,　⎬ Directors.
W. O. GILCHRIST,　　⎪
CHARLES PARBURY,　⎭
W. R. MEWBURN, Manager.
R. BUCKLER, Accountant.

We certify that the various securities held in London have been produced to us, and that we have examined the balance books of the several branches in the colonies for the six months ended 31st August, 1884, and the books and accounts of the London office for the same period, and, having compared the combined results with the above balance-sheet, have found the same correct.

FREDK. WHINNEY,　⎱ Auditors.
ALBERT DEACON,　⎰

London, 21st June, 1885.

II.—SOME LEADING BRITISH BANKS.

BRITISH LINEN COMPANY BANK (EDINBURGH).

We hereby certify that we have audited the books at the head office of the British Linen Company Bank, and the returns from the branches and the London office, and checked the cash and securities in Edinburgh and London; that the reserves and investments of the bank are correctly stated and vouched, and that the preceding abstract general balance-sheet as at 15th April, 1885, corresponds with the books of the bank.

WALTER MACKENZIE, C.A.
W. R. MYLNE, C.A.

CITY BANK (LONDON).

We beg to report that in our opinion the foregoing is a full and fair balance-sheet, properly drawn up, and that it exhibits a true and correct view of the company's affairs, as shown by the books of the company.

JOHN CURRY,
WILLIAM E. EAST. } Auditors.

BANK OF LIVERPOOL.

We certify that the above balance-sheet, in our opinion, is a full and fair balance-sheet, properly drawn up so as to exhibit a true and correct view of the state of the company's affairs, as shown by the books of the company, and that the profits, as stated in the profit and loss account, have been fully and fairly earned.

HARMOOD BANNER & SON, Chartered Accountants.
Liverpool, 10th July, 1885.

LLOYDS, BARNETTS, AND BOSANQUETS, LONDON.

We hereby certify that we have audited the accounts of the company, and that the above statement correctly sets forth the position of its affairs on the 31st day of December, 1884.

LAUNDY & Co., chartered accountants,
Auditors.

LONDON AND WESTMINSTER BANK, LONDON.

We have satisfied ourselves of the correctness of the cash balances, and have examined the securities held against the money at call and short notice and representing the investments of the bank, and in accordance with the provisions of the Companies' Act 1879, we have examined the foregoing balance-sheet and profit and loss account with the books of the company, and beg to report, that in our opinion, such accounts are properly drawn up, so as to exhibit a true and correct view of the state of the company's affairs as shown by the books of the company.

WILLIAM TURQUAND, }
EDWIN WATERHOUSE, } Auditors.

LONDON JOINT-STOCK BANK (LONDON).

We have audited the above statement of liabilities and assets, and we report that in our opinion it is a full and fair balance-sheet, properly drawn up so as to exhibit a true and correct view of the state of the bank's affairs, as shown in the books of the bank.

WILLIAM CROSBIE
(Quilter, Ball & Co.),
JOHN G. GRIFFITHS
(Deloitte, Dever, Griffiths & Co.), } Auditors.

LONDON AND COUNTY, LONDON.

We have examined the foregoing balance-sheet and profit and loss account, have verified the cash-balance at the Bank of England, the stocks there registered, and the other investments of the bank. We have also examined the several books and vouchers showing the cash-balances, bills, and other amounts set forth, the whole of which are correctly stated ; and we are of opinion this balance-sheet and profit and loss account are full and fair, properly drawn up, and exhibit a true and correct view of the company's affairs as shown by the books of the company.

FINLAY KNIGHT,
WILLIAM NORMAN, } Auditors.
RICHARD H. SWAINE, }

MANCHESTER AND LIVERPOOL DISTRICT BANKING COMPANY, MANCHESTER.

We have examined the accounts of the Manchester and Liverpool District Banking Company, Limited, and we hereby state that in our opinion the above is a full and fair balance-sheet, properly drawn up so as to exhibit a true and correct view of the state of the company's affairs as shown by the books of the company.

PETER G. CUNLIFFE, }
DAVID BANNERMAN, } Auditors.
GEO. STANLEY WOOD, }

Manchester, 11th January, 1886.

NATIONAL PROVINCIAL BANK OF ENGLAND, LONDON.

We beg to report that we have ascertained the correctness of the cash balances, and of the money at call and short notice as entered in the above balance-sheet, and have inspected the securities representing the investments of the bank, and found them in order. We have also examined the balance-sheet in detail with the books at the head office and with the certified returns from each branch, and in our opinion such balance-sheet is properly drawn up so as to exhibit a true and correct view of the state of the bank's affairs as shown by such books and returns.

EDWIN WATERHOUSE, }
ROD. MACKAY, } Auditors.

NATIONAL BANK OF SCOTLAND, EDINBURGH.

We, the auditors appointed by the shareholders of the National Bank of Scotland, Limited, beg to report—in terms of the Companies' Act 1879—that in our opinion the above is a full and fair balance-sheet, properly drawn up, so as to exhibit a true and correct view of the state of the bank's affairs at 31st October, 1885, as appearing from the books. We also report that we checked the gold and silver coin, and notes of other banks then on hand at the head office in Edinburgh, and at the London and Glasgow offices ; as also the certificates and vouchers of the balances with the London bankers, Government securities, and other investments of the bank, and found the same in order.

WILLIAM MACKINNON, C.A.
JAS. ALEX. MOLLESON, C.A.

Edinburgh, 8th December, 1885.

NATIONAL BANK (DUBLIN).

We have compared in detail the above balance-sheet with the books of the bank and the certified returns from each branch, and in our opinion such balance-sheet represents a true and correct statement of the bank's affairs, as shown in said books and returns on the 30th day of June, 1885. We have also examined the securities representing the investments of the bank, and found the same correct.

JOHN ABRAHAM, }
P. J. ROCHE, } Auditors.
JOHN F. SMITHWICK, }

ROYAL BANK OF SCOTLAND, EDINBURGH.

As auditors appointed by the proprietors of the Royal Bank of Scotland, we have checked the cash on hand at head office, Glasgow and London, verified the cash with London bankers, the securities for money at call and short notice, the Government securities and other investments, and examined the details of the other liabilities and assets set forth in the foregoing abstract state of affairs ; and we now certify that in our opinion said abstract state is a full and fair balance-sheet properly drawn up, and exhibits a true and correct view of the state of the bank's affairs, as shown by the books at 10th October, 1885.

THOS. G. DICKSON, C.A.
JAMES HOWDEN.

Edinburgh, 20th November, 1885.

STUCKEY'S BANKING COMPANY, LANGPORT, SOMERSETSHIRE.

Examined and found correct.

E. J. BOYLE,
W. T. SWAYNE, } Auditors.

Langport, 29th July, 1885.

UNION BANK OF LONDON.

We certify that we have verified the correctness of the cash balances, of the investments held by the bank, of the securities held against monies at call and short notice, and of the bills discounted; and having examined the foregoing balance-sheet and profit and loss account with the books of the company, we beg to report in accordance with the provisions of the Companies' Act 1879, that in our opinion such balance-sheet and account are properly drawn up so as to exhibit a true and correct view of the state of the company's affairs as shown by the books of the company.

R. MACKAY,
F. WHINNEY, } Auditors.

UNION BANK OF SCOTLAND, GLASGOW.

Glasgow, 15th April, 1885. — We, the auditors appointed by the shareholders of the Union Bank of Scotland, Ltd., beg leave to report—in terms of the Companies' Act, 1879—that we have examined the books kept at the head office of the bank, and the returns from the branches; and that, in our opinion, the above is a full and fair balance-sheet, properly drawn up, so as to exhibit a true and correct view of the state of the bank's affairs, as appearing from the books. We have also examined the securities representing the reserves and investments of the bank, including the balances at the Bank of England, and have checked the cash at the head offices in Glasgow and Edinburgh, and at the London office, and have found all to be in order.

JAMES HALDANE, C.A.
WILLIAM MACKINNON, C.A. } Auditors.

BANKERS' INSTITUTE OF AUSTRALASIA

[DECEMBER, 1886, pp.12-6]

BANK AUDIT

"BANK AUDIT."

In this short paper which I propose to read to you, it is my purpose to deal not so much with the actual auditing of the accounts, as with the principles on which it should be carried out to make it thoroughly efficient.

The question of audit has often been brought before the public, but beyond creating a stir for a short time, has not up to the present time had any practical effect in preventing inefficient and improper audits being made, by which in the end they themselves suffer. It is useless for me to recall to your mind the many instances in which very serious losses have occurred through insufficient supervision. But I think I may refer to the Commercial Bank of South Australia, where the most serious consequences have ensued, owing to the want of a proper system of audit.

The objects of auditing accounts are twofold. First, to see that no frauds have been committed, and that the business has been carried on with due regard to security and well within the powers under whatever act the company may be registered; and, secondly, that the balance-sheet may be made out so as to rightly represent the true position of affairs.

To enable these objects to be attained, it is absolutely necessary that every transaction should be examined and checked, the cash counted, bills and other securities examined, and due allowance made for bad and doubtful debts. Can an audit of this kind be made in connection with a bank or other institution, whose transactions are so varied and so numerous, in the ordinary way, that is every 6 or 12 months? There seems to me but one answer, and that is, that it would not only be impossible, but next to impossible to attempt. The only method, as far as I can see, would be under a system of continuous audit, that is an examination of the accounts going on from day to day and week to week.

The accounts of most companies are audited every six months, and I feel sure that it would be impossible for any auditor or auditors to thoroughly examine the multitudinous transactions that have taken place during that period under several months. The only instance which has come under my notice, though no doubt there are others, where the auditors make a continuous audit, is in the Comptoir d'Escompte de Paris. But in this instance the three auditors or censeurs are not merely auditors but are a permanent committee of inspection. They not only examine the books of the institution, but they attend all the meetings of the council of administration and of the committee. In fact the censeurs give their whole time to the affairs of the bank. This of course is possible with any other bank, but it is not perhaps advisable, except under a different form, to which reference will be made later on. There are many things that occur in a bank that it is not advisable for anyone outside of the bank officials to know, and, except in a case similar to the above, the auditor would not fully understand without being conversant with all the surrounding circumstances of the transaction.

In every Act or Statute under which a bank is incorporated, the auditing of accounts at least once a year is obligatory, and very rightly so. But the power of electing the auditor or auditors is left in the hands of the shareholders. The intention of this is to enable the shareholders to select men, independent of the board of management, who will consider their interests, and will report fully to them regarding the accounts. The duties and obligations of an auditor are hardly rightly understood by the public. While some think that he should, and does examine the accounts fully, which would be impossible for him to do, others look on it as a mere formality to be complied with. But to those who thoroughly consider the matter and examine the law on the subject, his position is clearly defined. Although the auditor is not expected to do all that some expect of him, yet he has certain specific duties to perform which require a considerable amount of special knowledge which can only be attained by special training.

Let us see, then, what are the duties of an auditor as laid down in the law. According to the most recent Act passed at home, a transcript of which is now before our Legislature, we find that the law does not expect of the auditor such supervision of the accounts generally as is looked for by many of the shareholders in these institutions. Sir Stafford Northcote, on moving for leave to introduce the bill on this subject, put the auditors' duties very concisely. He said :—" All we propose is that in every bank there should be a provision made for the appointment of an auditor or auditors independent of the directors, who should audit the accounts and publish the report which they will be called upon to make ; and in making the examination and drawing up the report what we call upon the auditors to do is to certify whether the accounts give correctly and disclose truly the state of the company as shown by its books. It is impossible for an auditor to go into the books and say whether this is a good bill or security. That is not only impossible to effect but almost to attempt. We keep free from that. What we propose in the bill is that a proper examination shall take place of the books, and that the auditors shall declare, assuming their correctness, if the statement of accounts properly put together does give a full and fair description of the state of the bank."

The clauses in the bill referring to audit were —First, that the accounts should be audited at least once a year, by an auditor or auditors elected by the shareholders in general meeting. Secondly, that every auditor should have handed to him a list of the books kept by the company, and that he should at all reasonable times have access to the books and accounts, and in relation to such books and accounts any auditor may examine the directors or any other officer of the company. Thirdly, that the auditor or auditors shall make a report to the members on the accounts examined on every balance-sheet laid before the company in general meeting during his tenure of office, and in every such report shall state whether in his or their opinion the balance-sheet referred to in the report, is a full and fair balance-sheet, properly drawn up, so as to exhibit a true and correct view of the state of the company's affairs as shown by the books of the company, and such report shall be read before the company in general meeting. Here the duties of an auditor are very clearly stated. He has simply to examine the books and accounts, and ask for explanations if necessary. At the same time he must examine carefully and see that none of the transactions of the bank are contrary to, or outside of, the powers taken out in the articles of association, and that every item in the balance-sheet is *bonâ fide*, and not represented by entries or paper promises. Besides this, the auditors should ascertain that the balance books and returns handed to them have, from time to time, been before the directors or board of management, and should take any other precautions they may deem necessary to make sure that the books handed to them are those which are actually in use for the purposes of the business of the bank.

To be able to do all this properly and efficiently, a thoroughly competent and reliable man should be selected. The shareholders have the right to elect these officers, and they should use their power more fully than they do in many instances, and insist on an auditor being elected for his actual qualification for the post, and not because he happens to be a shareholder, or has some influence either with the shareholders or directors.

According to the law, then, the auditor's duties are to a certain extent of a superficial character. How then are the affairs of the bank to be properly audited ? The responsibility of this, to my mind, rests with the permanent officials of the bank. This in my opinion is a most important point, and one which is hardly understood by the management of some institutions. These rely entirely on their system of book-keeping and their auditors. These have, time after time, been found to be insufficient, and frauds have been committed and sometimes carried on for a series of years without being discovered. A system under which such things can happen must be bad, and the only remedy that I can see, and one which should be insisted on, is that there should be a continuous inspection going on throughout the year. Many banks now have an inspector with a staff quite distinct from the other members of the institutions. By an inspector, I mean the head official on the permanent staff, whether under the title of superintendent, general manager, or inspector. This officer, being the supreme head, can and should examine all the books and accounts of the bank. As a member of the permanent staff, with a seat at the board of directors, he has a thorough knowledge of all the transactions of the bank. Besides being experienced in banking matters, he can at once point out any irregularities or deviation from the usual course. But to do all this thoroughly he must have a well-trained staff under his direct control, and separate from the general staff. If his inquiries are constant and searching, as they should be, he would at once be able to discover any manipulation of the accounts. Being a confidential officer of the bank, he would also have a right at any time to inspect the securities held by the bank, or any other matters affecting its credit, without any objection from the customers of the institution. There are of course many matters which the manager takes in hand without reference to the directors, and which may or may not be brought up at the next sitting of the board. Transactions of this kind can only be checked or watched by the inspector and his clerks. With a thoroughly efficient officer in this position, with a good staff of experienced men, it would be difficult for the other officials to manipulate the accounts or perpetrate frauds for any length of time, such as have often occurred up to the present. Considerable reliance must necessarily be placed in the manager of a bank, but neither the directors or auditors, unless continuously at the bank (which is inadvisable, and would interfere with the ordinary routine of business), could check his operations as efficiently as the inspector. Thus, for instance, at the meetings of the board, the manager brings forward any business that may have been undertaken since the previous sitting of the directors, or which has since been offered to him. The directors also have presented to them a list of advances and overdrafts, which they can, and usually do inspect. It is next to impossible for the directors to know whether the whole of the over-

drafts and advances have been shown in the list, but the inspector can easily have the list or book checked and see that they represent the true liabilities under these headings due to the bank.

A continuous audit conducted somewhat on the lines mentioned would certainly be effectual. With experienced and trustworthy men in charge of a bank, and with a good inspector's staff, it would be difficult for any defalcations to be long undiscovered. But if at any time one of these responsible servants of the institution determined to defraud the public, it would be next to impossible for the directors and auditors to discover the defalcations, which, however, could soon be discovered by the inspector. But it would be still more difficult to find out any such attempt should more than one confidential officer be implicated, as was apparently the case in the Commercial Bank of South Australia. But defalcations of this character are of comparative rarity. The higher officials of a bank are usually selected for their integrity and probity, as well as for their business capabilities, and rarely is this confidence of the shareholders and directors misplaced. In fact the same can be said of all the officers of banks, and, taking into consideration the large numbers employed in this business, the defalcations of the few weaker-minded men bring out in greater relief the probity of the rest.

I have tried to show that the duty of making an audit of a bank thoroughly efficient devolves on two separate and distinct persons. First, the permanent officials of the bank have to check and supervise all the work done in the bank ; while secondly, the auditor has to see that the books balance properly, and that the securities are all in possession of the bank, and that the balance-sheet rightly represents the true position of the institution. I have purposely avoided many side issues and details which are connected with this subject, and which I do not think come within the scope of this paper.

My object has been to show that although the auditor has considerable responsibility, a far greater weight of responsibility rests on the permanent members of the staff of the bank and on the directors. And I think that these officers sometimes do not fully understand this responsibility, and rely too much on their particular system of book-keeping, which, however, proves to be no safeguard against embezzlements and defalcations, and I think that under a thorough system of audit within the bank somewhat on the basis of what I have tried to sketch out, would not only enable the officials to discover wrong doing at the very commencement, but would also deter by fear of immediate detection any who might give way to temptation.

In conclusion, it seems to me that no audit of a bank can be thoroughly efficient without a continuous audit, and if the permanent officials of a bank and auditors do their duty thoroughly we should hear of far fewer cases of fraud, and the interests of the shareholders and the public would have every protection possible.

A discussion was initiated by Alderman Moubray, chairman of the Commercial Bank of Australia. He remarked that the interesting paper read by Mr. Turner on the career of Benjamin Boyd was more like a chapter taken from a book of romance, than what had occurred in real life within the memory of men now living and on Australian soil. The moral of the story, however, seemed to be, that bankers should keep on the beaten path, and well within the lines indicated by prudence and experience. With regard to the paper read by Mr. Biggs on Bank Audit, he had not sufficient knowledge of the subject to say whether the checks recommended by that gentleman would be an improvement on the systems now adopted. It was, however, desirable that the question of auditing the accounts of banks and financial institutions should be fully discussed, with the view of finding out and adopting the most efficient system. Mr. Biggs was to be complimented, as a young man, for the care and trouble he had taken, and also for the courage he had shown in submitting it for criticism to such an audience. This was one of the many advantages of the Bankers' Institute. Writers of papers who showed ability, or who criticised the papers of others with intelligence, would come to the front as surely as cork rises to the surface of water.

Mr. Robert Wallen asked the forbearance of the meeting for his addressing them. Although he was not a member of the Institute, he had been one of the earliest advocates of its formation in the editorial columns of the *Australasian Insur*-

ance and Banking Record. He had been informed that the Bankers' Institute of Australasia now numbered nearly 800 members, and he thought that there was, in this, ground for hearty congratulations when it was remembered that the Institute of Bankers of London, now for some time in existence, numbered about 1600 Fellows, Associates, and members; and, of course, in London there was a large leisured class, who, with ample knowledge, could contribute expert information. Mr. Moubray had spoken words of encouragement to young bankers, urging them to take all means to improve themselves in their banking knowledge, and this with a view to their official advancement. Mr. Moubray suggested that they should not hesitate to put on paper their views on banking subjects and bring them before the Institute. Now he (Mr. Wallen) wished to say, from his nine years' experience of editorship of the *Banking Record*, that nothing gave him such pleasure as to observe the anxiety of young bank officers in all parts of the colonies to improve themselves by addressing questions and seeking information upon matters of banking law and practice. It showed their keen interest in their occupation. He had had propounded to him banking conundrums of the most difficult kind, and he did not wish it to be believed that he had solved them unaided. He had had the assistance of banking authorities (some of them now present), and the responses had, he was glad to say, been generally uncontroverted. Passing to the question of audit, on which Mr. Biggs had read a paper, he (Mr. Wallen) considered that any absolutely perfect system of audit was impossible. No human ingenuity could prevent, or with certainty detect, deliberate fraud. It was quite right to endeavour to obtain the best possible approximation to perfection. There was in his mind no doubt that a system of inspection inside the bank, independent of the administrative management, was a good practicable system. The Bank of Australasia and some other banks had something of the kind. Mr. Turner had stated that, in his belief, bank auditors had never made any useful discovery. He (Mr. Wallen) could not agree with this. The Provident Institute of Victoria once issued a balance-sheet without the usual auditors' certificate appended. The speaker (then connected with the financial columns of a daily paper) pointed out the omission, with the result that the public justly took alarm. There was a run on the Institute, its doors were closed, and its directors punished. This was an instance of auditors declining to sign an incorrect balance-sheet with a useful practical effect. Besides, auditors may be presumed to have done good work which never meets the public eye. It may be supposed, for instance, that auditors have refused to certify balance-sheets unless alterations had been made in them by the management to comply with the auditors' requirements. The knowledge of an inevitable audit must have a constantly useful and, perhaps, deterring influence on the constructors of balance-sheets. Referring to the interesting historical paper upon Mr. Benjamin Boyd, there was this to be said in mitigation, that all he did, he did royally. It was certainly unfortunate that the London creditors of the Royal Bank of Australia suffered, but there could be no doubt that Benjamin Boyd had conferred undying benefits upon Australia. The stock he imported was of the highest class, and the BB brand was for a generation a name to conjure with. Benjamin Boyd was not the only smart financier the colonies had seen. He vividly remembered Mr. Thomas Mooney who, when Irishmen in the famine year were dying from bad potatoes, started an Agricultural Bank in Ireland. It came to terrible grief, and Mr. Mooney turned up in Canvas Town just across Princes Bridge, carrying on his old business of a baker. His credit did not exceed a single barrel of flour, which he himself trucked across to his bakery. Within a few months he built on credit the National Hotel in Bourke-street and the Princess Theatre in Spring-street—which only just now has given way to a structure on which £35,000 has been expended. He stood for Parliament, promising every citizen of Victoria "a vote, a farm, and a rifle;" but there seemed to be something so revolutionary in this, that successful efforts were made to keep him out, and he suddenly disappeared. Mr. Mooney in San Francisco subsequently started a "Mechanics' Bank," and, by a curious coincidence, the funds and the founder simultaneously disappeared. Mr. Wallen concluded by moving a vote of thanks

to Mr. H. G. Turner for his historical paper. Mr. Turner had always taken a lively interest in banking affairs generally, and he exercised a vivifying influence on the new organisation. On the title-page of the *Journal of the Institute of Actuaries* was the assertion that "every man is a debtor to his profession." Mr. Turner was one of those who discharged his obligations in full.

Mr. George D. Meudell (Savings Bank auditor) thought both Mr. Biggs and Mr. Turner had demonstrated the necessity for having an independent check on behalf of shareholders. Mr. Biggs had confused inspection and audit. The system of continuous inspection he had outlined was in operation in all the banks. For the protection of bank shareholders independent experienced auditors were absolutely necessary. Mr. Turner's paper well illustrated this, for if the directors of the Royal Bank of Australia in London had submitted Mr. Boyd's accounts to two auditors, that gentleman's career would have been summarily cut short. The defects of our audit system were due to a slavish imitation of the provisions of the English Companies Act. Here, in Australia, banking practice had altogether diverged from old-world principles, and our audit system should be more in consonance with these altered conditions. Continuous audit, by public auditors, was essential; and, in addition, he (Mr. Meudell) considered the Government should appoint a permanent official to scrutinise all balance-sheets and returns made under various Acts of Parliament by banks and mining and trading companies. Despite all precautions, while human nature remained the same, fraud would always be possible, for if a man wanted to be dishonest he would find the means.

Mr. H. D. E. Taylor had much pleasure in seconding a vote of thanks to Mr. Turner. It had always appeared to him that however high the standard the papers read before the Institute might attain, that the principal value of these meetings would lie in the discussion which afterwards took place, especially if that discussion was of the high character an Institute like theirs had a right to expect. He thought that the reason their discussions at previous meetings had been so short was that the papers read were all of an historical character. They could not very well discuss such matters, they certainly could not contradict history, they could only learn a lesson from it; and he noticed that Mr. Turner had attached a moral to his paper for our further consideration, one which would absorb a good deal of thought. It was somewhat remarkable (and Mr. Biggs would excuse him for saying this) that though Mr. Turner's paper possessed a higher literary merit and was more interesting, the discussion to-night had turned principally on the second paper. He ventured to hope that when the council came to exercise the power which they had retained for themselves of reading the papers before they accepted them, they would for the sake of the discussions to follow, choose those of a practical character, dealing with questions of present importance. Dealing with the question of audit, after referring to the able manner in which it had been discussed, and the present system defended by Mr. Meudell, there was one point which came out, viz., that after all the years of experience of the present system, both in this colony and at home (as shown by Mr. Wallen) it was proved to be an unmitigated failure. The history of bank audit might be read in the history of bank failures and bank defalcations. It was accepted as an axiom, in which he had to agree, that a perfect system of audit was unattainable, but surely some improvement of the present system could be effected. As the secretary had his name down for a paper on audit, when the council thought fit to bring this subject up again, he did not wish to say more on this subject just now, as he had no desire to cut the ground from under his own feet, and concluded by seconding the vote of thanks proposed by Mr. Wallen.

Messrs. W. Palmer (of Sale), and Mr. J. M'Cutcheon, manager of the Commercial Bank of Australia Limited in Melbourne, also took part in the discussion. The meeting closed with cordial votes of thanks to Mr. Turner and Mr. Biggs.

BANK AUDIT: CAUSES OF ITS INEFFICIENCY, AND SUGGESTIONS FOR ITS IMPROVEMENT

. . . the second lecture of the evening was read by Mr. H.D'E. Taylor, of the Savings Bank, on the subject of

"BANK AUDIT: CAUSES OF ITS INEFFICIENCY, AND SUGGESTIONS FOR ITS IMPROVEMENT."

In order to give as much interest as possible to my subject, and to stimulate discussion, I have decided to localise the scope of this paper, and to confine it to a consideration of the system we are familiar with, and of which we all have some practical knowledge and experience. As a justification for this course I may urge that if the principles to be set forth can be upheld for this limited range, they will be equally applicable to a larger one, and will be capable of extension from the city to the colony; from the colony to regions whose bounds are only limited by the banking organisations on which they depend.

At this early stage it may be as well to secure a clear understanding as to what an audit really is, to remove some misapprehension as to its scope, and as to the powers possessed by an auditor, which, it has been made apparent, exist in many directions.

After satisfying himself that the bank has kept within its powers, the duties of an auditor require him to conduct an examination of the books, to see that every entry necessitated by the transactions of the bank is made in them. that these entries are correctly carried through the bank's books, and that the results which they express are correctly set forth in the balance-sheets presented to the shareholders. If he can do this, if he can certify that the bookkeeping is absolutely correct, and that he has had cash, securities, and documents produced to him representing the value of the bank's assets according to its books, his work is done. In Mr. Biggs' paper on "Audit" you will find Sir Stafford Northcote's definition of an auditor's responsibilities. He has "to certify whether the accounts give correctly and disclose truly the state of the company as shown by its books." Now everything depends on this definition, "as shown by its books." To forget it is to have a false idea of an audit. To expect an auditor to certify beyond it is to expect an impossibility. Indeed, I venture to

say that no auditor should sign a balance-sheet without this proviso appearing over his signature.

It is no part of his duty to certify that the documents produced to him are of the full value they represent. He has nothing to do with the policy of the management, or the economy which is exercised in carrying it out. He is expressly debarred from inquiring into these points. Indeed, in nearly all cases a thoroughly competent auditor, from the nature of his training, his profession and his experience, would be anything but a reliable authority on such subjects.

This definition makes the examination by audit much more superficial, much less important than it is sometimes supposed to be. But it would be a great gain if a clear public understanding could be made to exist on this point. Much harm—very much harm— is done amongst investors who entertain exaggerated notions of an auditor's financial ubiquity; as, for instance, amongst those who imagine that the auditor's signature to a balance-sheet is a guarantee that all items set down as assets really possess the value set against them, whereas they only certify that these values appear against them in the books, and may be — in some semi-insolvent companies they are—gross overvaluations. Much harm is also done in a minor degree to auditors themselves, who on occasion are severely and ignorantly blamed for not doing something which they were never intended to do, and were quite unable even to attempt.

The history of Mr. Benjamin Boyd, which was recently before us, is a good illustration to bring into sharp contrast the actual duties and investigations to which auditors are limited, and the imaginary powers with which some people wish to invest them. In the discussion some severe reflections were passed upon the London auditors for not having "done their duty," and closed that gentleman's career in a remarkably short space of time. It was simply impossible for them to have done so. The utmost they could have done was to call the attention of the shareholders to the fact that certain necessary returns were not forthcoming. When Mr. Boyd forwarded them, the London auditors would simply have had to accept them as correct, even if every entry in them was a false one. They had no means of checking them, beyond the actual addition of the figures before them, no power to control any of his speculations, no possibility even of knowing that his returns were not cooked from top to bottom. That rested with his local auditors, supposing that there were any.

In common fairness to those who act as auditors, it should be realised that there are many kinds of defalcation which it is impossible for them to detect. Victorian banks have not yet adopted checks similar to those of some home banks to prevent tellers substituting or destroying credit slips. Auditors cannot detect frauds committed by these means. Where the fraud is committed before any entry is made in the books, and the first entry is made to conceal it, the auditor is powerless, but where the initial entry expresses the genuine transaction and subsequent entries are falsified to cover the delinquency, then the auditor should discover the discrepancy and detect the fraud. In many of the simpler frauds, and especially in those of a personal nature, the best auditor is the customer himself, and he does not seem to be made as much use of as he might be. A rigid insistance in banks of a rule that pass-books should be made up at frequent intervals, *being procured* when necessary, would have a deterrent effect on frauds of this description, and a similar reason could be deduced for compelling the customer's assistance by returning his cheques to him at short intervals.

Frauds, therefore, may be divided into two sorts, those which have been so effected that an audit will not discover them, and for which auditors cannot be held responsible; and those which can be prevented by a complete system of book-keeping and of check. Here I feel I must take exception to the dictum laid down at one of our meetings, that the great object of an audit is the discovery of fraud. The first object of an audit seems to me to be not so much the discovery of defalcation and error as the prevention of such misfortunes. Why, sir! the object of detecting fraud with certainty and with speed is to prevent its being attempted at all. Detection is more the *consequence* than the *object* of audit; its effect more than its cause; and "Prevention" not "Punishment" should be the aim and the motto of any association of auditors. The value of any system should be gauged, in the first instance, by the probabilities which it contains, and afterwards by the successes which it achieves in this latter direction. I take it that prevention should be the great object to secure, whether in the interest of the shareholders, who bear the loss; the management which suffers in reputation; the profession, whose corporate honour is held up to ridicule and reproach; the officers, on whom fall the penalties of guilt, carelessness, or inefficiency; and the innocent involved in the ruin which attends such lapses, and whose

sufferings and degradation are the keenest of all.

Having endeavoured to effect a clear understanding as to the aims and extent of an audit, my subject naturally divides itself at this stage into two parts—first, to show the inefficiency of the system existing at present, and the causes which are responsible for it; secondly, to offer for your consideration such suggestions as would appear to me to render it more complete and satisfactory. And here I wish to make this distinct proviso, that they are not expected or intended to secure efficiency beyond the lines already laid down, or to prevent any of those impossibilities which an audit is so often expected to perform.

The debate at the December meeting of this Institute has relieved me of a large portion of my responsibility in connection with the first part. A consensus of opinion on the part of leading and responsible authorities then presented showed that, amongst them at any rate, bank audit as at present conducted is looked upon very much as a farce. If bank auditors could retort when charged that they had failed to make any useful discoveries, that they had prevented there being anything to discover, the answer would be complete, and this paper would be unnecessary. But the experience of most of us, even that most recent, is that the bill is a true one, and that even the limited duties set forth in this paper they seem unable to fulfil. Amongst local banks the Oriental, the Provincial and Suburban, and the Commercial Bank of South Australia have been frequently instanced by competent authorities as examples of "neglect" or "flagrant incompetency" on the part of auditors. "It seems to us," writes the *Insurance Review*, "that in many instances where companies have at length failed, and the shareholders have had to pay their money, it is in nine cases out of ten the result of an inefficient audit, and by the *taking for granted the statements which are made by officials.*" Accepting explanations is the great rock on which auditors split over and over again. The latest number we have of the *Bankers' Magazine* declares audit to be a fallacy, and auditors to be a nuisance; while another publication has expressed the opinion that "auditing as a safeguard against defalcation seems to be a lost art, and exists only as a means of extracting guineas from shareholders."

The causes which combine to produce this state of inefficiency are known to all of you in a general way, but I shall make no apology for briefly directing your attention to the principal ones, because this course is really a statement of the errors which any efficient system should avoid. A consideration of them is therefore one of the main foundations upon which the closing part of my paper will be based.

First, there is the perfunctory character of an audit, which proposes to check the work of several months in a few hours. In such cases, totals and other accredited results have to be taken very much for granted. We all know, for they have been sworn to, some of the devices "*auditors*" have invented to get through their work in an expeditious manner. For instance, where many castings are involved, a kind of lottery is often instituted, one being checked here and there, on the chance that it may contain an error. If the few tried are correct, the rest are taken for granted. I have seen this done, and confess to a strong desire to suggest that the "auditor" should test the work by the arbitrament of a coin—should toss up. It is always urged as an answer to this allegation that the fees paid would not compensate the auditor for a longer examination. This is very true, but though unanswerable as an argument for not undertaking the duties, it is no excuse for half performing them. It involves this additional disadvantage—that the more efficient an auditor is, the more varied and complete his experience, the higher his business capacity and reputation, the less time he will have to devote to this work and the less likely he is to undertake it. And here is another cause of inefficiency. There is a danger—is it not more than a danger?—of this all-important work falling into the hands of some who have not had the preparation and the experience, or who do not possess the capacity which are necessary to qualify them to undertake it successfully. Unfortunately, auditing has never been raised to the dignity of a learned profession. Its professors need pass no examination, are under no compulsion, legislative or otherwise, to prove their fitness for their work before being allowed to enter on it. The doors are thrown wide open for anyone possessed of a self-confidence which may be either sublime or appalling, according to the temperament of the observer, to enter into the duties of a profession requiring, as much as any other, the possession of special faculties and their highest training—a training which at present, in many cases, if given at all, must be given at the expense and the risk of some monetary institution charged with the interests of hundreds of depositors and shareholders.

Such institutions seem to me to require the highest talent to certify to the correctness of their accounts, just as much as they require it to conduct their operations. It is like urging a truism to say that those who check should be equal in special knowledge to those who are checked and to those who prepare. There is an art—a little known art—in preparing a balance-sheet, which it requires an artist to understand. It would seem almost as wise to entrust this work to a junior clerk in such an institution as to place it in the hands of an "auditor" lacking the special training and experience necessary to fit him for the work.

Seeing the vast interests at stake, the number of persons whose welfare is involved, the misery

and ruin to individuals, the blow to a country's prosperity, and the shock to commercial credit which a serious bank failure involves, of all institutions in which an audit is necessary that of a bank should be the most searching, the most efficient, and the most unquestionable.

The last causation of failure to which I shall refer lies in the method by which auditors are appointed—by election by shareholders. Without discussing the arguments in favour of this system, it is a matter of experience that it is not favourable to securing the most efficient men in the positions. Rather, and in this it does not differ from nearly all elections, it decides too often in favour of the one who may have the most influence of a special character, the greatest number of active friends, who may be the most energetic, or who may advertise himself the most in ways which are known. Such methods of demonstrating that one's qualifications are higher than those of any other candidate enable men to be successful in many cases, because shareholders have to a very large extent to take a man at his own or his friends' estimate of his capability. They too often vote for some one whom they have never seen, perhaps of whose business capacity they are so ignorant as not even to have heard, except from a circular or a canvasser, which, of course, are the most reliable authorities known to business men. Again, they are compelled in many cases to choose between giving their votes to someone else to use for *his* friend, or to abstain from the poll altogether. Such considerations as these are sufficient to cause first-class men—men whose time is too valuable to be spent in canvassing for what, to them, are mere catchpenny positions; men whose professional standing and personal honour is too high to allow them to descend to touters' tactics, men whose business reputations might suffer from defeat, or who are unwilling to incur the annoyance which it causes—to abstain from the contests altogether.

The special reforms around which my suggestions will centre will therefore aim at securing the highest professional skill to conduct bank audit, and to ensure this will endeavour to provide:—Firstly, security of tenure; secondly, adequate remuneration; thirdly, exhaustive and continuous check; resulting, in the fourth place, in the prevention of certain classes of fraud from the difficulty of concealing them; and fifthly, in the immediate and unerring detection of all others which an audit can find out. Further, I hope to show that, put in operation, they would prove highly beneficial to the banks themselves, to the auditors who would be appointed under them, and to bank officers as a whole; in short, that the only interests which would not be advanced are those of the gentlemen acting as auditors at present.

In order to give security of tenure it will be necessary to do away entirely with the present method of election, and place it in the hands of some permanent and controlling body. Such a body exists in the Council, consisting of the representatives of the associated banks—the banking parliament, so to speak. The first suggestion I have to make, the basis on which all the others will be built up, is that the appointment and removal of bank auditors should be placed in the hands of this body.

The primary difficulty in the way of adopting this suggestion lies in securing the consent of the shareholders in the various institutions. Here we have to meet the struggles which will be made by the representatives of vested interests, actual and prospective, to preven such a reform. But I am sanguine enough to believe that if the directors of the various banks were to recommend its adoption as a means of securing a reliable audit, that a sufficient number would adopt their views, and that the remainder would shortly, from a consideration of their own interests and the pressure of public opinion, follow. The first exposure under what would be the old system would drive those who still retained it into the newer one. This difficulty (and all new propositions have to overcome initial difficulties) is by no means an insuperable one. The power of removing auditors should also be entirely in the hands of the same body. I consider this proviso most important, indeed *essential*, to secure thorough independence for their action and report.

They would know that if they found it necessary to present reports on any institution, which even the shareholders, to say nothing of the management, might resent, their positions would not be shaken thereby. Any challenge or charge against their capability, probity, or strictures would come before a board composed of experts, interested above all things in securing a sound financial position in every member of their body, and in maintaining the severest checks to secure it.

The positions of Inspector of the Clearing House and of the Secretary to the Associated Banks form precedents for placing such appointments in the hands of this body, and you all know the value placed on precedents by deliberative assemblies.

The next suggestion, in order to provide adequate remuneration, is that the official bank auditors shall be limited to a small number—for the purposes of discussion say one, two, or three—to be paid from a fund contributed to by the associated and such other banks as desire to secure their services. Such an auditing board charged with the responsibility of certifying to the correctness of the accounts of all the subscribing banks would require to be composed of men equal in ability to the managers and accountants they had to check. They should therefore be placed not only on an independent footing, but also on an equal one. The amount which they should receive will depend on the number of banks willing to combine in support-

ing such a scheme, and the amount each is prepared to contribute. I look upon £1000 a-year for each auditor as the least which should be proposed even at first, and that, as other institutions fell into the co-operation, this amount should increase to an extent only limited by the number and amount of the contributions. Salaries like these would secure efficient men, who would devote the whole of their time to their work. In such a provision lies one of the great guarantees for success in making an audit as perfect and efficient as possible. Auditors holding office under these conditions would become something more than auditors as we know them. They would become bank officials appointed by bank authorities, looking to banks for their remuneration, interested in banking successes, pledged to maintain bank secrets, placed in independent positions to secure financial soundness for banks, responsible to *two* public bodies, bank shareholders and a banking council—one a protection against harsh treatment by the other, the latter a security against unfairness or indiscretion in their reports. Under these circumstances their investigations might, by agreement, be extended deeper than the law actually allows at present, and an additional security for shareholders be obtained, which it is hardly possibly to provide in any other way.

In order to obtain continuous and exhaustive check, which all agree is necessary, the whole time of these auditors should be devoted to their work. In this provision lies one of the great guarantees for making the audit as perfect and efficient as possible. It should be an absolute necessity that one of such auditors should attend at each co-operating bank at very short intervals to check such cash, books, &c., as he considered necessary. This would prevent work accumulating, and to that extent render checking easier, and do away with any inducement to rush through it. It would also keep the audit close on the heels of the work and so discover any discrepancy almost immediately. Further, when the auditors reach the number of three, the same auditors should not always attend the same banks. They should interchange their work constantly, checking from the last signature of a colleague, having previously secured the date from him. It would also be advisable that the same two auditors should not sign successive half-yearly certificates. These smaller matters, and such little difficulties as several banks balancing on the same dates and requiring simultaneous audit, could easily be adjusted by previous arrangement. Indeed, from the continuous audit being brought up to within say a fortnight of the date of balancing, this particular portion of the work would be so lightened that this difficulty would to a large extent disappear. Under such a system and with such conditions, *false entries and such defalcations as an audit can disclose ought to be discovered within a few days of their taking place.*

This knowledge would go far—very far—to prevent their being committed at all, which I have before stated I take to be the highest aim to be secured. It is easy to realise that men occupying responsible appointments—permanent and highly paid—would study their duties, so as to retain them. They would know that every lapse coming to light while they retained office would be investigated as a charge of dereliction of duty, and that their positions would be imperilled if they had failed through their own *lâches* to detect it. If it arose from causes for which they could not be blamed, its discovery would prevent such a plea in the future. They would be on their mettle to suggest a method of preventing its recurrence, and place it out of the power of the auditors or bank officers (according to where the responsibility might lie) to put forward a similar excuse again.

In their own interests one of their first duties would be to study every case of defalcation in the past in order to learn the means by which it was concealed, and by the light of that knowledge to discover the checks which would prevent similar methods from being successful a second time. They would erect a structure of bank audit on a foundation of bank error and bank loss. Their time would be occupied in close investigation and analysis of the various systems of bank book-keeping, and of all the possible combinations by which they might be deceived, resulting in the development of a uniform system of bank books of the most perfect description obtainable; the rejection or alteration of any found to increase work without adequate return; and the development of their system of check to such a pitch of accuracy that false entries could never go beyond a short distance without declaring themselves.

It is a common saying that any smart book-keeper can deceive an auditor. Like many common sayings, it has a superficial smartness—a ring which causes it to be passed as genuine coin. Applied to the present method of bank audit it is quite true. Indeed the *Bankers' Magazine* declares that any smart clerk can do it. As an abstract objection against audit as a check, I do not believe it. For if the same amount of care, time, and ingenuity displayed in inventing systematic false entries were applied to prevent their being made at all, such sweeping conclusions would speedily be abandoned. But you can never expect these results to arise from the present want of system which employs a number of individuals, separate and disconnected, with interests opposed to each other, each full of his own occupation, of which bank audit only forms a small part, to which he can only give a few days, often snatched and grudged from his own business, and only performing, as men must only be expected to perform, as much (or as little) as will enable him to claim his cheque. These conditions are so well understood and accepted by shareholders that responsibility under the present system is a myth. The highest penalty that has yet been inflicted on any auditor is the loss of his audit, not a very heavy loss to a man even in moderate business, hardly a loss at all to a leading one. And even this is not inflicted. We find, under such circumstances, men re-elected again or re-appointed a little later on.

To secure the highest efficiency in bank audit it should be made a profession to be mastered only by a long course of study and training. As in other professions, it should be a man's accepted means of livelihood, to fail in which means loss of position, loss of *prestige*, loss of salary—in short, means failure in life; and which, therefore, contains the strongest incentives, the most imperative duty, to perfect himself in all its principles and details. Given these conditions, these interests, these incentives and these penalties, and I think that we should soon, as far as banks are concerned, read the proverb in a different manner.

But you may ask, where are the men who have the necessary training, who have gone through the course of study, who are competent for the work, who can be termed "professional" men in this sense? It is easy to answer. They are in the banks, and it is from the banks that such auditors as I have described should be appointed. The great prizes of the banking profession are few, and are confined to the general inspectors and managerships. To gain such a post requires special qualifications, quite different from those required by an auditor. The special qualifications for the latter are those which distinguish the inspector or the accountant (when the latter happens to be synonymous with the bookkeeper), whose knowledge of the bank methods, their capability and operation, their weakness and their failures should be complete to the smallest points. A faculty for organisation and for keen and lynx-eyed analysis, a thorough knowledge of the science of figures, a capacity for mastering detail, a painstaking correctness extending even to minuteness, together with the instinct of suspicion and the quality of caution developed to an unusual degree, are the characteristics to fit a man for such a post. A slow man, you say. Aye, but a sure one! Such qualities would never make a general manager. They are not wanted to. But I believe there are men in the profession possessing them—men who from the development of such valuable qualities are as practically shut out from its highest awards as are those who do not possess them at all. And here is another benefit—a great one, as I think it—which will be derived from the adoption of such suggestions as I have endeavoured to put before you. They will add valuable prizes to a profession which does not offer too many to those who have embraced it. They divide it into two distinct branches, with distinct ultimate honourable goals. The ablest men in the services, recognising the one for which they are best fitted, will specially prepare themselves for its highest offices. The aims of each will be recognized, a school of specialists will be formed in each branch, the competition for each office will be more limited, and the danger of placing a round man in a square hole will be decreased. The incentives to the younger officers, who, even now, have to look far more to their dim hopes of the future than to their present salaries and immediate prospects, will be doubled, and the most powerful inducement, *a practical one*, given to them to devote all their abilities and energies to attaining a mastery of that branch of the profession which must be their life study if they are to succeed in it at all. They will have a practical inducement to work for all those advantages, which this Institute was established to assist them to secure.

To effect this, means to raise the standard of the profession, not only inside itself, but with the public outside, from its lowest foundations to its highest pinnacles, than which no better object can engage our attention.

Any scheme which even remotely promises such results is well worthy of our deliberation, and when, in addition, it promises to decrease the perils of managers, to allay the anxieties of shareholders, and increase the confidence of the subscribing and investing public, it has established claims even to the consideration of that greater body which sits in judgment on the financial world — The Banking Parliament. There is no want like the want of backing up, and in bringing a subject of such importance before you I have ventured to hope for the influence of the Institute for such of these reforms as commend themselves to your approval, for such as appear likely to secure any radical, effective, and lasting improvement in what is admitted to be the most unsatisfactory branch of the banking profession.

Mr. Taylor's paper was discussed by several gentlemen, including Mr. H. G. Turner, general manager of the Commercial Bank of Australia Limited, Mr. A. Fraser (late of the Bank of Victoria), Mr. A. Skene (branch manager, National Bank of Australasia), and Mr. G. D. Meudell, public accountant and auditor. The opinion generally held was unfavourable both to the expediency and the practicability of Mr. Taylor's proposals. The meeting closed with votes of thanks to the lecturers and the chairman.

DUTIES OF AUDITORS

Duties of Auditors.

AT a meeting of the Incorporated Institute of Accountants (Victoria), held in Melbourne on 22nd September, an interesting discussion was conducted on the important question of the " Scope and Limit of the Duties of Auditors." The proceedings of the meeting have not been reported, but the subject was one deserving the attention of the members of the Institute. Generally speaking, the public does not possess a very clear understanding as to the position which auditors of the accounts of companies should occupy, and in the prevailing uncertainty directors frequently share. Some authoritative statement from the Council of the Institute might give greater definiteness to the status of auditors, and form a guide to directors and others upon this important matter.

Directly and impliedly the Companies Statute endows auditors with far more discretionary power than is generally suspected. In many cases the accountancy of institutions operating under this Statute is so well conducted that there is no occasion for the auditor to take up any higher ground than that involved by the checking of figures, and by other processes of a routine character. In other instances, however, an excess of prudence deters the auditor from taking exception to matters of more consequence than mechanical details. Confining himself merely to the testing of the accuracy of figures by books and vouchers, he does not venture to advise on the form of the accounts, or on the principles which should be applied in making a valuation of impersonal assets, or on points where it may be questioned whether the prescriptions of the law are followed with sufficient fidelity.

Amongst higher matters which may be considered as falling within the scope of the duty of auditors may be mentioned the question whether the transactions for the period under review have been kept within the four corners of the memorandum of association. The " objects" of a company are generally sufficiently wide and diverse in character to make extraneous operations undesirable, and possibly illegal. It would be quite proper, for instance, for an auditor to express his doubt as to the right of directors of a company, formed for the purpose of trading, to enter into " cornering" transactions for the purpose of artificially controlling markets. Such " corners" are quite likely, and as often as not do end in disaster. Another matter upon which the auditor should be ready to speak as occasion may require is that of valuation, which necessarily includes allowances for depreciation. He may not be able to affirm that the stock is accurately valued throughout, but he should be in a position to vouch for the soundness of the methods by which the appraisement has been made. Doubtless in many, perhaps in the great majority of cases, the directors have exercised a matured judgment in valuing their assets, but where they have, either ignorantly or in order to "find a dividend," inflated values, the auditor can hardly be considered presumptuous if he recalls them to a proper sense of their duty. In a sense, the auditor watches on behalf of the possible investor besides holding a retainer for the actual holder of shares in the company. As regards dubious practices in the compilation of balance-sheets, such as the inclusion of nominal capital or subscribed capital as a liability, or unissued or uncalled capital as an asset, the auditor is justified in tendering his advice. Other matters may arise in which he should be prepared to recommend better methods by which to state accounts, so that they may not mislead by complexity or by want of coherency.

Considerable advantage may, as we have already said, result from a professional statement of the scope and limit of the duties of auditors as interpreted by themselves. There is one thing, however, which they cannot very well suggest, but which should be referred to. The employment of non-professional auditors has had much to do with the encouragement of whatever disposition may exist to belittle the duties of the office of auditorship. A large number of balance-sheets necessarily come under our inspection, and we almost invariably notice that where crudities or irregularities appear, the auditors are non-professional. Now, it must be quite plain that the audit of a professional man, whose reputation and emoluments are at stake, is likely to be more efficient than that of an amateur, who jeopardises nothing but a few occasional guineas in declaring the accuracy of misleading or incorrect figures. Shareholders as a body will do well to give preference to professional auditors, but not necessarily to those who are members of the Incorporated Institute of Accountants. The main thing is to elect men who are not only responsible, but have sufficient reason to be alive to their responsibility.

THE DUTIES OF AUDITORS.—THE ANGLO-AUSTRALIAN BANK

The Duties of Auditors.—The Anglo-Australian Bank.

AN important correspondence between Messrs. LANGTON, HOLMES and M'CRINDLE, the well-known firm of public auditors in Melbourne, and the directors of the Anglo-Australian Bank Limited, has been recently placed before the shareholders of the company by the firm named, and, in self-defence, the directors have also sent out a circular letter, to which are appended letters from the present auditors of the company. Some interesting issues are raised by this correspondence. Messrs. LANGTON, HOLMES and M'CRINDLE have taken a departure new to Australian financial circles, but which, so far at least as the motives which have dictated it are concerned, is to be approved. We do not, by this expression of opinion, necessarily beg the questions between them and the directors of the Anglo-Australian Bank Limited, but we do say that by the action they have taken they have justifiably repudiated the notion often held by directors of companies, that the functions of auditors are confined to merely vouching the arithmetical accuracy of the entries in a statement of accounts. There has been by far too much subserviency to this view of the duties of auditors shown by the profession in Australia. Had Messrs. LANGTON, HOLMES and M'CRINDLE assented to the request, that they should give "a certificate "of the clerical accuracy of the books," they would have ignored the spirit of the 140th article of association of the company, which sets forth—

That the auditors shall make a report to the members upon the balance-sheet and accounts, and in every such report they shall state whether in their opinion the balance-sheet is a full and fair balance-sheet, containing the particulars required by the regulations of the company, and properly drawn up, so as to exhibit a true and correct view of the company's affairs, &c.

The article does not, however, go so far as the 94th article of Table A of the Companies' Act, which proceeds after the word "affairs" as follows:—

And in case they have called for explanations or information from the directors, whether such explanations or information have been given by the directors, and whether they have been satisfactory.

But Messrs. LANGTON, HOLMES and M'CRINDLE did not hesitate to call for "explanations or information," and the disagreement between them and the directors arose.

In proceeding to review the specific points raised by the firm in connection with the accounts of the Anglo-Australian Bank Limited, we desire to avoid adopting any statements of an *ex parte* character. The first question raised regards the paid-up capital, which in the accounts to 30th September, 1890, submitted to the auditors, was stated at £100,317. Of this two shareholders held £90,280, as follows:—A, 8180 shares paid up to £5, £40,900; B, 39,464 shares paid up to £1 5s., £49,380. There does not appear to be any dispute as to these amounts. But Messrs. LANGTON, HOLMES AND M'CRINDLE proceed to say that—

A's [shares] were originally held by C as 42,360 shares paid up to £1, but only £5000 was ever paid upon them, the balance being provided for by a debit to C in his current account. These 42,360 shares were then transferred to A, and after allowing for several small transfers are now represented by the 8180 shares paid up to £5 abovementioned. But beyond the £5000 already referred to no other money has ever been paid to the company on account of these shares, the debit to C's current account having been transferred to that of A, where it now stands at £37,060 2s. In the face of these facts we cannot recognise these shares as having been paid up to £5. Nor can we see our way to recognise the 39,464 shares of B as paid up to £1 5s., seeing that there is a debt due upon them to the company of £33,538 8s. 9d., unless, indeed, it can be shown to us that for this advance the company holds substantial security.

The directors by their chairman meet the foregoing with the following explanation :—

It is a part of the bank's business, as defined in its memorandum of association, to make advances on *all descriptions of shares.* In this particular case [that of B's shares] the shares were *fully paid-up at the time of issue,* and no advance was made against them for fourteen months after their issue. To challenge the bank's right, as you virtually do, to make advances on shares is, in my opinion, to go behind and attempt to override its memorandum of association. The same remarks apply to A's shares, the only difference being one of time, the advance being made sooner in the latter case than in the former. The bank's vouchers prove that the shares were genuinely and *bond fide paid-up,* and the advances made by the bank were subsequent acts.

The two statements are reconcilable so far as B's shares are concerned, but with regard to A's shares they do not correspond, the technical question being whether the shares held by A were only partially paid on account, the balance being treated in current account, or whether they were actually paid up, and afterwards advanced against. Whatever the correct reply may be, we gather that the "paid-up" capital of the Anglo-Australian Bank Limited is made up as follows :—

	Debit in Current Account.	Amount Clear from Advances.	Total.
A's shares ..	£37,060 2 0	£3,839 18 0	£40,900
B's shares ..	33,538 8 9	15,791 11 3	49,330
Other shares (assumed not to be under advances) ..	—	10,087 0 0	10,087
Total	£70,598 10 9	£29,718 9 3	£100,317

Thus out of a paid-up capital of £100,317, more than seven-tenths are under advances, leaving an unencumbered balance of less than £30,000. Now we are not going to question the right of the company to make advances, but it may reasonably be doubted whether it is quite prudent to advance so large a proportion of the "paid-up" capital to two shareholders holding nine-tenths in value of the stock. Nor can such advances be quite satisfactory to the depositors and debenture-holders of the company, who at the last balance stood on its books for £110,339. There is another aspect of

the question to which it is fair to the directors of the bank to refer. The directors allege in support of their policy that . they are empowered under their memorandum of association to "advance money without any security "whatever." This is actually the case, for the "objects for which the company is "established" include the following :— "8. To lend money . . . without taking "security." But whatever consolation the directors may draw from this provision, it is in our opinion only just that depositors, especially in the United Kingdom, should be informed that they are asked to lend money to an institution which has the power to relend it "without "taking security." The most valuable safeguard to which the depositor is entitled is expressly abolished.

A subsidiary point in connection with the share register is the inclusion of 109 shares, upon which it appears to be admitted that no money has been paid. Messrs. LANGTON, HOLMES and M'CRINDLE declined to recognise these shares as having been legally issued. In reply, it is stated that the shares in question were bonus shares given in lieu of commission. It is not quite clear on the surface how these shares came to be issued, but the holders of them can doubtless make the matter plain in the event of the necessity arising.

The second point raised by Messrs. LANGTON, HOLMES and M'CRINDLE regards the balance at the company's bankers of £8405 9s. 7d. on 30th September, the allegation being that, with the exception of £68 14s. 5d., it was made up by paying in two cheques on two current accounts in the company itself on 30th September, which were retired the next morning by the company's cheque upon its bank. The bank has, however, given a certificate to the effect that on 30th September the balance was £8405 9s. 7d., so that it is to be concluded that on this point Messrs. LANGTON, HOLMES and M'CRINDLE'S case may, from a purely technical point of view, hardly be tenable. The bank could hardly go back upon its certificate.

The third objection is one of great moment. The firm of auditors found that the amount of the freehold properties of the company, viz., £329,118 2s. 8d., included interest, £22,034 14s. 4d., written up during the year, and naturally decided—

That unless this addition of interest to the amount of the assets can be sustained by clear evidence of an equivalent increase of value we. shall not be able to certify to its correctness.

To this the chairman of directors of the company replied—

That the question of charging properties with interest *is entirely one of policy.* The directors have, I contend, exercised a wise discretion in charging properties with interest, in one case charging only 3 per cent., in another 6 per cent., and in the third 10 per cent. In this last case the value of the property has been much enhanced during the past twelve months by the erection of a railway station in the centre of the estate, thus bringing almost every portion of it within a few minutes' ride of the city. In the case where we have charged the property with 6 per cent. interest, we have a valuation made after the collapse of the land boom, showing a surplus of about £30,000. This valuation has been more than confirmed by subsequent sales of portions of the estate.

We place the two views upon the policy of writing up interest on properties fairly before our readers. But we must confess that we consider the policy of the directors to be a rather dangerous one, in view of the depression in the real property market in Melbourne. We would rather be disposed to applaud the policy of writing down valuations than of adding interest. However that may be, assuming Messrs. LANGTON, HOLMES and M'CRINDLE's figures to be correct, and the directors of the company do not say they are not, there is material for amplifying the company's balance-sheet (which appeared in the *Record* for January, page 31). In the first place the *in globo* asset in the balance-sheet divides itself as follows :—

Freehold properties	£329,113	2	8
A's and B's current accounts against security of their shares..	70,598	10	9
Bills receivable, advances, loans on mortgages, and other securities	204,468	7	8
Total, as shown in the balance-sheet	£604,180	1	1

Turning to the profit and loss account, we find that for the year the net profit was £9141 1s. 6d. But interest written-up on properties, according to Messrs. LANGTON, HOLMES AND M'CRINDLE, was £22,034 14s. 4d. for the year. Some further elucidations regarding the profit balance seem to be necessary. Generally, the accounts of institutions which deal in real property would be more instructive to the investing public if the exact amount of interest written-up on the properties were stated separately.

We do not in the slightest manner desire to suggest that the probity of the board of directors of the Anglo-Australian Bank Limited is to be doubted. The matters with which we have dealt are questions of policy, upon which difference of opinion may arise. But we cannot agree with the policy which has been adopted, and we certainly think that Messrs. LANGTON, HOLMES and M'CRINDLE were fully justified; in assuming the position they did. Their action was one to be expected from a leading firm, which is not afraid to discharge all the duties of auditors.

AUDIT

Audit. WE have received from Mr. GRAN-VILLE S. PRICE, public accountant, Melbourne, a reprint of a letter upon audit, from his pen, which appeared in the Melbourne *Argus* of 10th October, 1885. In all essential respects we agree with Mr. PRICE's admirable presentation of what audit and the auditor ought to be. But there is one thing to which we must take serious objection (and the objection is applicable to a good deal of the newspaper correspondence and writing that has lately appeared), viz., that inadequate pay is in the remotest sense a justification, or even an excuse, for bad auditing. We admit freely that in many instances the auditor is greatly underpaid for the work he is required to do. But we hold that once the job is accepted the auditor is bound to discharge the duties he has undertaken to the fullest extent of his abilities, whatever the fee may be. We have no sympathy whatever with the growing notion that responsibilities are to be measured by monetary considerations alone. If an auditor thinks his remuneration too little, and directors will not better it, then obviously the proper course is that he should decline the work rather than yield to any temptation to " scamp" it. The conscienceless board and the labour-evading auditor are about on a par.

THE AUDIT OF INSURANCE COMPANIES ACCOUNTS

The Audit of Insurance Companies Accounts.

A DISCUSSION on the scope of the duties of auditors of the accounts of insurance companies has recently taken place in Melbourne. The directors of the Guardian Accident and Guarantee Insurance Company called a meeting of shareholders to receive an *ad interim* report upon the operations for the half-year, and to declare a dividend. The statement of accounts was submitted to the two auditors, who for certain reasons refused to sign. One of the auditors appears, however, to have subsequently waived his objections. The meeting of shareholders was held, notwithstanding that the accounts had not been certified. At the instance of one of the auditors, however, a special meeting was held on 27th ult. to consider a protest which he had raised against the payment of the interim dividend. A long discussion took place, but the shareholders refused to appoint a committee of investigation, and endorsed the action of the directors. Several interesting points have presented themselves during the course of the controversy, and upon these we propose to comment. But before doing so we ought to state that the directors were not compelled by the articles of association to present any statement of accounts at all to the shareholders at an interim meeting, the period prescribed being yearly, *i.e.*, to 31st May. The directors could have taken the responsibility upon themselves, after personal inspection of the accounts, to simply declare the interim dividend. Had they done so nobody could very well have complained. But they had a formal statement drawn up, and submitted it to the auditors for examination.

Having taken this step it was not, in our opinion, prudent or seemly for them to take up the position that if the auditors would not certify without certain objections being met, they would ignore them altogether. It would have been better to take a qualified report from the auditors, and to give the necessary explanations to the shareholders.

Of the three objections raised by the auditor, we can hardly think that two of them were supportable, and possibly a conference might have led to their withdrawal. The first objection was that an asset amounting to £980 4s. 1d. improperly included £404 14s. 9d., the amount of certain outstanding cheques and over-due promissory notes. Now, there does not appear to have been sufficient ground for this objection, especially as nearly the whole of the sum called in question was paid shortly after the ordinary meeting of shareholders. The second objection was raised against the inclusion as assets of two receipts for deposits with institutions which have recently failed in Melbourne. Again, the objection was groundless, for the simple reason that there was positively nothing to show that the company is likely to lose any portion of the money, much less the whole. Both the objections we have referred to related, as we think, to matters upon which auditors are not called to decide. Their responsibilities, properly viewed, are quite heavy enough without their seeking to add to them unnecessarily. Such points as those brought in question are for the consideration of directors alone, for it is their duty to make a proper estimate of the assets.

The third objection which was raised stands, however, on a very different ground, and we think that the directors might have given it more consideration. The auditor thought insufficient provision was made for unexpired risks. The Guardian Accident and Guarantee Insurance Company has now stated its accounts for a year and a-half (or, more exactly, seventeen months), to 30th November last. During that period it has received £11,945 in net premiums, and it has paid away in claims £3948, or say nearly one-third of the premiums. But the proportion for the six months of its existence ended 30th November last exceeds 50 per cent. It would at first sight appear doubtful, therefore, whether an adequate reserve has been made by the company for unexpired risks, especially as against the balance at credit there is a considerable amount of preliminary expenses still to be dealt with. But we will assume that the directors of the company have taken this point into intelligent consideration, and that they are satisfied that their undivided profits adequately provide for the unexpired risks. The abstract question arises, whether an auditor of the accounts of an insurance office is justified in seeking to be satisfied that the liability on unexpired risks is fully covered before a distribution of profits is made? We hold that he is; that if an auditor passes a statement of accounts which ignores the liability referred to, he is partly responsible if dividends are paid out of capital, notwithstanding an apparent profit balance. Many an insurance company has failed to achieve success because it has ignorantly assumed that the credit balances of its earlier statements justified distributions, while current liabilities under policies were treated as if they had no existence. The controversy has once more raised the question, at what rate preliminary expenses should be extinguished. In the case of an insurance company the item is one which should be dealt with as promptly as possible, and one which

certainly should not be added to after the company starts operations. In the case of the Guardian a large deduction was made in the first year, and doubtless the directors will make a further reduction at the second annual balance. There is one important matter in accident insurance business which always demands careful handling. We refer to the payments made by life members and to the guarantee premiums received. The proper and really the only safe practice is to treat these items as liabilities, on a suitable basis. They should certainly not be merged in the premium income for the twelve months, as contributing to their full amount to the profit balance. The New Zealand Accident Insurance Company has adopted the right method of treatment, and their balance-sheet, which appears elsewhere, shows the liability "Life members' account and guarantee premiums account, £5939 7s. 11d.

Reviewing all the circumstances of the disagreement between the directors and the auditor of the Guardian Accident and Guarantee Insurance Company, we are inclined to think that, with the exercise of a little more forbearance and consideration on the one side, and a little less captiousness on the other, an amicable understanding might have been come to. But the controversy has been instrumental in recalling attention to two or three important points in insurance practice.

AUDIT

Audit.

(FIRST ARTICLE.)

THE disasters which have recently overtaken some of the financial institutions doing business in Melbourne and Sydney, have caused the subject of audit to be brought more prominently before the public than has hitherto been the case. At some of the meetings of shareholders which have been held it has been more than hinted that collapse could have been averted had the auditors appointed to examine and certify to the correctness of accounts performed their duties in a less perfunctory manner. The time, therefore, seems opportune to examine the whole question of audit with a view of ascertaining in what particulars the present system is defective, and, if possible, devising remedies. A perusal of the published reports of the meetings referred to indicates that the two principal charges laid at the door of auditors are :—(1) Inability to discover frauds committed by managers or secretaries, and concealed from the knowledge of directors ; and (2) contributory negligence to such frauds through looseness of the method employed in the examination of books, vouchers, and securities generally.

As to the first of these charges, it may be fairly argued that the detection of a dishonest chief official is, from the very facilities he enjoys, extremely difficult. The manager or secretary is the head and front of a public company, possessing an intimacy of knowledge of its affairs through daily working, to which a board of directors, however conscientious in the performance of its duties, rarely attains. The relationship between the board and its manager must, therefore, in the nature of things, be one • of mutual trust and confidence, otherwise the business of the institution could not be carried on. Take, for instance, the associated banks. In these institutions

lists of overdrafts are laid at least weekly before their respective boards, for the correctness of which the manager is responsible. The duty of the directors does not extend to the comparison and verification of the items in these lists with the actual books of account, for in a large institution such routine work would be absolutely impossible. In the case of one of the recent failures, however, it would appear that neglect to ascertain from the proper books, independently of mere statements or abstracts, the true position of customers was the faulty link in the chain which admitted of the fraudulent appropriation of the bank's funds. Had the directors of the Land Credit Bank taken the trouble, if only occasionally, to compare the ledger balances of current accounts with the weekly statements put before them by the manager, that official's career of duplicity would have been nipped in the bud.

Now comes the auditor upon the scene. The insinuation against him is virtually failure to discover that false information had been periodically supplied to the directors, who were consequently unaware of the individual indebtedness to the bank of its own customers ; and also inability to detect that certain entries in the books were made without the cognisance of the board or in direct opposition to its instructions. The reply to this, from the point of view of the auditor, is as to the loaning of money to certain individuals, that it is no part of his duty to query a balance merely because of its magnitude, the allowance of such a balance being a question of policy to be determined by the directors, and not coming within his province; and, as to the book entries, that if vouchers are produced for these, signed and verified in the usual manner, his function as examiner then ceases.

From this statement of one of the charges brought against auditors, and the reply thereto, it will easily be perceived that the first weak spot in our present system is the uncertainty as to where the duties of directors end and those of auditors begin. There is no precise definition as to this, and as a consequence directors frequently seem to regard attention to certain matters, or knowledge of certain facts, as coming within the scope of the auditors' duties, which those officials in their turn assume have already come under the consideration of the board and received its sanction.

The second charge, that of contributory negligence arising out of a hurried or imperfect examination of books, vouchers, or securities, is of an altogether different nature. The comparison of vouchers with entries, of deeds with security registers, and an ocular demonstration that for every entry in the books of account there is a proper voucher, and for every entry in the deed register a corresponding security, is to a great extent a mere mechanical process. No auditor is therefore justified in taking a manager's word or accepting his assurance either that a suspicious entry is capable of satisfactory explanation, without such explanation being then and there forthcoming, or that deeds and documents not produced at the time of audit are in some other person's custody, even if that person be the solicitor of the company. In this latter case nothing short of an actual inspection of the deeds at the solicitors', or if lodged at the Titles Office, a certificate in writing from the solicitor to that effect, should be accepted. No auditor should, in fact, take anything on trust. His primary duty is that of verification, and no verification can be satisfactory unless based on personal knowledge. It is not for us to allege that as regards this mechanical part of their office the auditors of some at least of the institutions now in trouble have failed to acquit themselves with credit. In this particular the public, with the knowledge

obtained from recent lamentable revelations, will be sufficiently competent judges. Suffice it to say that in one instance at all events, that of the South Melbourne Building Society, had the audit been of the thorough nature we have indicated, that institution would have been in a very different position at the present moment, and much of the misery and suffering which have fallen upon innocent individuals would have been averted.

Having briefly dealt with the charges which have been made against auditors, there remains another aspect of the question which demands attention, in view of the action recently taken by some of the building societies and investment companies. The institutions we refer to are those which, finding themselves in difficulties, have asked their depositors (that is to say their creditors) to grant them what virtually amounts to three or four years' time in which to discharge their indebtedness. Although in many instances a considerable amount of capital is still callable, it is not proposed that shareholders should make sacrifices to defray the just debts of the institution with which they are connected, but the depositors who, be it remembered, have specific contracts with it, are asked to suffer all the inconvenience and perhaps loss which the delay in payment of their claims entails. If the unfortunate depositors display any reluctance in complying with this somewhat arbitrary request, they seem in many instances to be regarded as enemies of the general welfare, and legislation in the shape of voluntary liquidation Acts is literally hurled at them to prevent enforcement of their rights. Now, seeing that large bodies of depositors are put in this false position through the *laches* of officials somewhere, the question arises as to whether in the selection of auditors—that is persons whose special office it is, or should be, to detect and prevent irregularities—the depositors as well as the shareholders should not have a voice.

We can quite understand that as long as shareholders are prepared to meet all the claims upon them they should have the sole right of appointing such officials. When, however, they ask depositors to bear with them the consequences of bad management or improper practices, it seems but reasonable that the latter should at least have a representative to watch their interests in the periodical investigations of the affairs of the company which holds their money. The fundamental error seems to have been the allowing of companies or societies to take deposits unless substantial reserves of coin were held against them. As, however, the error has been committed and the evil consequences demonstrated, we think that in future legislation the claims of depositors in the direction we have indicated should not be lost sight of.

In a second article we purpose dealing with the question of reform of our present methods of audit, with the view of aiding in the prevention of another series of scandals, discreditable alike to our reputation for business acumen and our commercial morality.

$$\text{-----}\blacklozenge\text{-----}$$

AUDIT

Audit.

[SECOND ARTICLE.]

IN a previous article we drew attention to what appeared to us to be serious defects in the existing methods of auditing the accounts of public companies, and pointed out that the collapse of two at least of the many institutions now in difficulties in Melbourne, if not directly traceable to these defects, could probably have been averted had a better system of check upon the actions of the managing officials prevailed. We now purpose indicating what in our opinion should be a few of the safeguards to be insisted upon in the elaboration of any more efficient scheme for protecting shareholders against fraudulent manipulation of accounts, misappropriation of securities, or *laches* on the part of those to whom the conduct of the business of the institution in which they are interested is entrusted.

This involves the consideration (1) of the objects of a public company, and (2) the status of its officials.

Now, for whatever special purpose a company is formed, it will not be denied that the primary object of its existence is to produce the best possible results for its shareholders. Their money is in the concern, and they have the right to demand the best return for their investment of capital. To ensure this there should be three forces continually at work. These are—A board of directors to initiate enterprises, determine questions of policy, and issue instructions for carrying on business generally ; a manager or secretary to act as the executive officer of the board ; and an auditor or auditors to check the operations of the company in order to ascertain that they have been conducted in accordance with the articles of association, that the instructions of the board have been carried out by the manager, and that no frauds have been committed.

An audit may therefore be defined as " a complete examination and verification " of the whole of the transactions of a " public company for a given period by a " person or persons totally independent " of the company, and not subject to the " control of the directors or officials." The more closely an audit approaches to this standard, the more satisfactory will it be (while of course the converse is true), so that it is evident that the officials whose duty it is to make such an examination, must as far as status goes, be placed on a level with directors and managers, and considered as answerable to the shareholders only.

We are quite aware that these views as to the duties and position of auditors are in advance of those at present generally prevailing. Auditors are too frequently regarded as merely servants of directors, and so little importance is attached to the examination they are called upon to make, that instances are not unknown in which balance-sheets have been submitted without passing through the hands of auditors at all, and if the omission has been pointed out, a gentleman has perhaps been called in hurriedly for a few hours, at a remuneration of a guinea or two, to go through and certify to the operations of a company extending over a period of six months ! This idea of the inferior status of auditors, widespread though it may be, is altogether wrong. We cannot too clearly point out that auditors are the servants of shareholders and not of directors. Auditors are not responsible to directors, but equally *with* them to the shareholders within their respective spheres of duty.

Turning now from the question of the status of auditors to the safeguards which we advocate, we are confronted at the outset by the oft-urged difficulty— " Given your auditors and granting them " the equality of position you claim, what

" guarantee have you that they will per-
" form their duties efficiently? In other
" words, auditors, like other individuals,
" are only fallible mortals after all, and
" how is it proposed to check or super-
" vise *them*, the very officials that are
" appointed to check the operations of
" others?" The most feasible way of
meeting this difficulty appears to us to be
to insist on the compulsory retirement of
one of two auditors every six months, and
the appointment of a fresh one; that is
to say, to establish practically a rotation
of auditors. One of the gentlemen
occupying the position during the first
six months of the financial year should
not be eligible during the second, and so
on. Of course, it is not intended to permanently disqualify any auditor, but
merely to ensure a constant rotation, so
that what is virtually an independent
examination of the books should be made
during each half-year. This system, if
adopted, would, we think, be the means
of ensuring as perfect a check as it is
practically possible to obtain. Experience
in connection with financial institutions
has shown that an occasional change of
officials in any department, even if it
only be for a time, is on the whole
beneficial; and we think that this is a
rule which would apply with special force
in the case of auditors.

Given then a system of rotation of
auditors, it is in our opinion highly
desirable that the duties and powers of
directors and auditors respectively should
be specifically defined, if necessary, by an
amendment or extension of the Companies Act. In particular, power should
be given to auditors to inspect and
examine the books or ledgers containing
the individual accounts of customers—a
privilege which in many cases is at present denied them. It is chiefly by the
manipulation of customers' accounts in
some way or another that the more
skilled among dishonest officials operate,
and not by the mere vulgar abstraction
of cash from the safe or till. If auditors
are debarred from checking these accounts,
half their utility as detectors of fraud
vanishes. They should, therefore, have
the privilege of inspecting every book of
account kept by the institution without
exception, and should further be requested
to report in writing to the directors upon
any dangerous feature in the business of
the institution which such inspection
may reveal.

We think, also, that an audit, to be
thoroughly effective, should be practically
continuous, or as nearly so as possible.
The ordinary half-yearly audit, the time
for which is generally a matter of arrangement between company-managers and
auditors, is in the majority of instances
altogether too hurried and superficial.
Besides this, it puts a manager who may
be dishonestly inclined on his guard, and
gives him an opportunity of manipulating
his accounts in such a way as to deceive
even very experienced men. Thus the
debit balance of a customer may be for
the nonce converted into a credit, and
the true state of the institution thereby
concealed, or securities may be hurriedly
borrowed from an accommodating friend,
to be returned immediately after the
audit is over; in fact, a hundred and one
deceptions may be arranged which the
auditors would find it difficult to detect.
The only remedy for this is either the
adoption of the continuous audit which we
advocate (and which already obtains in
some of the best regulated institutions)
or a system similar to that of bank
inspection—that is, audits made without
notice and at irregular intervals. There
is no force in the argument that audits of
this latter class would render the proper
conduct of business impossible. They
obtain in all the associated banks of Melbourne without causing undue inconvenience, and could easily be carried out in
such a way as not to interfere with the
legitimate daily operations of any society
or company.

In order that nothing in the progress
of an audit may be left to chance, we

would suggest as a minor safeguard the adoption of a general printed form showing the exact information to be obtained and the best manner of obtaining it—a similar form, in fact, to that used by most bank inspectors, and known, we believe, as the "Inspectors' Return." We do not hesitate to say that many auditors elected under the present system enter upon their duties with a very imperfect conception of what these really are. By the general adoption of the form we advocate (devised after a consultation between company managers, bankers, and other experts in this city, which we have no doubt could be easily arranged), the duties of auditors would be very clearly pointed out to them, and any neglect on their part could easily be sheeted home.

Finally, we are of opinion that the time has now arrived when an Institute of Auditors could be established with much advantage to the community generally. We have, it is true, an Institute of Bankers and an Institute of Accountants, but auditing proper is neither banking nor accountancy. Like these professions, it demands a special training, and the object of such an institute as we suggest would be to provide that training, and also to study the whole question so as to devise from time to time such special checks or safeguards as might be required to meet special cases. It is obvious that such a body would speak with an authority which no private individual can command, it would afford a source from which to obtain a perpetual supply of competent men, and, most important of all, it would silence the clamour of those who, looking upon the "Government" as the fountain head of all knowledge and wisdom, now loudly demand, as a panacea for the (financial) ills from which we are suffering, the appointment of more Government officials in the shape of "Government auditors."

As to the mode of election of auditors, we think a distinction should be made between institutions taking deposits and maintaining a gold reserve against their liabilities (in other words "banks"), and institutions which, although accepting deposits, maintain no gold reserve. In the case of the latter, it seems to us that some means should be devised by which the depositors might be assured that a proper use was being made of their funds. The simplest way of achieving this would be to give them a status (in some manner to be hereafter determined), so that they might have either a special representative in the examination of accounts, or share in the selection of the auditing body.

To briefly sum up. In substitution for the present indefinite or happy-go-lucky methods of auditing, we advocate :—

1. An enactment that the status of auditors is equal, so far as their special duties are concerned, to that of directors.

2. Compulsory rotation of auditors.

3. Definition by enactment of the specific duties of directors and auditors respectively.

4. The inauguration of a system of continuous audit, or audit at irregular periods, as well as at the half-yearly rests.

5. The adoption of a general printed form, giving particulars as to the information required of auditors and the best means of obtaining it.

6. The establishment of an Institute of Auditors.

7. An improved method of election of auditors in the case of companies taking deposits and not holding a gold reserve.

We think we are safe in asserting that if the suggestions embodied in the foregoing list are carried out there will be fewer complaints of ineffective audits, and the community generally will not again be scandalised by the discovery of gigantic frauds of the character of those for which the past year has acquired so unenviable a reputation.

AUDIT

SIR,—The community are indebted to you for the excellent ideas contained in the articles under this head in your leading columns of February and March.

I entirely agree with the seven clauses in your summing up, especially with clause 6, advocating the establishment of an Institute of Auditors in Melbourne. Such a society, conducted on impartial lines, with the necessary machinery for educating the younger men in our profession, would indeed be a boon. I trust some capable men will take up and carry out your suggestion.

I need scarcely say I am not in any way reflecting on the Institute of Accountants in Victoria. I cannot do so because I really know very little about that body.—Yours, &c.

C.H. DAVIS, F.S.A.A., Eng.

Melbourne, April, 1892.

THE BANKERS' MAGAZINE OF AUSTRALASIA

[NOVEMBER, 1893, pp.219-23]

AUDITORS: THEIR RESPONSIBILITIES AND DUTIES

In these times a little information on these points will be useful. Dicksee has the following on the responsibility of auditors for errors: Having now considered the practical extent of the auditor's certification of correctness, let us consider what will be his liability in the event of his investigation having failed to detect errors or frauds.

Having regard to the weighty responsibility resting upon the auditor, and the enormous power—for good or evil—exercised by him, it is reassuring to find that there exists no single instance of a competent and conscientious auditor having been held liable to reproduce moneys that have been lost to his clients by his inability to detect an error in the accounts he has certified.

The decision of Mr. Justice Stirling, in *The Oxford Building Society* case, is perhaps one that more nearly affects the profession than any yet given. The head-note of this case reads as follows:—

"Held that it was the duty of the auditor in auditing the accounts of the company, not to confine himself to verifying the arithmetical accuracy of the balance sheet, but to inquire into its special accuracy, and to ascertain if it contained the particulars specified in the articles or association, and was properly drawn up to contain a true and accurate representation of the company's affairs."

The portion of the judgment which more particularly affects auditors enforces the same doctrine in even more definite terms:—

"In each of (these) years, L. (the auditor) certified that the accounts were a true copy of those shown in the books of the company. That certificate would naturally be understood to mean that the books of the company showed (taking for example the certificate for the year 1879) that on the 30th April, 1879, the company was entitled to 'moneys lent' to the amount of £29,515 15s. od. This was not in accordance with the fact; the accounts in this respect did not truly represent the state of the company's affairs, and it was a breach of duty upon L.'s part to certify as he did with reference to them. The payment of the dividends, directors' fees, and bonuses to the manager actually paid on those years appears to be the natural and immediate consequence of such breach of duty; and I hold L. liable for damages to the amount of the moneys so paid."

The futility of an auditor attempting to escape his just responsibilities by a limitation of the scope of his certificate is here most forcibly demonstrated; there are, however, two other points, which must not pass unnoticed.

Firstly, there was no question, in this case, as to the accounts being false. The matter in dispute was no moot question of depreciation, or of apportionment between capital and revenue; the accounts were indisputably false, and it was not even suggested that the auditor had done his best to verify their accuracy. Had there been any possible doubt upon this score, and had the auditor conscientiously attempted to perform his duties, it is not unreasonable to suppose that he would have received the benefit of any doubt that might have existed.

Secondly, the immediate result of his neglect was a payment of dividends, directors' fees, and bonus. Had no such result taken place, it is by no means so certain that any liability would have accrued. It would probably be considered a question open to argument, as to whether the failure of an auditor to detect fraud was the direct cause of loss to his clients; so far as the money already stolen was concerned, it would appear that the cause cannot well be preceded by its effect, while it is not quite obvious that even subsequent frauds would be the direct result of the auditor's neglect. The point is rather a nice one, and—as far as the auditor's knowledge is concerned—still undecided.

Before dismissing this case altogether, it may be well to remark that L. was allowed the benefit of the statute of limitations; but—inasmuch as this point was not disputed by plaintiffs' counsel, and was consequently not before the court—it does not follow that a like plea would avail upon another occasion.

To sum up, then, it does not appear that the conscientious and capable auditor, who has endeavoured to conduct his audit upon the lines laid down, need feel the least apprehension as to the legal consequences arising either from a *bona fide* error of judgment, or from his inability to discover an exceptionally clever fraud. On the other hand, it would doubtless be greatly to the advantage of all properly qualified auditors if even more were expected from them, for there might, then, be some chance of scaring out of the field a too numerous class of so-called auditors, whose extreme ignorance of the veriest elements of their profession is only equally by their utter inability to appreciate the moral responsibility of their position.

Pixley on Auditors says, It is not often an auditor comes into conflict with the directors. Both they and he have, as a rule, the same interests at heart, namely, the prosperity and welfare of the company, and in his capacity as an ally and assistant of the directors in all matters concerning the welfare of the shareholders, an auditor has many opportunities of pointing out to them various improvements which might with advantage be adopted, not only in the book-keeping department, but also in the general routine work of the office.

As already stated, in many companies, more especially in large ones, the amount of detail passed and repassed through the books is wholly unnecessary, and an efficient auditor has many opportunities of suggesting alterations, which would, if adopted, greatly lessen labour, and, consequently, expense.

It is very important that, in his anxiety to do his duty towards the shareholders, the auditor should be careful not to interfere in the management of the company by insisting on the adoption of any of his propositions as to the system of book-keeping, the interior economy of the office, or in any other matter. He should endeavour to introduce his reforms by friendly suggestions, and by putting them forward gradually.

The directors are the managers of the company on behalf of the shareholders, to whom they are alone responsible, and the strict duty of the auditor is to ascertain that the accounts, as presented to the latter, show accurately the result of this management. It is by performing this duty conscientiously and efficiently he can best discharge his obligation to those who have elected him to his responsible position.

The real value of a thorough and systematic audit of the accounts of public companies is not, however, at present adequately appreciated by shareholders, but the very severe lessons the investing public have learnt through the failures of the last few years are certainly causing them to pay more attention to the qualifications of those who undertake the duties of auditors.

This fact is so well recognised by promoters that nearly all the prospectuses of new companies now include among their officers the names of professional accountants as their auditors, while the older companies are gradually replacing the shareholder auditor by a professional one.

Mr. A. Lyell, the eminent Melbourne auditor, lately said in a lecture before the Victorian Institute dealing with the question of desirable amendments in the practice of auditing, I think that this Institute would do really useful work if it were to devote some time to discussing exhaustively, and in detail, the whole question of auditing, with the view of establishing, as far as it may be deemed practicable, some uniformity of practice in relation at all events to points of vital importance.

As practice at present prevails, great differences exist as to the details of the work which ought to be included in audits.

In some companies the work is practically limited to checking the total stated cash receipts with the moneys lodged in the bank account, the stated cash disbursements with the moneys withdrawn from the bank account, verifying the correctness of the ledger bank balance with the actual bank balance, checking all the vouchers for disbursements, checking the additions of the ledger, and verifying the different balances brought down with the balance-sheet, and verifying the correctness of the profit and loss account.

In other words, the work is limited to checking the vouchers, and verifying the apparent correctness of the position of the company, as stated in the balance-sheet, with the balances brought down in the ledger, and the correctness of the profit and loss account with the ledger, without checking the entries which record the operations of the company from the date of the preceding balance, and which have led to the position and results shown at the end of the period which is covered by the audit.

And I may here remark that in many instances the remuneration of the auditors has been fixed on a scale which does not admit of more work being done and adequately paid for.

Of course the amount of work which ought to be done by auditors must necessarily differ according to the nature of the business transacted by different companies, but I cannot help thinking that the experience of different members of this Institute, in relation to the audit work which they are from time to time called upon to do, might advantageously be made use of in an attempt to classify, in some degree, the work which ought to be regarded as necessary to be done in auditing different kinds of companies.

At present I think it might be said, that we have no sufficiently recognised standards of practice in relation to audits to guide members of the Institute, and more particularly to which we can refer the more inexperienced of our members for guidance.

An auditor has either to be guided by what his predecessors have done, or partly by what his own judgment and partly perhaps by what the judgment of his co-auditor may suggest as being necessary, in doing the work of different audits. No doubt there are some published works on the subject, such as Pixley's, but valuable as such works may be, they do not seem to me to throw sufficient light upon details of audit work to be as useful as they otherwise might be in educating our members to be efficient auditors, and for that among other reasons I advocate very strongly an attempt being made by the Institute to establish standards of practice for guidance in auditing.

Another reason is this, that if the members of the Institute were first to establish some recognised standards with which the work of auditing companies should comply, as far as the nature of the transactions of each company would permit, and then to act unitedly in requiring compliance with these standards, it would greatly improve the average of the remuneration now paid for auditing.

On many occasions I have had great difficulty in bringing boards of directors to take even equitable, far less liberal, views on the question of what was a fair remuneration for an auditor, and I have frequently had to draw up a schedule of the whole work which ought to be done in connection with each of the books and records of the company to ensure an effective audit, in order to enable them to form a proper idea of the time required to do the work justice.

On other occasions I have submitted such a schedule, and arranged to keep a record of the time occupied over the first audit, and the fee to be fixed afterwards upon fair terms for that and subsequent audits. On a recent occasion I felt constrained to resign an audit, because, although I showed from the time occupied what would be a fair fee, the directors fixed an inadequate amount. In resigning, I pointed out to the board that it would have been quite easy for me to have cut down the work to suit the fee fixed, and to have impared the efficacy of the audit, without their knowledge.

In this instance my co-auditor elected to retain the position at the reduced fee, and although I felt that I was not entitled to take exception to his so doing, it appeared to me that this case illustrated in a practical way the desirability of some action being taken by this Institute in the direction I am now advocating.

THE INCORPORATED INSTITUTE OF ACCOUNTANTS, VICTORIA

THE INCORPORATED INSTITUTE OF ACCOUNTANTS, VICTORIA.

ADDRESS delivered to the members of the Incorporated Institute of Accountants, Victoria, by Mr. Thomas Brentnall, President, on Friday, 13th October, 1893 :—

I have often thought that the first business meeting of the Institute, after the annual meeting of members, ought to be regarded as the special prerogative of the retiring President, at which he would be afforded an opportunity of reviewing the work of the past year in somewhat fuller detail than is admissible in the report to the members; and also of commenting upon any items of interest to the profession which may have been suggested as the result of his personal experience, but which do not particularly come within the scope of the Institute's operations.

I ought here to explain that in initiating this practice (which, I trust, will be deemed obligatory by my successors) I lay myself open to the charge of usurping a function which properly belongs to my colleague the Hon. Edward Langton, who, last year, at the pressing solicitation of the council, accepted the position of president. But the acceptance of the office by Mr. Langton was made conditional upon his being relieved from the details of the executive work, in consequence of the heavy demands upon his time, and·it, therefore, devolved mainly upon me, as the senior vice-president, to act as his viceroy during the past year.

This is "the head and front of my offending," and I pray you, therefore, bear with me for a while till "I, a plain, unvarnished tale unfold." I have first to congratulate the members upon the increased and ever-increasing recognition of the Institute's position and influence. The council, in its report, has referred to the opportunities which have been afforded it of making suggestions in regard to various bills submitted to the Legislature.

The time, I trust, is fast approaching when here, as at home, the propriety, nay, I would rather say the necessity, for the legal recognition of the status of our profession will be admitted ; and when *ipso facto* none but duly qualified practitioners will be authorised to append the definition to their names which should be the imprimatur of competency and ability and our passport to the confidence of the public. In order to do this I need hardly say it behoves us to see to it that our standard of competency is of the highest possible character; and, in view of this, I would earnestly impress upon members the wisdom of strengthening the hands of those who wish to do what is needful to attain this high ideal.

In this connection let me commend to you all, both old and young alike, the pertinent remarks made by Mr. Edwin Waterhouse—than whom no man in the profession is more entitled to be listened to with respect—speaking as president of the Chartered Institute of Accountants in England and Wales on the occasion of the annual meeting of members held in London in May last. *Inter alia*, he said :—" The growing importance of our profession, and the increased responsibility which appears daily to be laid on our members, are quite sufficient justification for the legislation which we seek. It is as important for the commercial and investing public as it is for ourselves that those who have acquired the knowledge necessary to undertake the very varied duties which fall to the lot of public accountants should be clearly designated, and it is of paramount importance to all, that when occasion arises, means should be at hand to clear the register of practising accountants of the name of any person, who, in the opinion of a judge of the High Court, has committed an act discreditable to his position."

Arising out of this proposal for legislative enactment, which would place public accountants on the same plane and in the same category as legal or medical practitioners, it may be as well to point out the salient features of the proposal, so that we may mark the lines on which they at home are seeking to deal with this important question.

I am the more anxious to do this because a certain feeling of discontent has been, I know, engendered in consequence of a declaratory resolution of the council of this Institute in regard to the progression of an Associate to the degree of Fellow having been circulated amongst the members. I want you to see the restrictions which have been deemed wise by the Institute at home in the matter of the admission of both Fellows and Associates.

At present all members of that Institute must enter by one door only—that of examination ; and a *sine qui non* is that an applicant must be either a practising public accountant, a clerk to a public accountant, or have served his articles to one.

Three examinations have to be passed—a preliminary, intermediate, and final, the last of which, at the end of a five years' probation, is a severe test of both practical and academic knowledge. The applicant may then be admitted as an Associate if he has served for five years as a clerk in a public accountant's office, or has been in private practice for the same period.

He can only be admitted as a Fellow when he has been continuously in practice for five years as a public accountant, so that he may have to practically serve an apprenticeship of ten years to pure accountancy work before attaining this position.

From a somewhat lengthened and varied experience, I hold that this is none to long a term for any man, however capable, or even brilliant, he may be.

But mark the difference which the English Institute wisely recognises between the man with such a training as the above course involves, and the man who has probably only turned his attention to accountancy at a later stage in life. In such a case they suggest in their new bill that, if examinations be remitted, an applicant must have been in public practice for ten years before he can be admitted as a Fellow, and as an Associate only if he have been ten years a clerk in a public chartered accountant's office and passes the intermediate and final examinations, and in each case they must be at least thirty years of age. This distinction is a proper one, and, in my opinion, not a whit too drastic. We must always remember that the possessions which have been acquired with most difficulty are those which we, as a rule, most highly prize, and, depend upon it, the ultimate value to the owner is proportionately enhanced.

It only remains to point out that under the bill which it is intended to introduce into the British House of Commons all existing members of certain defined societies of accountants in Great Britain will be eligible for recognition as chartered accountants, and, for one year, any accountant (not a member of these societies) who may have been in public practice for five years will be eligible for admission as a Fellow, and for two years as an Associate, on payment, however, of a fee of twenty guineas in the former case and ten guineas in the latter. This extremely liberal provision for the admission, for a short term only, of practising accountants outside of the pale of recognised institutes is, doubtless, included in the bill as a matter of expediency for the purpose of disarming opposition and removing any feeling which might exist as to its object being the creation of a close corporation for the sole

benefit of the comparatively select few who have already identified themselves with one or other of the accountants' societies. To my mind, this must necessarily be an element of weakness, but one which time will cure.

As I have before said to my young friends in this Institute, it is they who will reap the ultimate advantage of what may appear to be, at the time, somewhat harsh restrictive measures to conserve its best interests, and I was glad to see that Mr. Wingfield, speaking as a junior member of the Institute at home, also pointed out the same fact in his remarks to the meeting of accountants in London.

Such restrictions cannot of themselves be of any direct advantage to us older members, but, believe me, they will prove of inestimable benefit to those of you who are steadily working your way up the ladder.

I fully recognise that in a young country like this the conditions of life and business experience are vastly different to those which obtain in older communities, and, therefore, I do not see my way, at present, to go to the same lengths in limiting the membership of our Institute as can safely be adopted at Home. For instance, I would strongly urge that for a few years yet the Associateship should be open to any intelligent man of good repute—whether he come under the strict definition of a public accountant or not—who is able to pass our examination for that degree. But there I would stop; and limit the Fellowship to those only who practise the profession of a public accountant.

The question of age, too, is a most important one, and I am very hopeful that the good sense of our members will be exhibited by agreeing, when the time comes for the question to be dealt with, to an increase in the limit of age. It goes without saying that in a profession embracing such a wide scope of subjects as come into an accountant's practice, proficiency and competency to deal with them can only come from fairly long experience. When, apart from pure accountancy in the ordinary acceptation of the term, it is remembered that our assistance is sought on questions of insolvency, partnership company law, mercantile law, arbitrations, and the like, it must be patent to all that the experience necessary to advise on these various subjects, with all the ramifications involved therein, cannot possibly be acquired in the four years set out in our Article 6, section c, as a condition precedent to the application for the promotion of an Associate to a Fellow being entertained.

Hence the council, as I contend, wisely determined that a longer term of active practice should be disclosed before granting the step to the higher degree. It is all-important, in my opinion, that this principle be heartily endorsed by the members, and that a defined limit be clearly set forth in any revision of our articles.

These and other very important subjects are now receiving the earnest consideration of the revision of articles committee; the result of their deliberations will in due course be reported to the council, and thereafter full opportunity will be afforded the members for discussing their recommendations in detail, before they can be embodied in a permanent legal form in our articles.

I have often been asked, and, doubtless, many of my colleagues have had the same experience, to advise our younger members on questions which presented points of difficulty, and it is needless to add that it has always given me pleasure to afford any assistance in this way, and I only mention this here to remind not only the junior members of the Institute, but also the senior members, that the council will, at any time, be glad to consider any question of practice which may be submitted to it, and by this means, in course of time, a series of ex cathedra decisions may be compiled for the uniform guidance of the profession.

Probably members will expect to hear from me some explanation of the views which I had an opportunity of publicly enunciating when under cross examination in the Mercantile Bank case, but as the case is, unfortunately, still *sub judice*, I can only comment in general terms on some of the opinions which I then expressed.

There can be no question that the scope of the duties and responsibilities of an auditor are very vaguely understood by the investing public, and it must have amazed the minds of most of you to learn what tremendous issues, according to the views of some of our candid critics, hang upon the *ipse dixit* of the auditor of a company. To fulfil the functions expected from such a paragon, one must be almost omniscient. To a special knowledge of accounts would fall to be added that of a skilled valuator of all kinds of properties, stocks, and investments generally. The latter, I contend, is by no means a necessary qualification, although the possession of special knowledge outside of his own work will of course be of undoubted benefit, and often enable him (an auditor) to grasp with greater precision and clearness the correctness of the setting forth of the accounts. But, primarily, one must be largely, if not solely, dependent upon the certificates of experts as to the question of values. His position enables him to insist upon these being furnished to his satisfaction, but beyond this his responsibility ceases. Take, for example, the case of a manufacturing concern where stock consists mainly of goods in the various stages of completion. An auditor is almost absolutely at the mercy of him who compiles the stock sheets, and, as you know, it is a comparatively easy task for an unscrupulous valuer to completely alter the aspect of a company's operations; whilst the auditor, who may have absolutely no means of checking their correctness, will, most probably, have to bear the brunt of the blame for the dishonest manipulation of the figures.

Again, in the case of a bank, how utterly impossible it is for an auditor to verify even the possession, to say nothing of the values of the securities held, leaving out of view the fact that it is not even obligatory that an advance be covered by any security at all. It is almost supererogatory to remind you that to examine the securities, simply as documents, of almost any bank in this city with its branches would require a continuous inspection from 1st January to 31st December, whilst to attempt the Herculean task of assessing their values would be nothing short of crass folly. All this is properly the work of the bank's own inspectors, and if the system of supervision and report be carried out faithfully, as in all well-ordered institutions it is, then the responsibility for advances made rests where it properly should rest, with the directors and management of the bank, and not with the auditor.

It is, of course, out of the question to attempt to lay down the exact lines upon which different classes of audits should be conducted. Varying circumstances necessitate varying treatment; some kinds of companies require and admit of more inquisitive examination than others. For instance, the details of a building society's operations can and should be followed with infinitely more exactness than that of a bank. In the one case the rules rigidly prescribe the class of advances which may be granted, and lay down the procedure which has to be followed in relation thereto, and it is the duty of the auditor to see that all this has been fully complied with; but, in the other, the power of the management is almost unlimited, and practically unquestionable, except in case of fraud or criminal negligence.

Then, again, a company dealing in articles of its own manufacture requires an entirely different system of supervision from that which is sufficient in a concern acting mainly as the agent, say, for the sale of natural products.

Again, a mining company admits of the absolute verification of operations which would be impracticable in the case of a squatting company, and so on.

It will be seen, therefore, how difficult, even if it were desirable (which I gravely doubt), it is to formulate the exact method and scope of an audit. A great deal must necessarily be left to the judgment and experience of the auditor, and it by no means follows that exactly the same procedure must be followed even in dealing with the accounts of similar companies.

During the current year, through the exertions of your business meetings' committee, a series of papers on interesting subjects will be read, and I trust that members will use every effort to make the meetings a great success. One of the subjects, the notice of which appears in the circular convening to-night's meeting, is of especial interest at this juncture. I mean that on " What is Profit ?" by Mr. Morton.

Those of you who have perused the bill, now before the Legislative Council, to " further amend the Companies' Act, 1890," will see that sub-section 2 of section 34 provides that directors shall be subject to a penalty not exceeding £500, or, in default, imprisonment for not exceeding twelve months (in addition to the civil rights of creditors to recover from them any amount so paid away) if they " pay dividends other than out of the profits arising from the business." " Aye, there's the rub."

Some of the members of that august body, in addressing themselves to this particular clause, appeared to think that the stating of a profit and loss account in, say, a trading or manufacturing company, could be defined with the same exactitude as a problem in euclid, losing sight of the fact that a number of the constituents of that account can, of necessity, only be a matter of supposition—as, e.g., the valuation of book debts, apportionment of expenditure between capital and revenue, depreciation, values of stocks, &c. All these must be, to a large extent, matters of opinion, which may, honestly, differ at the time when they are being dealt with, and which may be subject to unforeseen and violent fluctuations.

Yet, the arbitrament of difficult questions of an intricate and technical character, involving the personal liberty of the accused, is to be left, if this bill becomes law, to a jury, possibly months afterwards, which may not contain a single member qualified for the task of comprehending them. As for the poor auditor who signs a balance-sheet containing a supposed fraudulent profit and loss account, the opinion of the framer of the bill is that he must go to prison for not more than two years, without the option of a fine.

Then, a fortnight hence, we are to be instructed by Mr. Jowett on the complex subject of "Bimetallism," in its relation to that extremely painfully personal aspect of the case represented by the prevalent shortness of cash in our own pockets, to say nothing of those of other people.

Having been comforted in this direction, although our pockets may have been still further depleted by the intervening dissipations of Christmas, Mr. F. G. Wood will still further revive our drooping spirits by advising us " What balance-sheets should contain, and how far auditors should be responsible therefor."

In the meantime we can only fervently hope that Parliament, in its wisdom, may not have settled that question by enacting the second question of the third schedule to Hon. Mr. Wynne's Companies Act 1890 Amendment Bill.

To set out a balance-sheet in the form prescribed in that schedule would probably be a thousandfold more damaging and baneful in its effects on the general investing public than even the non-publication of any balance-sheet at all.

To specify in separate lines " Money lent on mortgage," " Money lent on other security (specifying nature of security)," and " Money lent without security," would, to a vast majority of shareholders, convey an absolutely alarming impression of the position of a company ; and, whilst it can answer no good purpose, must only be extremely mischievous in its effects.

After Mr. Wood has settled this vexed question, Mr. Hooke has promised to deal with the subject of " Building Society Audits," to be followed later on by a paper on " Railway Figures," by Mr. Walker, when it doubtless would be a gain to the community if we could have the presence of the Railway Commissioners and a few members of Parliament, not to mention the plaintiff, defendant, and leading counsel in that *cause celèbre* which bids fair to beat the record in the matter of the time occupied in its discussion in the law courts.

Although I have had occasion to criticise adversely some of the provisions of the Hon. Mr. Wynne's bill, which, notably in the provisions relating to directors, auditors, and as to dealings in shares, bears the unmistakable evidence of " panic legislation," yet I am fain to admit that there are in it many desirable amendments and additions to our present Companies' Act which it would be a great gain to have on our statute book, and none, in my opinion, of more importance than those referring to the " Alteration of Objects or Constitution of a Company."

Clause 51 of this division, if enlarged as suggested by the laws' committee of this Institute, will prove a most useful and valuable addition.

In this regard members will have been interested in the case and opinion lately furnished to them on the subject of dealing with forfeited shares. The difficulty has presented itself to some of us in our professional work to advise what is the proper course to adopt in the case of shares forfeited to a company in consequence of breach of covenants or other causes.

Hitherto there has been a wide divergence of opinion amongst accountants as to the proper legal disposition of such shares.

Another aspect of the case came under my notice only within the past few weeks, when a vendor, who held a large number of paid-up shares as part of the purchase money for his property, expressed his willingness to surrender as many of them as was represented by the item of "goodwill" on the assets side of the balance-sheet, and there was absolutely no legal means of giving effect to his generous wishes except by putting the company into voluntary liquidation, and forming a new one.

Another example of the insufficiency of the existing Act to meet the not unusual exigency of lost capital was presented to me a short time ago, where, in consequence of large and unpreventable shrinkage in values and losses by death of live stock, a considerable portion of the original subscribed capital had disappeared; and, although the shares were all fully paid-up, and the shareholders—comparatively few in number—were willing to write off the debit at profit and loss account by *pro tanto* reducing the nominal value of their shares, by which means the company could have resumed the payment of dividends on the reduced capital, yet under the existing Act legal effect could not be given to the unanimous wish of the shareholders except by the somewhat dangerous process, in these critical times, of voluntary liquidation.

The divisions in Mr. Wynne's Bill relating to winding-up, defunct companies, foreign registers, contain little which is not distinctly valuable, and the addition proposed and carried in the House on Wednesday night last at the instance of Sir Frederick Sargood (to whom, I should like to interpolate here, this community is deeply indebted for the earnest and thorough attention which he invariably gives to all the details of the various bills submitted to the Chamber, of which he is one of the most distinguished members), providing that all mortgages or assignments of uncalled capital must be authorised by special resolution passed and confirmed in the manner prescribed by the Companies Act 1890, is unquestionably, to my mind, a fair and proper provision.

Recent instances have exemplified the necessity for this, where, until the company has been forced into liquidation, no means existed for the detection of the fact that the uncalled capital had been pledged, and the creditors, relying in most part on the fancied security of this asset, have found themselves helplessly left out in the cold.

The one proposed amendment which was strangled, as it deserved to be, before it came to birth, was to the effect—

"1. That a companies' audit board be constituted.

"2. That no one should be eligible to act as an auditor to any company registered under the Act of 1890 who had not previously passed an examination to the satisfaction of this board, save an except (and this is where the comical effect of the suggested clause appears) the local government auditors who have passed in the three subjects—bookkeeping, auditing, and local government law."

It would be intensely funny to think that whilst some intelligent young accountant of, say, twenty-one years of age, who had passed the simple examination required under the Local Government Act, but with probably no practical knowledge whatever of the duties of an auditor, would be regarded as a fit and proper person to examine the intricate accounts of some large trading company, whilst practitioners of 15, 20, 25, 30, nay, even 40 years' standing would be deemed unfit to undertake these responsibilities until they had submitted to an examination by—whom?

The idea had only to be mentioned to be laughed out of court.

The clauses in the sixth schedule, bearing upon the procedure at and before meetings of creditors and contributories, in the matter of proxies appear to be arbitrarily restrictive, and one fails to see what good purpose can be attained by the preventing of solicitation for proxies by candidates for the appointment of liquidator.

Within the last few days a deputation waited upon the Minister of Public Works to urge upon him the unfairness of the proposed reduction of Government auditors' fees from £2 2s. and 10s. 6d. per diem expenses to £1 11s. and 7s. 6d., more particularly in view of the fact that after remonstrances by the local auditors their fees had been retained at the higher figure.

A very strong case for reconsideration was made out by the representatives of the Government auditors, but the Minister was immovable, and would not consent to recommend any alteration of the Order-in-Council.

The most objectionable feature of this reduction, in its ultimate effect, is the danger that the lessened amount may come to be regarded as adequate remuneration to skilled men for a day's work of seven hours.

During the past few weeks a movement has been set on foot, and appears likely to be brought to a successful issue, for the establishment of a "Tribunal of Arbitration," on the lines of the London Chamber of Arbitration. If would-be litigants can only be brought to see the advantage of such a natural and simple method of settling their disputes it will prove as great a boon here as it has at home. The Council of your Institute has been invited to co-operate with the Chamber of Commerce (which body has initiated the scheme) in selecting specialists to act as arbitrators in this tribunal.

I will only refer to one other point and then I have done. If has long been felt, and in various quarters expressed, that the position of the Institute and its work is not sufficiently in evidence—that no report of our proceedings, except the annual meeting, ever appears in the public press, and, consequently, that a very large section of the community are unaware that such an organisation has an existence. To a certain extent this may be perfectly true ; although one would have liked the Institute to have been spared some part of the unfortunate notoriety which has attached to it, not so much on account of the actual laches of its members, as of the irresponsible, and in most cases unfounded, utterances of those who, perhaps smarting under losses to which their own greed of gain has mainly conduced, regard the auditor—especially if he be an F.I.A.V.—as a convenient scapegoat to bear his sins, and, if they had their wish gratified, to carry them even into the desert of Pentridge.

The council, at its meeting yesterday, decided to furnish the press with a summary of the proceedings at its monthly meetings, so that not only will the public be able to know that we are doing some work, but our own members will also have an opportunity of seeing that the executive is never idle, and, I venture to add, never neglectful of the best interests of the Institute.

I have by no means exhausted the many topics, germane to our profession, which afford subject for comment, but I am also anxious not to exhaust your patience, and will, therefore, close my remarks with a word of congratulation and welcome to the Associates who have recently been admitted into our ranks.

Although the standard of the entrance examinations has been gradually raised, the quality of the papers sent in during the last two years has also been relatively higher, and in several instances reflected very great credit upon the examinees.

We extend to you the right hand of fellowship, and only ask that you will remember that a grave trust has been confided to you—the good name and honour of our corporation—which, I fear not, it will be your constant aim to cherish and zealously guard as you would a precious jewel.

LIABILITY OF DIRECTORS AND AUDITORS

Liability of Directors and Auditors.

THE judgment delivered by Mr. Justice VAUGHAN WILLIAMS on 21st December *in re* the London and General Bank Limited has attracted much attention, defining, as it does, the responsibility of directors and auditors where unearned dividends are distributed, such dividends being really paid out of the capital of the company. The judgment further deals with the troublesome question—What are profits for distribution? The London and General Bank Limited was one of the "BALFOUR group" of companies which has obtained the same kind of notoriety as certain groups of companies formed in Melbourne. It was the discount and overdraft centre of the BALFOUR group, just as a Melbourne bank now in liquidation was the centre of attraction of a number of revolving minor luminaries. The largest part of the funds of the London and General Bank were, according to Mr. Justice VAUGHAN WILLIAMS, used from the very first for the purpose of making loans or affording discount conveniences to the Liberator Building Society and its satellite companies, and therefore the profits of the bank would consist mainly of interest or commission payable by this group of companies. Generally the current account of the borrowing company was debited with the interest on the loans and other charges, and the amount so debited was regarded as profit by the London and General Bank, forming, indeed, nearly the whole of its profit. But the current account was kept in credit from time to time by loans, and Mr. Justice VAUGHAN WILLIAMS held that the bank obtained the interest and charges only from loans which it granted to the borrowing company. In other words, the bank made a profit only by ad-vancing money to the debtor company, so that it could pay the interest and charges and keep his current account in credit. This is a far different conception from that which has influenced decisions in Melbourne in similar cases. But in Melbourne the loan account and the current account were not kept distinct, and, with simply an overdraft account, the real nature of the transactions did not stand out clearly. Yet an advance, even under the form of a book entry to a debtor to enable him to pay the interest he owes to the company making it, cannot have the effect of making the interest secured as profit. The underlying doctrine is calculated to have wide consequences, especially where securities for an overdraft are insufficient. It is evidently the opinion of Mr. Justice VAUGHAN WILLIAMS that if interest is not absolutely secured, it cannot be regarded as realised profit. That is, he looks to the adequateness of the security, and in reference to this highly important point he said—

Moreover, even assuming that investigation establishes that the interest received by the bank was paid out of money lent by the bank directly or indirectly to their customer liable for such interest, this may be perfectly legitimate banking business in certain events, and certainly would be so if the loans in question were made on fresh security of a substantial character, and might be so even when there was no fresh security, and the loan was a mere act of grace, if the margin of security already held was proved to the satisfaction of the directors to be amply sufficient to cover the new loan.

This dictum necessarily involves a thorough investigation, and this, in the case of the London and General Bank, Mr. Justice VAUGHAN WILLIAMS proceeded to make, commencing with a critical examination of the articles of association which referred to the declaring of a dividend. The articles of the bank provided that the dividend declared annually should be paid out of profits, and that the interim dividend should be paid out of "estimated" profits. Following a previous judgment, His Honour held that "realised" profit is the direct converse of "estimated" profit, and, therefore, that in the case under his consideration, while for the purposes of an interim dividend (limited by the articles to 6 per cent. per annum) profits for the six months might be "estimated," yet for the annual dividend they must be "realised." The means for paying dividend out of "real-"ised" profits need not be actual cash in hand, but must at least be tangible. His Honour's views of what constitutes realised profits appears to us to be perfectly conclusive, and it is only to be regretted that the judgment was not delivered ten years ago, so that the question of the so-called profits of the Melbourne property institutions could have been definitely answered in good time.

Having elucidated the subject of "realised" as opposed to "estimated" profits, Mr. Justice VAUGHAN WILLIAMS asked himself two questions, viz.:—1st, Were the profits declared by the bank in the years 1888 to 1891 realised so as to justify the dividends declared? and, 2ndly, If they were not so realised, were the profits so earned as to justify the directors in recommending to the general meeting the declaration and payment of dividends which were declared by the company, or in declaring the interim dividends which they did declare and pay? In dealing with the first question, His Honour reverted to the mode in which credit was taken for interest, &c., debited to customers. He said:—

It seems clear that it was paid in form, because, for the most part, it was paid by debiting the current account of the customer with the amount of the interest and commission, and, generally speaking, the account of the customer was in credit at the time of the debit of the interest and commission. *Primâ facie*, such a debit to an account in credit would constitute payment just as real as the payment of the interest and commission in coin of the realm would have done, but an examination of the books has led me to the conclusion that in many cases, and indeed in most cases, the account of the customer was put in credit for the express purpose that it might truly be said of the account that it was in credit at the moment that it was debited with the interest and commission; but this credit it will be seen, was really, to a great extent, if not entirely, of a temporary and fictitious character.

His Honour then proceeded at considerable length to show how the accounts were put into credit, continuing as follows:—

I have now dealt with the principal companies of the Balfour group, and the conclusion at which I have arrived is that the credits at the end of each year were generally credits created temporarily for the purpose of audit, and that such credits, in the majority of cases, were created either by the discounting of bills of companies like Hobbs and Co., which constituted a mere paper asset, or by loans, direct or indirect, from the bank itself, the bulk of which were ill-secured.

The second question next engaged his attention, and the conclusion he arrived at is expressed as follows:—

On the whole, it seems to me that the securities taken in the Balfour group were not of such a character that the interest carried to profit could be treated by prudent men as realisable assets. Nay, more, so far as the securities were concerned, there seems to have been no such likelihood that the principal and interest of the loans would be even ultimately realised, that a prudent man would treat the debt, principal and interest, as a good debt.

Having arrived at conclusions adverse to the policy of declaring and paying the dividends, His Honour had next to consider how far the directors and the auditors were responsible. As regards the directors, he admitted what has been laid down before, that for errors of judgment, even if grave, they would not be responsible. But if they surrendered their judgment to others, immediately they would become responsible. This is another distinction which in similar cases in Melbourne the courts have appeared to ignore or to lose sight of. The accounts which were laid before the shareholders year by year were, in His Honour's opinion, utterly illusory, in that they did not afford the shareholders any material on which they could really judge of the state and condition of the company. The habit of directors generally in seeking to shelter themselves behind the certificates or reports of auditors does not exculpate them. As to the auditors, it is clear from His Honour's statements regarding their certificates and recommendations that they were consenting parties to the deception practised upon the shareholders. One of the auditors is a chartered accountant, and His Honour thought that he had taken a very low view of his functions. But that is by no means a rare thing, either in London, Melbourne, or Sydney. The decision of the Court was that the directors were liable to make good to the assets of the bank the amount of the annual dividends declared for 1890 and 1891, and the interim dividends of 1890, 1891, and 1892, and that the auditors were also liable for the two annual dividends, but not for the interim dividends.

The judgment is as flawless as it is clear and luminous, and it defines the law upon the most important points. In future it will be understood that profits must be realised in cash or be covered by securities, and that if dividends are declared out of illusory profits, responsibility will attach to those answerable for the improper distribution.

AUDITORS AND THEIR CERTIFICATES

FROM THE "JOURNAL OF COMMERCE," MELBOURNE

There is perhaps no more important subject requiring the consideration of the investing public than the extent of the responsibilities of auditors, the professional gentlemen to whom, as we think, shareholders of companies or tax-payers are entitled to look for protection. To thoroughly thresh out the whole matter would require more space than is at present at our command, and therefore only a few of the difficulties can be submitted for consideration. Recent legislation, or, perhaps we should say, recent interpretations of the law, have made it plain that auditors are considered responsible for not exercising sufficient care, or for performing their duties by rule. We have before alluded to a judgment given in the English Courts by Mr. Justice Vaughan Williams, and in another place we print a fairly full report of it, because to us it seems to have established a precedent which is all-important to those concerned, whether auditors or the public. In holding the auditors of the London and General Bank Ltd. guilty of misfeasance in regard to the paying of a dividend, his Honour said, "that they ought to have known the real condition of the company; ... they should have taken care that the balance sheet, which bore their names, was in a form which would have enabled the shareholders to judge of the propriety of a dividend," and he adjudged the auditors to be liable for the dividends paid in 1890-1 and 2. Now it seems clear enough from this judgment that auditors have something more to do than merely certify to the arithmetical correctness of a balance sheet. Yet that restricted view of the matter is often held. Not so long since the Corporation of Birmingham declared that "the elective auditors had nothing whatever to do with the 'detailed items' of municipal expenditure, and that those functionaries have simply to check 'the arithmetical accuracy' of the treasurer's accounts." A shrewd clever merchant and a bank director in a neighbouring colony is related to have turned the page of a ledger half down, and, pointing to the figures only, instructed the auditor, in a certain case, that to check the addition was all he had to do. This, of course, is a very nice definition of auditors' duties for directors of companies or municipal councillors to accept, and it may be perfectly agreeable to a large number of junior accountants, who run after audits with great keenness and accept utterly inadequate fees for thorough work, but we have a sufficiently good opinion of many in the profession to believe that they would not be so restricted in their investigations. "Examined and found correct" is about the most brief certificate we have seen attached to a balance sheet, and, we take it, implies nothing more than that the figures of the balance sheet have been checked with those in the books. But that is not sufficient to protect auditors, if it be subsequently found that the accounts in themselves are wrong. Other certificates are much more complete, and generally directors of companies are anxious for reports. Here auditors are likely to fall into a great error unless they are very, very cautious; for we have seen certificates so full that it was quite impossible for them to be founded on the absolute knowledge of those giving them. Take, for instance, that appended to the accounts of one bank in Melbourne. It runs that the accounts of the bank have been examined, together with the profit and loss statement and aggregate balance sheet, and that the balance sheet is full and fair and properly drawn up so as to exhibit a true and correct view of the bank's affairs. Now, we take it, that such a certificate guarantees that the balance of profit was correct and had been earned, and yet it was manifestly impossible for the auditors to examine the thousands of accounts to ascertain if interest taken to credit had actually been paid and earned. We are much afraid that the gentlemen giving such a certificate would be in a difficulty if it should prove the profit distributed had not been earned. Of late there has been a tendency to so frame certificates that while apparently full they in their strict wording convey much less. This, no doubt, arises from the fear of trouble, joined with a desire to go as far as possible to meet the views of directors; but it is as well that it should be clearly understood that there is little protection in a careful choice of words if the public is likely to be deceived. On this point Mr. Justice Williams was very explicit. He said the auditors ought to have known the interest given as profit was not paid, and that the securities on which advances were made were insufficient. "The fact that they had knowledge of the state of the company was demonstrated by their each year appending a varied and more cautious certificate to the balance sheet."

There was a gradual alteration in these certificates, and it seemed made, not for the purpose of giving information to the shareholders of the declension in the estate and condition of the bank, but of making the auditors safe. *"Therefore the graduation of the certificate was not a matter which could be relied upon in favour of the auditors."* And we know that his Honour but voiced a well-known fact. Therefore it is clear that however a certificate may be worded, unless it clearly conveys to the persons most concerned what the accounts do represent, auditors, however guarded in their reports, may be held responsible.

In taking up this rigid view of auditors' duties, it must not be supposed that we are ignorant of the difficulties and troubles of these officials. Many directors presume to dictate what auditors shall do and not do, and are not above threatening. The auditors know to their cost that such threats are not mere idle words; that, in fact, their services may be summarily dispensed with, or their re-election prevented by the board, without, in the great majority of cases, shareholders taking the least trouble to support those who have been, or are to be, sacrificed for the honest discharge of their duties. Again, fees are cut down so low by boards, or by shareholders, that it is actually impossible for any man of experience to honestly do all that is necessary if his certificate is to be anything else but a mere voucher for the agreement of the balance sheet with the books. Further, there is often a difference of opinion as to whether an auditor is required to satisfy himself as to the correctness of the profit and loss account. We have even seen the balance sheet certified to, but not the profit and loss account; and we do know as a fact that in many, very many, cases directors resent any inquiry into the "detailed items." But granted all these difficulties, it is for accountants to remember that they are servants of shareholders, not of boards of directors. They are elected to supervise the actions of the latter in the interest of the former. Granted that they are most ungraciously and ungratefully treated, they have yet to think not only of their own honour and professional reputation, but of the civil or other liability which may accrue from an ineffective investigation. A well-known Scotch chartered accountant, in a paper read before the Glasgow Institute of Accountants, said: "Do not let the fear of the loss of the fee payable to the auditor, do not let the arguments of interested officials, do not let the arguments of directors whose pockets as shareholders may suffer, induce you for one moment to swerve from your duty as a chartered accountant and auditor. Use your own judgment, and do not allow one penny to be taken credit for that you do not honestly and conscientiously believe will, and that without delay, be received." This, of course, is a standard which it may be difficult to attain, especially in this young community; but surely it is possible for the various associations of accountants to take some steps to protect auditors in the discharge of their duties, and at the same time to make it clear to their members that they must do what common sense and the honour of their profession demands.

The Sydney Institute of Public Accountants.

AN ADDRESS

DELIVERED BY THE PRESIDENT

(MR. JOHN B. C. MILES),

AT

UNITED CHAMBERS, HUNTER STREET, SYDNEY,

ON

THURSDAY EVENING, 28TH NOV., 1895.

"CONCERNING AUDITING."

WHEN the Council, in despite of all my entreaties, "buckled honor on my back," and "enforced me to a world "of care" by conferring upon me the distinction of the Presidential office of this Institute, I felt that it was incumbent upon me to manifest my appreciation of that mark of favor, and my apprehension of the duties it involved, in some manner more conspicuously than by merely presiding at the monthly meetings of the Council, and at the annual meeting of the members.

It was not long before a suitable opportunity for that manifestation presented itself.

The subject of the delivery of lectures before the Institute engaged the attention of the Council, and it was cogently urged that the first lecture ought to be delivered by me.

In recognition of the propriety of that suggestion I am here to-night to address to you some observations which, I trust, you will deem interesting.

I renounce all intention of claiming for this address the designation of lecture, conscious that the desultoreous remarks which will fall from me are unworthy of that dignified appellation.

One of the objects for which the Institute was established is " To support and protect the character and status " of Public Accountants."

I am impressed by a strong conviction that of the various means by which that highly desirable object may be promoted, a just conception, and a steadfastly honest discharge, of the responsible duties of an Auditor are the most influential ; and, therefore, I have chosen Auditing as the theme of my discourse this evening.

As you are not neophytes I am spared the necessity of declaring and solemnly exhorting you to rigidly observe all the elementary articles of our professional faith which are contained in the authentic gospels according to those eminent evangelists of our sect, Saint Dicksee and Saint Pixley.

Even if I could concentrate all the ideas which are enrolled in the precise definition of the correct procedure to be followed in conducting audits, and parade them in skilfully marshalled array, time would not allow me to display the imposing spectacle.

But my belief is that such a demonstration is not possible. Speaking on this subject at the Fourth Provincial meeting of the Institute of Chartered Accountants in England and Wales, held at Liverpool, in October, 1894, the President said : "Appeals have been made to the " Council of the Institute to promulgate rules for " the guidance of its members, and long and " anxious consideration has been given to this " subject. It has, however, been found undesir- " able, and, in my judgment, having regard to the " diverse circumstances of certain audits, well nigh " impossible, to lay down any fixed rules applicable " to the circumstances of each audit. For the " present, at all events, the conduct of audits and " the duties which they entail, must rest largely on "the individual decision and responsibility of the "auditors who carry them out. Some may be "stronger of will and purpose than others, and "have more resolution in enforcing their opinions." And the same gentleman said, at the Annual Meeting of the Institute, in May last, in London : "Those duties are "so multifarious and so varied that it is not pos- "sible to outline them in any precise way ; and in "addition they were all aware, from experience, that "there were many and varied features in different "audits. The audit of a railway company, for "instance, was a very different matter to the audit "of an ordinary commercial business." To which I now append the supplementary observation that the accounts of a mining company, or of an institution having large advances on Australian pastoral properties, present very dissimilar phases for the investigation of an auditor.

I think it a fair assumption that, without exact defini- tion of the requirements of each case, auditing may be safely left, with a large measure of confidence, to the dis- cretion of an auditor whose experience, acquired in the first place by clerkship in the office of a public accountant, has been enlarged by the study necessary to successfully pass examinations prescribed for admission to the Institute, and matured by vigilant observation of the daily occurrences of commercial life.

I shall now hasten to narrate some incidents which lucidly illustrate several of the most important functions of an auditor, which clearly show the serious responsibili- ties they involve, and authoritatively declare the penalties which attach to even a negligent performance of them.

In August, 1887, the case of the Leeds Estate, Building, and Investment Company *v* Shepherd, was heard before Mr. Justice Stirling. This was an action by a Company, which had gone into liquidation, against certain of the former Directors, the representatives of a deceased Director, the Manager and Secretary, and the Auditor of the Company, seeking to render them liable for, among other things, breach of duty in making payment of dividends out of capital, and in receiving remuneration to which they were not entitled.

This case is peculiarly interesting to us from the circumstance that it was the first occasion on which an Auditor was made defendant to such a suit.

The following provisions were comprised in the Articles of Association of the Company:—" That when, and so " long as, the Company shall pay a dividend of " 5 per cent. per annum, each Director present " should receive 10s. for each weekly meeting " of the Board, and when, and so long as a " greater dividend should be paid a further sum " of 2s. 6d. for every additional 1 per cent. of " dividend."

" Once at least in every year the Directors shall lay " before the Company in General Meeting a state- " ment of the income and expenditure for the " past year, or for the past half-year, made up to " a date not more than one month before such " meeting."

" The statement so made shall show, arranged " under the most convenient heads, the amount of " gross income, distinguishing the several sources " from which it has been derived, and the amount " of gross expenditure, distinguishing the expenses " of the establishment, salaries, and other like " matters. Every item of expenditure only charge- " able against the year's income shall be brought " into account, so that a just balance of profit and " loss may be laid before the meeting."

" A balance-sheet shall be made out in every year " and laid before the Company in General Meeting, " and such balance-sheet shall contain a summary " of the property and liabilities of the Company, " arranged under the heads appearing in the form " annexed to table B of the Companies' Act, 1862, " or as near thereto as circumstances permit."

The Company was formed in 1869, and carried on business till October 1882. The defendant Crabtree was originally a Director of the Company, but in February 1870, shortly after its career began, he was appointed Secretary and Manager at a salary of £200 per annum, and in 1872 a resolution was passed that he should be paid a bonus of £25 in every year in which sufficient profits should be realised to enable the company to pay a dividend exceeding 5 per cent.

Under the generous stimulation of the articles and the resolution just mentioned, dividends of from 5 to 10 per cent. per annum were paid every year until 1882; the Directors drew their correspondingly augmented fees, and Crabtree received the benefactions prescribed by the liberality of the special resolution.

The report of this case is very imperfect, for it does not recite the diverse methods of falsification which had been utilized, but it states that the investigation of the Official Receiver proved that with the exception of one year, when the Company made a small profit of less than 5 per cent., no profit had ever been earned by it, and that its business had been really carried on at a loss.

The statements of accounts laid before the shareholders in General Meeting were prepared by Crabtree, but they were not in conformity with the provisions of the Articles.

Those accounts had been audited for the last ten years of the Company's existence by a Mr. Locking, whose certificate for the last six of those years ran thus :—

> " I certify that I have examined the above accounts,
> " and find *them to be a true copy of those shewn in the*
> " *books of the Company.*"

to which words your thoughts will naturally revert when listening to an extract from Mr. Justice Stirling's decree in this case, and to an extract from Mr. Justice Lindley's judgment in Mr. Theobald's appeal in another case, which I shall quote in two or three minutes hence.

Mr. Locking, the auditor, to whose case I shall confine myself, pleaded that he had not seen the Articles of Association of the Company, but admitted his knowledge of their existence. He also pleaded the Statute of Limitations.

In pronouncing his decree Mr. Justice Stirling said :—

> " It was in my opinion the duty of the Auditor not
> " to confine himself merely to the task of verifying
> " the *arithmetical* accuracy of the balance-sheet, but
> " to enquire into its *substantial* accuracy, and to
> " ascertain that it contained the particulars specified
> " in the Articles of Association (and consequently
> " a proper income and expenditure account), and
> " was properly drawn up so as to contain a true and
> " correct representation of the state of the Com-
> " pany's affairs."

" Mr. Locking stated in his evidence that he did
" not, during the period of his auditorship, see the
" Articles of Association of the Company. This
" statement, if true, appears to me to afford no
" excuse for him, for he admitted that he knew of
" their existence."

The finding was that the payment of the dividends,
Directors' fees, and bonuses to the Secretary and Manager
were the *natural and immediate consequence of the Auditor's
breach of duty*, and that he was jointly and severally liable,
with the other defendants, in damages to the amount of
the moneys so improperly paid, except so much thereof
as was barred by the Statute of Limitations.

Probably the most recent judicial decision on the
subject of the liability of Auditors is that of the Court of
Appeal in *re* the London and General Bank, one of the
notorious Jabez Spencer Balfour group of Companies. The
gravamen of this case was that debts which *must* have been
known to be irretrievably bad were treated in the balance-
sheet as thoroughly good. In the Liberator Building
Society case the gravamen was that the book values of
properties were arbitrarily enhanced by entries specially
designed for the production of factitious profit and loss
accounts.

An order had been made by Mr. Justice Vaughan
Williams declaring that Mr. Theobald an auditor, and the
directors of the bank were jointly and severally liable to
pay to the Official Receiver of the bankrupt Company two
sums, £5,946 12s. and £8,486 11s., being respectively the
amounts of dividends declared and paid by the bank for
the years 1890 and 1891, *plus* interest on the same. That
order was made against Mr. Theobald on the grounds that
those dividends had been paid out of capital, and that
they had been so paid pursuant to resolutions of the
shareholders based upon recommendations of the Directors,
and upon balance-sheets prepared and certified by Mr.
Theobald, which did not truly represent the financial
position of the bank.

On appeal, by Mr. Theobald, the order was varied by
discharging him from liability for the dividend for 1890,
for the reason that will be mentioned further on, but the
order in respect of the dividend for 1891 was sustained.

Mr. Theobald was an auditor of the Bank from its registration in 1882 down to and including the audit for 1891, and, therefore, ought to have had full information of its business and position.

When the audit of the accounts for 1891 had been finished, the auditors, Messrs. Theobald and Timms, addressed a special report thereon to the Directors, the unfavorable character of which may be deduced from one of its sentences, which said : " We cannot conclude without " expressing our opinion, unhesitatingly, that no " dividend should be paid this year," and to their usual certificate, annexed to the balance-sheet, which was a mere statement that the balance-sheet was a correct summary of the accounts as recorded in the books, and that the value of the assets as shewn in the balance-sheet was dependent on realization, they proposed to add : " On " this subject we have reported specifically to the " Board," but in an evil moment they, at the persuasion of Mr. Balfour, struck out the aforesaid clause from their report to the Directors, and eliminated their proposed addition to their certificate on the balance-sheet.

Mr. Theobald and his co-auditor were present at the meeting of shareholders at which the balance-sheet and profit and loss account for 1891 were adopted, and remained silent when the dividend, recommended in defiance of their judgment, was declared. Merely incidental reference was made by the chairman, Jabez Spencer Balfour, to the auditors' special report to the Directors, without divulging its purport, and in the auditors' certificate on the face of the accounts printed for circulation among the shareholders there was no hint of their belief that the Bank was in a perilous position.

Mr. Justice Lindley in delivering his judgment said :—
" It is no part of an auditor's duty to give advice either
" to directors or shareholders as to what they ought
" to do. An auditor has nothing to do with the
" prudence or imprudence of making loans with or
" without security. His business is to ascertain
" and state the true financial position of the Com-
" pany at the time of the audit, and his duty is
" confined to that. But then comes the question,
" how is he to ascertain such position ? The answer
" is, by examining the books of the Company.

" But he does not discharge his duty by doing this
" without enquiry, and without taking any trouble
" to see that the books of the Company themselves
" show the Company's true position. He must take
" *reasonable* care to ascertain that they do. His first
" duty is to examine the books, not merely for the
" purpose of ascertaining what they do show, but
" also for the purpose of satisfying himself that
" they show the true financial position of the Com-
" pany. An auditor, however, is not bound to do
" more than exercise reasonable care and skill in
" making enquiries and investigations. He is not
" an insurer. He does not *guarantee* that the books
" *do* show the true position of the Company's
" affairs. His obligation is not so onerous as this.
" Such I take to be the duty of the auditor; he
" must be honest, that is, he must not certify what
" he does not believe to be true, and he must take
" reasonable care and skill before he believes that
" what he certifies is true."

" What is reasonable care in any particular case
" must depend upon the circumstances of that case.
" Mr. Theobald's evidence satisfies me that he took
" the same view as myself of his duty in investi-
" gating the Company's books, and preparing his
" balance-sheet. He did not content himself
" with making his balance-sheet from the books
" without troubling himself about the truth of
" what they showed. He checked the cash,
" examined vouchers for payments, saw that the bills
" and securities entered in the books were correct,
" took reasonable care to ascertain their value,
" and in one case obtained a solicitor's opinion on
" the validity of an equitable charge. I see no
" trace whatever of any failure by him in the per-
" formance of this part of his duty. It is satisfactory
" to find that the *legal* standard of duty is not too
" high for business purposes, and is recognised as
" correct by business men. The balance-sheet and
" certificate of February, 1892, that is for the year
" 1891, were accompanied by a report *to the Direc-*
" *tors* of the bank. Taking the balance-sheet, the
" certificate, and report together, Mr. Theobald stated
" *to the Directors* the true financial position of the

" bank, and if this report had been laid before *the*
" *shareholders,* Mr. Theobald would have com-
" pletely discharged his duty to them. Unfortu-
" nately, however, this report was not laid before the
" shareholders, and it becomes necessary to consider
" the legal consequences to Mr. Theobald of this
" circumstance. A person whose duty it is to con-
" vey information to others does not discharge that
" duty by simply giving them so much information
" as is calculated to induce them, or some of them,
" to ask for more. Information, and means of in-
" formation, are by no means equivalent terms.
" Still there may be circumstances under which
" information given in the shape of a printed
" document circulated amongst a large body of
" shareholders would, by its consequent publicity,
" be very injurious to their interests, *and in such*
" *a case I am not prepared to say that an auditor would*
" *fail to discharge his duty, if, instead of publishing his*
" *report in such a way as to ensure publicity, he made a*
" *confidential report to the shareholders, and invited*
" *their attention to it, and told them where they could*
" *see it.* The auditor is to make a report to the
" *shareholders,* but the mode of doing so, and the
" form of the report are not prescribed. If, there-
" fore, Mr. Theobald had laid before the *shareholders*
" the balance-sheet and the profit and loss account
" accompanied by a certificate in the form in which
" he had prepared it, he would, perhaps, have done
" enough under the peculiar circumstances of the
" case. I feel, however, the great danger of acting
" on such a principle, and in order not to be
" misunderstood I will add that an auditor who
" give shareholders *means* of information instead of
" information in respect of a company's financial
" position does so at his peril, and runs the very
" serious risk of being held, judicially, to have
" failed to discharge his duty. In this case I have
" no hesitation in saying that Mr. Theobald did
" fail to discharge his duty to the shareholders in
" certifying and laying before them the balance-
" sheet of February 1892, without any reference to
" the report which he laid before the Directors, and

" with no other warning than is conveyed by the
" words : 'The value of the assets as shewn on
" ' the balance-sheet is dependent upon realization.'"
" It is a *mere truism* to say that the value of loans
" and securities depends upon their realization.
" We are told that a statement to that effect is so
" unusual that the mere presence of those words is
" enough to *excite suspicion.* But, as already stated,
" the duty of an auditor is to convey *information,*
" *not to arouse enquiry,* and although an auditor
" might infer from an unusual statement that some-
" thing was seriously wrong, it by no means follows
" that ordinary people would have their suspizions
" aroused by a similar statement if, as in this case,
" its language expresses no more than any ordinary
" person would infer without it."

Then coming to the subject of the last dividend declared,
that for the latter half of 1891, His Lordship said :—" A
" dividend of 7 per cent. was, nevertheless, recom-
" mended by the Directors, and was resolved upon
" by the shareholders at a meeting furnished with
" the balance sheet and profit and loss account
" certified by the auditors, and at which meeting
" the auditors were present, but silent."

" The balance sheet and account certified by the
" auditors as showing a profit available for dividend
" were in my judgment *not the remote, but the real*
" *operating,* cause of the motion for the payment of
" the dividend which the Directors improperly
" recommended. The auditors' account and certifi-
" cate gave weight to such a recommendation, and
" rendered it acceptable to the meeting. As to this
" part of the case *res ipsa loquitur.*"

The reason for the discharge of Mr. Theobald from
liability for the 1890 dividend, as before mentioned, is thus
declared by Mr. Justice Lindley : " This part of the case
" is very near the line, but having carefully con-
" sidered it, I do not think that the evidence is
" sufficiently strong to establish a case of misfeasance
" on the part of Mr. Theobald in February, 1891.
" I am not satisfied that he was then guilty of more
" than an *excusable error of judgment* ; although now
" that all the facts are known the error is seen to
" have been very serious in its consequences. As

"to the sum of £5,946 12s., therefore, the appeal
"must be allowed. As regards costs, Mr. Theobald's
"appeal has resulted in reducing the sum for which
"he has been held liable ; but in other respects,
"and as regards his main contention, it has failed.
"Under these circumstances he ought not to receive
"or pay any costs of the appeal, and the only order
"as to costs will be that the Official Receiver be
"paid his costs out of the assets of the Company."
I cull the following from an article in *The Investors'*
Review of May last, entitled, "J. Spencer Balfour and
"Liberator Finance " :—"The most concise description of
"his financial methods is that contained in the evi-
"dence of his nephew. That showed how properties,
"originally costing moderate sums, had been written
"up and up by adding, not only the interest paid
"on the original purchase price to the capital value
"every year, but by imaginary large 'unearned
"'increments' to suit the exigencies of a balance-
"sheet which was bound to display a handsome
"profit for distribution. Hundreds of thousands
"in this way grow into millions without making
"the Companies one penny the richer in cash. To
"howl curses against Jabez and pay no attention to
"the warning conveyed by his methods of finance
"is silly. Punish him by all means if he has sinned
"to deserve it, but see also that the other offenders,
"of whom there are legions, are warned by the
"fate which overtakes him to amend their
"behaviour. We have never thought J. Spencer
"Balfour the greatest criminal by any means
"among the Company, and balance-sheet fabrica-
"tors of our day, reckoning only those who have
"failed and passed into retirement in recent years.
"And if he is the greatest of all the fabricators of
"unreal profits, he is followed by a mighty host
"who, year in and out, do as he did with less
"boldness." Mark this next sentence—"Many
"private owners of businesses follow the same
"road ; but of late years, when the end drew near,
"they have turned their concerns into joint stock
"companies on the basis of the false profits they
"took to themselves, leaving the foolish public

"to reap the harvest of ruin sure to come. The
"sins of the Company Director and promoter and
"false balance-sheet fabricator will not, then, be
"washed away by visiting them all on the head of
"the miserable being now to be placed in the dock,
"nor shall we demonstrate our commercial probity
"as a Company fabricating and subscribing people
"by merely cursing his name, or shouting for
"vengeance on his carcase. He went too fast and
"was found out too soon; but there are thousands
"in the land as bad as he is. We rub shoulders with
"them in the city every day in the week—honor-
"able men all, and sleek and self-satisfied. They
"have not been found out, or they have been able
"to slip away in time, and leave others to squat
"over and cover up the heaps of abominations they
"left behind them."

"That other characteristic of Liberator finance—
"the private deals behind the door—whereby a
"profit was obtained for individuals between the
"passage of a property from one Company's owner-
"ship to another, is also as common as daisies in
"the grass; but we cannot go into illustrative
"particulars from the Liberator group's history on
"this point now, because it is only just that the
"accused man should have a fair trial."

One of the "Fugitive Notes" of last Saturday's *Herald*
says :—"After a pleasant and extended trip abroad. during
"which he had unrivalled opportunities for studying
"the criminal codes of various nations, Mr. Jabez
"Spencer Balfour has at length been kind enough
"to vacate the stage, leaving it clear for the next
"star. It may be that it will be some time before a
"successor considered worthy to bulk with equal pro-
"minence in the public eye will be found, although
"Mr. Balfour's rôle is one that is becoming more
"common as time goes on. He was an essentially
"modern scoundrel—a type of swindler only evolved
"by these latter days. In the bad, silly, unpro-
"gressive days of old, Mr. Balfour might probably
"have gone abroad as a soldier of fortune, or have
"taken to the road, and so on to Tyburn; but
"those were the days when people were willing to

"go into the profession of stealing and take
"enormous risks for absurdly small gains. We
"have changed all that, and no artist in any
"particular walk of crime can hope to succeed
"unless he assimilates the leading characteristics of
"the virtuously eminent of the hour. He must be
"prominent in religious movements, he must be
"conspicuous in good society, he must be charitable,
"and intensely devoted to the cause of his fellow-
"man, and he ought to be in Parliament, and have
"a town house. Then, and only then, the multitude
"will press round him, making offerings of silver
"and gold, yea, bank notes and rich securities, and
"he may proceed to open his oyster at his leisure
"and as he wills. Jabez Balfour was all this, and
"acted accordingly, and it was only one of those
"unforeseen hitches that brought the Liberator
"tumbling about his ears. Now he takes a com-
"plete rest in prison; but, after all, this is only one
"of the liabilities of success. And for every
"Liberator fraud who is fast by the heels, there are
"a hundred, perhaps, who still offer the general
"public in various parts of the world enormous
"facilities to invest its hard-earned savings."

I have no doubt that some zealous disciples of the arche-
types portrayed in these sketches live and move and have
their being in the City of Sydney.

In the criminal records of our own and of a neighbouring colony may be read the mournful histories of several
financial institutions, wrecked three or four years ago by
the incompetency and rascality of their management. The
discovery of the unlawful practices resorted to by the men
directing the misfortunes of those Companies provoked
the indignation of their dupes, and led to the successful
prosecution of several of the offenders. It may be said of
some of those who were then convicted that they were
men possessed of but little education, whose commercial
experience was limited to the vicissitudes of the comparatively insignificant businesses in which they had been
engaged for years on their own behalf, and who were
greatly controlled and misled by the dishonest subtlety of
some knavish officials of the institutions in whose ruin
they assisted. Although those extenuating pleas were

urged and considered, condign retribution was meted out to most of the guilty ones. Insulted commercial morality appears to have been amply appeased, and outraged justice completely vindicated by the imprisonment of a few men of mean natural, and almost entirely uncultivated parts, and utter inexperience of mercantile affairs of magnitude.

It must not, however, be supposed that those cases which have been investigated under the inquisitorial light of Australian criminal tribunals are the only examples of institutions nefariously managed in the colonies, whose lives, short as they were, were extended by the artificial aliment of money deposited with them by deluded investors.

At the time of the convictions to which I have alluded, people spoke wherever they met "in holy anger and pious grief," of the wrongs done by a few ignorant men, and of the painful necessity for avenging them; but wrongs of the same type, and on a more stupendous scale, have eluded "the passing tribute of" denunciation.

There have been fraudulent balance-sheets fabricated and circulated year after year by men who cannot plead innate ignorance, neglected education, or inexperience of of active personal participation in extensive and varied mercantile transactions, who must now be enduring much mental disquietude, and very anxious "searchings of heart" from the recent intelligence of the conviction of their Grand Master in fraud, Jabez Spencer Balfour.

There is no need to leave Australia on a voyage of discovery of profit and loss accounts munificently endowed by audacious estimates of alleged increased, but unrealised, values of assets, the distribution among unsuspicious shareholders of the intangible, and never afterwards realised profits so delusively exhibited, being facilitated by the possession of deposits obtained from confiding investors who were beguiled by the crafty simulation of prosperity displayed in the fallacious balance sheets to constitute really bankrupt companies the depositaries of the meagre fortunes of scantily provided widows and children, and the hard earned savings of diligent and thrifty artisans. Highly cultivated and well-developed specimens of indigenous growth of this order of profit and loss accounts are not rare in this metropolis.

Of course the published accounts of those companies which adopt that, and other equally flagitious means of betraying and plundering a trustful public, conceal those practices by deliberately misdescribing the sources from which the turgid streams of their treacherous profits take their rise.

The impassive demeanour and almost unbroken silence in which creditors are watching the tedious liquidations of some Australian companies once in high repute, depressed by dreadful apprehension that some sections of themselves will be left without an atom of a dividend when the lamentably disastrous realisations of assets now proceeding shall be completed, may, at some day not very remote, when the dire results of the liquidations shall be definitely ascertained and proclaimed, be succeeded by an ebullition of justifiable resentment, and a stern and loud demand for merited vengeance which, though tardy, shall not be denied.

I ask you to excuse a short digression, *en passant*, to the grave responsibilities of Liquidators. Notwithstanding the reticence of Liquidators, I cannot believe that the failures of all the Australian financial companies, on whose affairs neither a civil nor criminal judicial determination has been expressed, are attributable solely to the destruction of schemes perhaps rashly conceived, but honestly conducted, by fortuitous encounters with adverse circumstances. Before long, some exasperated creditor may enquire whether a company in which he had invested some of his means, now obviously irrecoverable, had paid dividends out of capital (or perchance out of borrowed money), demand and insist upon an unequivocal answer.

If it be found that dividends were so paid, and that a Liquidator, who was necessarily well aware of that incriminating fact, has withheld the information from the defrauded creditors, I think the position of that Liquidator is calculated to fill his mind with an agitating solicitude which will not be easily allayed.

In the *Australian Insurance and Banking Record* of August last, I find this paragraph :—" The proceedings "against the Directors and officials of the New "Oriental Bank Corporation in liquidation, for "dividends paid by the bank in, and prior to, July, "1891, have resulted, according to a cablegram "dated 13th inst., in a compromise by which the

" proceedings have been abandoned on condition of
" the Directors and officials concerned paying the
" sum of £18,216."

For some days I sought in vain for particulars relating
to this case. At a late hour to-day I was shewn a copy
of the report of the special committee of creditors upon
which the proceedings were based, and I am happy to say
that the auditor is completely exonerated from blame.

The allegations in this case are so astounding that I
shall use diligent endeavours to collect a full report of it
for the information of our members.

An unprofitable career, followed by an unpropitious
liquidation does not necessarily establish a charge of
unscrupulous conduct, or even of negligent management.
Investments prudently made may entail heavy losses by
a calamitous depreciation of their value, and a partial
subversion of their marketableness in a time of panic,
and in the dull, and probably long, season of depression
succeeding it.

After the recitals of flagrant enormities perpetrated by
coteries of pharasaical rascals, one's confidence in the
existence of some honesty in human nature is restored
when meditating upon a disaster which was not projected
by flagitious agencies.

My own experience has recently gathered the pleasing
facts which I shall now relate.

The Directors of a certain Building Society in the
County of Cumberland, without any pressure from their
creditors, authorised a Public Accountant to make a special
investigation and report of the position of their society.
The integrity of the Directors, who assiduously and
faithfully discharged their duties, was revealed in
every page of the books, and nothing but two
small items provoked the hostile criticism of the special
auditor. The value of two small unsold properties
had been increased by amounts transferred to profit
and loss account. A searching inquiry into those
matters proved that those increases were not arbitrary
caprices designed for the deception of the depositors and
members, but could be conscientiously ascribed to simple
error of judgment. In acknowledgment of the correctness
of the Auditor's remonstrance against such a breach of
principle, the items objected to were written back without
delay, and a complete disclosure of those and all other
matters on which the Auditor expressed his opinions and

advice was furnished to the members by the circulation under the Directors' orders, of printed copies of the Auditor's report, and by verbal statements made by the Chairman of the Society at a special general meeting of the members convened by the Board for that purpose.

When reviewing the devastation which overwhelmed so many financial companies here within the last few years one cannot fail to be impressed by the low average standard of their Auditors' qualifications. Yet in all those instances the Auditors were elected by the shareholders, whose self-interest would, one would naturally suppose, dictate the selection of none but men thoroughly well qualified by ability and integrity for the satisfactory discharge of their important functions, and whose vigilence would be constantly fanned by a salutary desire to preserve an unsullied professional reputation.

Many of those so-called auditors then held, or had formerly held, good appointments in commercial establishments, which fact disentitles them to claim exemption for the inefficient performance of their duties on the plea of ignorance. The fact is that the audit fees, though not large, were a grateful accretion to their incomes, which they, being totally oblivious of the moral responsbility of their position, were pleased to secure at the low cost of as little trouble as possible. They had no public professional credit to maintain by diligent examination of the accounts submitted to their inspection, and by strenuous protests against, and intrepid exposure of, the ruthless violation of honest principles which was perpetrated in those accounts ; and they were, in all probability, friends of the Directors, whose acquiescent minions they voluntarily became.

Year after year there are still re-elected as auditors of banking and other large financial institutions men utterly incapable of writing up an ordinary cash book, and of constructing a proper balance-sheet even if supplied with a list of ledger balances. The audits done by such men are valueless. They accept, without demur, any explanation which the permanent officials deign to supply in response to some (probably stultifying) enquiry ; sign whatever documents have been prepared to receive embellishment by their autographs, pocket the fees, which, although inadequate for efficient services, profusely recompense them for their worthless labours, and cheerfully make before a

Justice of the Peace the declaration which conveys to the shareholders the exhilarating assurance that their company is in a highly prosperous condition.

Shareholders possess the remedy for this state of things, but they do not apply it. The desirability of an audit is spontaneously avowed, but the fees awarded indicate, unmistakably, that a really serviceable audit is not expected. Hence few professional men seek for those appointments, and the onerous and responsible positions of auditors in some institutions dealing with vast sums of money, are held by shareholders who have retired from the petty businesses in which they accumulated their modest fortunes, and whose ludicrous assumptions of the influence of a station, and an opulence far exceeding the reality of their acquisitions, amuse those who are cognizant of their social career, and of the limited extent of their means. Perhaps in course of time shareholders will perceive the advantage of choosing as their auditors none but men having a perfect knowledge of book-keeping in all its ramifications, and an intimate acquaintance with a variety of business affairs of distinctive characteristics, and of scope and dimensions which are not contemptible, and bestow commensurate remuneration for their services.

Unfortunately, poor pay may tempt men of weak principle to leave undone many things which they ought to do. On this subject the *Australasian Insurance and Banking Record* of January, 1892, contains a very proper denial that the inadequacy of fees " is in the remotest sense a " justification, or even an excuse, for bad auditing," and adds " we admit freely that in many instances " the auditor is greatly underpaid for the work he " is required to do. But we hold that once the job " is accepted the auditor is bound to discharge the " duties he has undertaken to the fullest extent of " his abilities, whatever the fee may be. If an " auditor thinks his remuneration too little, and " Directors will not better it, then, obviously, the " proper course is that he should decline the work " rather than yield to any temptation to scamp it. " The conscienceless board and the labour-evading " auditor are about on a par."

Among the members of our Institute can be found examples of the self-respecting retirement of auditors under circumstances precisely similar to those stated in the hypothetical case in the extract just read from the *Record*.

A brief allusion to a rather phantasmal asset known as " goodwill," and to the necessity for a liberal provision in profit and loss accounts for depreciation of plant and other wasting assets, is indispensable.

In my opinion the practice of allowing " goodwill " to remain for many consecutive years as an undiminished asset is a hideous defacement of balance-sheets, and deserves severe reprobation. When business has been unprofitable there is usually an indisposition among officials to make sufficient allowance for wear and tear of machinery, and other adjuncts of plant. No determinate rule can be devised which would apply equitable treatment to all cases under these heads. Auditors in dealing with these items must be governed by the special conditions peculiar to each case, *always remembering* that regular and ample contributions from profit and loss account are obligatory for the gradual total extinction of " goodwill," and for the reduction of the amount standing against "plant " to its impaired value, which is the natural result of deterioration by usage.

Our earnest efforts ought also to be devoted to ensure the proper segregation of items on both sides of balance-sheets and profit and loss accounts, so that shareholders and investors may be supplied with that reasonable and useful information which is their due. That end may not be achieved without frequent reiteration of protests against the scandalous incongruities and reticence in the present style of many published accounts; but an improved mode of construction will assuredly be esteemed by shareholders generally, notwithstanding their apparent indifference to the matter as may be implied from the uncomplaining manner in which they accept the meagre statements which are provided by the pernicious system of the day.

A passing reference may be made here appositely to press criticisms, which have some kinship with auditorial functions. It is to be deplored that the daily commercial press of this city devotes but little attention to the examination and criticism of the published balance-sheets of local Companies, and of prospectuses of new enterprises designed to decoy the unwary, and to satiate the rapacity of merciless promoters. I feel that it is my duty to acknowledge that the only press criticisms of value which I have read here have been published in the columns of the *Bulletin*, where frequently well conceived, and perspicuously and forcibly expressed comments may be found bearing an unmistakable impress of their emanation from an observer of keenly penetrative acumen.

When I first approached the preparation of this address I did not fully comprehend the vast dimensions of my subject. I knew that in the narrow space at my command to-night I would have to leave unnoticed many important elements concerning auditing. I selected, therefore, for consideration a few salient points, the supreme importance of which has been emphasised by the recent events which have illustrated my remarks; but even on those time has allowed me to descant merely in a diffusive and inconclusive manner.

I trust that it is not undiluted egotism that provokes the surmise that in some future hour of reverie our minds will recur to the proceedings of this evening, and when, perchance, " by lonely contemplation led " to muse upon what has been said, other features not reviewed to-night will present themselves to our imagination, on which our thoughts can expatiate at leisure to the improvement of our faculties, and to the advantage of our patrons, the public.

Grave and onerous as are the responsibilities of an auditor, they will not be felt oppressive by men of healthy and robust principles, and the faithful discharge of their obligations will always be honoured by compensating rewards.

To elicit the respect and confidence of the community we must be assiduous and punctual in the performance of the routine of our work; we must be unceasingly vigilant to repel assaults upon our honest judgment by the sophistical cajoleries of plausible and designing men, and we must perpetually maintain and exercise an inflexible resolution to expose every abuse at which we may be tempted to connive. Unrelaxed adherence to those vital principles will be quickly recognised by the multitude of investors, who will then unreluctantly acknowledge that we have indeed

" Something attempted, something done "

for the security of the public, and for the support, protection, and elevation of the character and status of Public Accountants.

THE COMPANIES ACT, 1890, FURTHER AMENDMENT BILL. AS AFFECTING AUDITORS, WITH OBSERVATION ON THEIR FUNCTIONS AND FUTURE SCOPE

AS AFFECTING AUDITORS,
WITH OBSERVATION ON THEIR FUNCTIONS AND FUTURE SCOPE

(To the Editor of the Bankers' Magazine of Australasia.)

Dear Sir,—Pending the passage of this Bill through the Legislative Council, it may not be inappropriate to venture a few remarks on the general scope of the measure in its relation to auditors, prior to it, or any modification thereof, passing into law. The Bill, as it left the Assembly, presumably limits the selection of auditors and accountants for the auditing of public companies to be made only from the "Societies of Accountants and Auditors, or from any institute, society, or association approved, etc.," and thus apparently excludes all those accountants and auditors who do not happen to be allied to any of these bodies.

Now, if this portion of the measure should become law, it will disqualify all those who do not belong to such societies, and thereby inflict grievous, and, in many cases, irreparable injury upon a number of capable and respectable men—men equally as competent and possessed of as wide and varied experience and practice as those members *of originally self-constituted* bodies, which authorises them to affix the magical letters to their names.

It surely cannot be the deliberate intention of the Legislature to disfranchise such a large number of auditors, and by one "fell swoop" deprive them of the means of earning a livelihood! Such a proceeding would be a violation of all British traditions of fair play and even-handed justice.

Whatever may be now the curriculum whereby one may be admitted within the pale of these associated bodies, it is an admitted fact that not more than one-half their present number underwent an examination. Seeing, therefore, that a certain number of men did originally combine to form the parent association in this colony without examination,—indeed, who could examine them?—and without legal recognition or status, where can be the equity now of refusing to recognise the claims of those who do not happen to be identified with such association, especially in the face of the fact that there is not at present any legally recognised test or standard whereby to judge of their respective qualifications and general fitness for auditing the accounts of public companies?

With a knowledge of these facts, it does strike one as being somewhat arbitrary and one-sided to find Mr. Brentnall advocating the exclusion of the Associates of the Bankers' Institute from auditing the accounts of public companies (*vide* his evidence before the select committee of the Legislative Council), because the one has as much right to style itself "Incorporated" as the other.

Doubtless there are some very able men connected with the Incorporated Institute of Accountants, Victoria, but neither that nor any other kindred association monopolises all the ability to be found in the colony, hence it would be very partial legislation to recognise only those bodies and exclude *outside* talent. In this connection it may not be inappropriate to cite a paragraph from the "Argus" of July 24, 1894, as follows:—

"We have received a copy of the new rules proposed by a minority of the Council of the Incorporated Institute of Accountants, Victoria, for adoption by the members. The objects sought by these rules are frankly stated, being first the maintenance of what is called 'the integrity of vested interests;' and second, the 'raising the standard of the Institute.'

"Now, any endeavour to raise the standard of a profession is highly commendable, and if public accountants and auditors, as a body, can be educated to serve the public better in future than they have in the past, everybody will be glad.

"But obviously, efforts to raise the standard of ability should not be *confined merely* to the members of the Incorporated Institute of Accountants, but, to be of any substantial service, they should *embrace the whole of the profession*. This brings us to the first object sought by the promulgation of the new rules, viz: 'the maintenance of the integrity of vested interests.'

"Now, we hold in common with the majority of the mercantile community that there *ought not to be*, and *cannot* be, any vested interests in accountancy and auditing, and that to advocate the maintenance of its integrity is really to advocate the upholding of a professional union on the Trade Union model."

Again, the "Argus," in its mercantile columns, of February 12 last, has the following remarks:—

"A good deal of dissatisfaction has been occasioned by the 32nd section of the last companies' Bill introduced into the Legislative Assembly, which relates to the qualifications of auditors of companies. Now, while we have always strenuously upheld the importance of the auditor's office, and the emancipation of the auditor from the often sinister control of the directors, we have never approved of the attempts which have been made to convert the auditor's profession into a species of Trade Union.

"There is a Trades Union in Melbourne designed the 'Incorporated Institute of Accountants, Victoria,' whose members generally sign themselves F.I.A.V.

"In New Zealand there is a similar body, the members of which signed as F.I.A.N.Z.; and in Brisbane is to be found a narrower sect, which signs F.I.A.Q. The question may well be asked, In what does incorporation consist? The answer is that it consists in nothing but in compliance with certain provisions of the Companies Act, and that there may be an incorporated association of carpenters or blacksmiths, as well as an Incorporated Institute of Accountants.

"As to the value of the mystic letters referred to, anyone who has studied balance sheets certified in Melbourne since 1887 can hardly avoid the conclusion that the certificates of members of these corporations afford no special security as against the certificates of accounts who do not belong to them. The provision in the new Bill, to which we have referred, imposes limitations as to the persons who may act as auditors of companies, all in the Trade Union direction. But the proper course is to leave the room open for the employment of efficient persons, although they may not be members of the trades union. The proper rule, especially in a democracy, is to leave the career open to ability, and not to *subordinate* ability to artificial rules intended to secure advantages for a limited number of persons."

It is to be devoutly hoped that the Legislature in its wisdom will see fit, even in the eleventh hour, to expunge from the present measure all clauses confining the selection of auditors to associated bodies, and leave their qualifications, standing, and appointment to the judgment of shareholders themselves, who, as partners, ought to be more vitally interested, and consequently the fittest tribunal as to what they require. Let talent, whether *incorporated or not*, have a "fair field and no favour." It is generally conceded that the less governments interfere with the management of companies—especially trading companies—the better. When the question of amending the Law of Limited Liability was being considered by the House of Lords nearly a decade ago, Lord Bramwell, in an address to the English Institute of Bankers, on July 23, 1888, "protested most strongly against Government interference, urging that it would be absolutely mischievous."

As previously remarked, shareholders are neither more nor less than partners, just as much so as if they are members of a private firm; and if they neglect the obvious duty of electing only competent auditors, the consequences must and indeed do fall upon themselves.

It has recently been ruled in England that auditors are "officers," and if such be the case the Government has no more right to approve of, or, as some people recommend, appoint them to their office than it has to appoint any other "officer," such as managing director, manager or secretary. It forms no part of the duty of the state "to stand between a fool and his folly." But suppose, for the sake of argument, that it is right that Government should interpose, there is at present no department of the state specially qualified to critically examine and report on the character and scope of prospectuses of new companies, nor at present is there any one of its officers specially trained to examine into the qualifications of auditors. To create a department for these purposes would be a most costly as well as tardy operation.

In the meantime sufficient protection is already available to the public in the shape of trained and experienced accountants and auditors, and if the promoters of each new company were compelled to submit their prospectuses to the investigation of accountants of repute and standing for verification, and report as to whether there would be a reasonable chance of such company succeeding in its projects, before promulgating the scheme, the public would be, as a rule, sufficiently protected, because no accountant who valued his reputation in the least would give his "Hall" stamp of approval to a Bogus company.

In taking a retrospective view of the commercial storm which has swept like a furious tornado through this colony, and uprooted so many institutions, the question may be asked, Can any section of the community be specially selected for blame? It may be answered that a good part of the blame does indirectly rest on the shareholders themselves, because it was clearly their duty, as well as their right and privilege, as "partners" to scan closely, nay, even suspiciously, those cleverly constructed balance sheets and flowery reports that were put before them during that period of commercial madness, with a view of discovering—bearing in mind the time honoured axiom that "high rate of interest means bad security"—whether those tremendous dividends were justified. But probably few in those palmy days thought of considering the position; doubt or misgivings slumbered; and the *crash came.*

Then they rose up in their wrath and sought victims to their rage; they hit out at all and sundry, and doubtless the present drastic legislation is the outcome of their neglect to perform a very palpable duty. This may be a "hard saying," but who could, or who can even now safeguard their interests so well as themselves. It may be urged in extenuation that many of the unfortunate and badly used shareholders did not possess the requisite experience to criticise a balance sheet effectively, but on the other hand there must have been others who possessed the necessary acumen and business ability to discern the danger. However, it is somewhat late in the day to refer to this, and one can only join in the tribute of praise and admiration paid to those who have gone down in the storm, and who have learnt "How sublime a thing it is to suffer and be strong." Guided and warned, however, by the awful effects of this storm—of madness—shareholders should henceforth take a more lively interest in the management of the several institutions to which they belong, and every future balance sheet and report issued to them should command their closest attention and scrutiny.

Before closing this part of the subject, the question might well be considered whether it would not add to the confidence of the public if directors in issuing their reports were required to annex a declaration thereto, to the effect that to the best of their knowledge and belief the dividend recommended had been fairly earned, and was absolutely payable out of bona fide profits; and again: it would be a distinct move in the right direction if solicitors to public companies were asked to annually examine and report upon deeds and other securities held, which also should be appended to the report.

STATUS OF AUDITORS.

They should be absolutely independent, and, if necessary, be in a position to speak their minds as freely as a member of Parliament. No kootooing nor patronage nor nomineeism, but perfect independence.

They should not be looked upon by one section as "nuisances armed with a pen and a bottle of red ink," to be tolerated; and by the other section, the shareholders, they ought to be regarded as their "bulwark and shield;" and receive from them, so long as they merited it, their full and loyal support. Indeed, so absolutely independent ought an auditor to be, that a case might arise in which he would be brought into direct conflict with the shareholders themselves, in having to veto the payment of a dividend recommended by the directors, but not, in his opinion, justifiable. The proposal that auditors should be changed frequently is not a judicious one, as who so capable of grasping the position of a company as the one who had been some years in office, and had acquired a thorough knowledge of all its affairs.

If this proposal were put into practice generally, it would not be to the advantage of the shareholders.

AUDITORS' FUNCTIONS.

Mr. John Mather, F.C.A., says: "If I were asked to describe the accountant's mission in the world, I should say it is 'to right the wrong and to keep what is right from getting wrong;' and again he says: "While the law very properly assumes every man to be innocent until the contrary is proved, in the practice of accountancy we are not allowed to take anything for granted, and however repugnant to our amiable feelings, we have to proceed upon the opposite assumption." "The auditor's mission should be to prevent litigation and dishonesty, and all large concerns should subject their books to the investigation of an auditor."

An auditor should not be regarded so much as a "*detective*," but as a "*preventive*" officer, and as his audits should be continuous, but *without notice*, the moral effect of this course would be incalculable, because very few men, even though they were on the lookout for an opportunity of wrong-doing, would have the hardihood to begin a course of swindling when they knew that the auditor might surprise them at any day or hour.

FUTURE SCOPE FOR AUDITORS

As the commercial community generally becomes more alive to the value of audits, so will the scope for employment become enlarged, and very shortly there will be work enough for every man of talent whether "incorporated" or "non-incorporated."

There is a wide field open embracing:—

1. Increase of audits among private firms.
2. Investigation of prospectuses of new companies.
3. A more general investigation of books prior to any one taking a share of a partnership.
4. Settlement of disputes arising out of accounts.
5. Arbitration in relation to accounts.
6. Advising as to whether investments are judicious or otherwise, and generally.
7. Accountancy in every branch and audits *ad infinitum*.

Just one more word before closing on—

FEES.

As it is presumable that both directors and shareholders are desirous of obtaining the best talent and the most efficient and exhaustive work, it follows that they must be prepared to pay fees commensurate therewith.

Auditors are only human, and it is not at all surprising to occasionally find them measuring their time according to their pay, but, as a body, they are endowed with a fair share of honour, and often give a *maximum* of time and attention for a *minimum* of pay.

As, however, their responsibilities and risks are becoming great, so must their pay be.

Melbourne, Nov. 3, 1896.   WM. HOLT.

THE VICTORIAN COMPANIES ACT 1896

The Victorian Companies Act 1896.

FOR many years the colony of Victoria was behind every other colony in the assimilation of its company law to that of the mother country. To every expressed desire that legislation should be brought up to date, both Government and Parliament turned their deaf ear. The frightful abuses of the provisions of the Statute by many of the bubble land and finance companies, which were at the height of their power for mischief in 1887 and 1888, made no impression. For the neglect of Parliament to deal eight or nine years ago with a matter of vital importance, more than compensation has, however, been taken in the enactment of the measure which became law on 24th December last. Whatever credit attaches to the reform is due primarily to the Legislative Council, which, two or three sessions in succession, passed a serviceable bill, only to endure the mortification of its being allowed to fall through by the Legislative Assembly. A comprehensive bill was at last introduced into the Legislative Assembly by the Attorney - General, who is possessed of a great deal of acumen and force of character, but of no practical mercantile knowledge. From the time of the introduction of the bill the extraordinary position was taken up that it was the best measure that could possibly be devised, and that criticism of its provisions could only proceed from sinister counsels. The Legislative Assembly, not at the best very

competent to deal with great measures, accepted it by compulsion of the mechanical operation of the Government majority; the Legislative Council was threatened with all sorts of pains and penalties if it dared to amend. The Council did, however, make some valuable improvements, but it is to be feared that it failed to make others because it was too tender to expose itself to unmerited reproaches. What was really wanted was that the bill should be patiently and laboriously considered in every detail without party feeling. That it was not so considered in the Legislative Assembly is to be regretted.

Division I. of the Act provides for the regulation of " No-liability Trading Companies." The provisions are, however, mere surplusage, for under the principal Act companies can call up all their capital, the shareholders bearing no further liability. It is hardly necessary to say that no-liability trading companies will not be entitled to any credit beyond that for which they can actually deposit undeniable security. Their very constitution will be a warning to lenders.

Division II. (subdivision 2) makes provision regarding the " Constitution and Incorporation of Companies." The leading section is as follows :—

21. (1) A company limited by shares shall not commence business or exercise any borrowing powers unless and until one-third of the shares shall have been subscribed for and one-fourth of the subscribed capital shall have been actually paid up in money or value received and statutory declarations made by the manager and not less than two directors shall have been filed with the Registrar-General verifying such subscriptions and such payment and setting forth—

(a) The number of shares in the company and the amount of each share.

(b) The amount paid up per share in money or value received.

(·) The number of shares subscribed for.

(d) The names and addresses and occupations of the shareholders ; and

(e) The number of shares held by each shareholder and the whole amount paid up in money or value received.

(2) The Registrar-General shall on the filing of the said statutory declarations certify that the company is entitled to commence business, and such certificate shall be conconclusive evidence that the company has complied with the provisions of this section.

(3) Nothing in this section shall prevent any company from paying or contracting to pay any preliminary expenses but any other contract made by a company before the date on which it is entitled to commence business shall be provisional only and shall not be binding on the company unless adopted by the company after that date.

It will be readily seen that in the expression "value received" the section itself provides for the evasion of its main intention. Promoters experience no difficulty in making up a "value received," but the case is often different when it is sought to obtain cash over the counter for shares. Any amendment of the law should have prescribed the proportion to be actually received in cash. Preliminary expenses may also be made to mean a great deal. Subdivision 3 of Division II. has respect to the "Statements, Books, and Accounts," the proposals of the English Bill (clause 28) regarding the shareholders' balance-sheet being adopted. Whatever the form of that balance-sheet may be, it is to show in every case—

(2) The shareholders' balance-sheet shall be in such form as is directed either by the articles of association or by a resolution of the company and shall show in every case –

(a) The amount of share capital issued and the amount paid up thereon distinguishing the amount of share capital paid up in money and the amount paid otherwise than in money and the arrears of calls due.

(b) The amount of debts due by the company distinguishing the amount of mortgages debentures and floating charges over the general assets of the company.

(c) The amount of debts due to the company after making a proper deduction for debts considered to be bad or doubtful.

(d) Whether the assets other than debts due to the company are taken at cost price or by valuation or on what other basis they are stated and whether any and if so what amount of percentage has been written off and what other provision (if any) has been made for depreciation.

(e) The actual amount of the reserve fund (if any) and the mode in which it is used or invested ; and

(f) The amount by which the gross value of the assets of the company has been increased since the last balance-sheet in consequence of any increase in the valuation of real or personal property belonging to the company.

(3) The shareholders' balance-sheet shall be accompanied by a certificate signed by one or more of the directors on behalf of the board stating that in his or their opinion the balance-sheet is drawn up so as to exhibit a correct view of the state of the company's affairs and such balance-sheet shall be in one of the forms in the third schedule to this Act or to the like effect, and shall be accompanied by a certificate of not less than two directors that in their opinion the statement is correct.

Subsection 3 is one which will give companies a considerable amount of trouble. The balance-sheet, it says, "shall be in one of the forms in the "Third Schedule to this Act, or to like "effect, &c." The forms are ill-fitted to cover the circumstances of either banks or other companies, but we think that the words we have italicised justify some departure from them on proper grounds. So far as the banks are concerned, only those with head offices in Victoria are obliged to comply with the requisiti on. And those of them which do busines s in other colonies are hardly called upon to publish an unnecessarily cumbrous form with a string of declarations and certificates outside Victoria. As to the form itself, it is inferior in clearness, and will convey less information than that used since 1893 by either the Commercial Bank or the National Bank. An illustration of its application will be found in the balance-sheet to 31st December, 1896, of the Bank of Victoria, which is presented on another page.

The 25th section prohibits the publication in any form (as from 24th June, 1897) of the amount of the reserve fund of a company (if any) unless such reserve fund is actually existing. The representation is, moreover, to be "accom-"panied by a statement showing whether "or not such reserve fund is used in the "business, and, if any portion thereof is "otherwise invested, showing the manner "in which, and the securities upon "which the same is invested" The provision is only of academic interest where, as is largely the case at present in Victoria, no reserve funds exist. But it is totally unnecessary.

Subdivision 4 of Division II. relates to "Audit and Auditors," but its provisions are not applicable to life assurance companies, " or to any proprietary company, or to "any company incorporated outside Vic- "toria and not having its head or prin- "cipal office within Victoria." Auditors are required to state in their certificates whether they have observed or become acquainted during the audit with any breach of the Companies Acts committed by the company, or any director, manager, employee, auditor, or shareholder thereof. That is to say, the auditor, in addition to his proper duties, is to sit in judgment upon the legality of the acts of the management. Surely the Attorney-General must be aware of the fact that evil-doers taking advantage of the Companies Acts have paid scrupulous attention to technicalities. In their case the injunction to auditors is absolutely unnecessary; in the case of honestly-conducted institutions it is a grave reflection. As to the qualifications of auditors, it is evident from the persons who belong to various professional societies or institutes, some good, some quite indifferent, being regarded as eligible, that the Victorian Parliament is not particular about quality. A board of three persons is to be appointed to formally indorse the qualifications of auditors. It is to inquire into general conduct and character, but it will no doubt construe this injunction liberally, for we do not see how it can shelter itself, more than any other organisation or person, from the consequences of a wrong conclusion in so important a matter. The whole of the provisions regarding the qualifications of auditors should have been struck out. They benefit nobody, whether the capable auditor, - the incapable auditor, or the company employing either one or the other. Fortunately the company retains the privilege of selecting its own auditor. The subdivision provides pains and penalties for improper conduct on the part of auditors, but the difficulty of proving default will still exist. And the difficulty as it presents itself to an ordinary Melbourne jury is almost insuperable.

Subdivision 5 of Division II. (sections 36 to 43) provides for "Special Audit" at the instance of "members not indebted "to the company holding not less than "one-tenth part in number and value of "the whole shares of the company for "the time being issued." We do not think, with some objectors, the provisions for a special audit will encourage un-called-for interference. In all probability they will become a dead letter. Their enactment is a work of supererogation.

Subdivision 6 forbids companies from advancing on their own shares, and sub-division 7 provides that a return of advances to directors and officers, and to firms with which they may be connected, shall be filed with the Registrar-General. Under the provisions of subdivision 8, companies must, in advertising their capital, describe the term capital, whether nominal or authorised, subscribed and paid up, and the amount of any charge on the uncalled capital. Subdivision 9 relates to dividends and premiums, but as the principal provision regarding dividends is that none shall be payable excepting out of *profits*, and the vexed question what is profit has not, and probably will never be settled, it is so far useless. So also is the restriction that "the directors of any "company shall not make a first or any "issue of shares in such company at a "premium until the company shall have "been established at least twelve "months." The intention is laudable enough. But directors of questionable companies will only be tempted to do what was freely done in Melbourne in 1888, viz., to make fresh issues to them-selves or their friends at par, and im-mediately place them on the market at a premium for their own special benefit, although the benefit should accrue to the company. The section is a piece of child's play. Subdivision 10 restricts the use of the word "savings" and similar words, as well as of the word "bank" and similar words. Subdivision 11 relates to evidence.

The highly important subject of mortgages created by companies is dealt with at great length in subdivision 12 (sections 53 and 54). The first three subdivisions indicate the character of the legislation. They are as follows :—

53. (1) Every mortgage created by a company after the commencement of this Act, and being—

(a) A mortgage of uncalled or unpaid capital of the company; or

(b) A mortgage of any other property created or evidenced by an instrument which, if executed by an individual, would require registration as a bill of sale or under the Book Debts Act 1896 ; or

(c) A mortgage for the purpose of securing any issue of debentures ; or

(d) A floating mortgage on the undertaking or property of the company, not being a mortgage subject to any other part of this subsection, and not being a lien by law or a mortgage created in the ordinary course of business—

shall be subject to the following provisions of this section.

(2) No such mortgage shall be operative or have any validity at law or in equity unless the same be in writing and unless the same be registered in the office of the Registrar-General by lodging in such office the mortgage or a copy thereof accompanied by an affidavit of the execution of the mortgage, and in the case of a copy also verifying it as a true copy of such mortgage. Such mortgage or copy shall be so lodged within thirty days after the date of the creation of such mortgage. For such registration there shall be paid to the Registrar-General such fee as may be prescribed.

(3) No mortgage created by a company of its uncalled or unpaid capital shall be operative or have any validity at law or in equity unless previously authorised by a special resolution of such company passed and confirmed in the manner provided in the principal Act.

The provisions demand the careful study of all companies which have given mortgage charges upon their assets. Generally these provisions are valuable, for the secret pledging of assets, and of uncalled capital has been a crying evil. In borrowing, the company should be left to its own discretion; but every preferential debt that is created ought to be registered.

Subdivisions 13, 14, and 15 relate to statutory meetings, extraordinary general meetings, and extraordinary resolutions respectively. The allotment of shares is regulated by subdivision 16, the proposals of the English bill being adopted.

Division III. is in two subdivisions, (1) referring to branch registers (which should be consulted by companies having branches in other colonies), and (2) to foreign companies and societies. In the latter it is provided (section 75) that "no company shall be deemed to be "carrying on business within the mean-"ing of this Act by reason only of its "investing its funds or other property in "Victoria."

Division IV. relates to "Alteration of "Objects or Constitution of a Company," and Division V. to "Reduction of Capital "and Shares by a Company." The provisions of Division V. will enable banks and other companies to write down capital in order to provide for losses, and, unfortunately, will be of considerable use. The methods that have to be followed are rather cumbrous. Provision is made for permitting the reduction of uncalled liability, but the policy involved is open to question.

Division VI. defines the "Liability of "Directors and other persons with regard "to Companies and Societies," and embodies English legislation, accomplished and projected. In view of what has taken place in Melbourne in the past, we do not think its provisions are open to serious objection. Directors will show their good sense in not taking umbrage at them, for they are only called upon to do now what obviously devolved upon them before, viz., to discharge the duties of their office with straightforward honesty and to the best of their ability. Penal threatenings, however irritating from their paltriness, will then have no terrors for them.

Division VII. provides winding-up procedure, mainly according to English precedent. It is satisfactory to note that on the report of an official liquidator the Court may order an examination of the directors and officers without being compelled to first impute fraud. But voluntary winding-up will be resorted to in the future as much as in the past.

Divisions VIII., IX., and X. are entitled respectively — "Defunct Com-"panies," "Acquisition of a Business "by a Company," and "Miscellaneous."

We hope next month to deal purely with some legal aspects of the Act as to procedure, &c.

———————◆———————

INADEQUATE AUDIT

Inadequate Audit.

WHAT is called the "Millwall Dock "Scandal" has called attention in London to the question of audit, and, we may add, the position and qualification of auditors. The Millwall Dock Company rejoiced in the possession of a *rara aris* in dock management, Mr. BIRT, who was appointed to the position of superintendent in 1868, and in the course of time became managing director. It was Mr. BIRT's business to earn the interest for debenture-holders, standing for £493,457, and the dividend for the stockholders, standing for £1,526,350. Much was expected of him, and he rendered much. By the simple process of falsifying the ledger accounts of the customers of the docks—the indoor superintendent, and the chief clerk at the docks entering into connivance—the balance-sheet was made to show a large current indebtedness to the company. The profit and loss account was proportionately swollen, and in the end dividends were paid out of a fictitious profit and loss credit balance. It would be highly improper at this stage to suggest even in the most remote manner, while the case is still *sub judice*, that Mr. BIRT directly benefited pecuniarily from the falsification. Indeed, it may be regarded as certain that he did not. But having once commenced to "doctor" accounts in order to show a profit, and justify directors and shareholders in regarding him as the prince of dock managers, he had to go on or to face the alternative of disgrace. The step once taken could not be retraced, for the operations of the company yielded much less than the amount of the dividend distributed. Hence the item, outstanding accounts, constantly increased, until, by the accident that was sure to occur at some time or other, its overgrown dimen-

sions were discovered and the pricked imposture collapsed. Not, however, until the deficit in the item had reached about £200,000. With respect to the two accessories it is to be soundly assumed that having once been induced to sanction the falsification, they could not turn back. To expose the misdoing would have probably entailed instant dismissal. So they had to do what they were told by their superior officer until the discovery was made.

The case, it will be seen, is not one of defalcation or malversation of moneys, but one of falsification of ledgers. The parties who have benefited from the falsification are not the falsifiers, but the shareholders of the company, who have received dividends that were never earned. But the benefit has been evanescent, for the capital has been impaired precisely to the extent to which dividends have been overpaid. As creditors have not suffered, the question is one between shareholders and directors, and it is very difficult to see how the directors can be compelled to refund improperly-paid dividends to the very persons who have received them. If, however, the public have been induced by the dividends paid to purchase shares in the company, they might have a just cause for an action for damages.

But if Mr. BIRT managed to impose silence upon his subordinates, or tools, how did he contrive to impose upon the credulity of his co-directors, and of the auditors? The deputy-chairman, at the meeting held on 27th February, did not, however, appear to consider such a question worth entertaining, for, he said :—

It is not the duty of directors - for no director would undertake the duty—to examine from their origin the accounts of the company when prepared and certified by competent officers appointed for that special purpose, and in our case also by Mr. Birt, in whom everyone had the greatest faith as our managing director and chairman; and if the principal officers of a company combine to present fraudulent accounts the directors and the shareholders are at their mercy. How can it be otherwise! . . . . I must not be understood to mean that the directors have not been anxious upon this subject of the outstandings. On the contrary, they have repeatedly questioned Mr. Birt upon the subject, but they have always been assured by him that the increase was due either to increase of trade or to the variations which from time to time have taken place in the class of trade, or by other similar explanations, which, in view of their absolute confidence in Mr. Birt's honour, they were bound to accept as genuine. I venture to say that everyone who knew Mr. Birt, and who knew his integrity and honour, as was supposed, would have done exactly as we did.

All this means that the very magnitude of an item exciting a feeling of doubt should cause directors to exhibit greater confidence than ever in the person without whose knowledge the improper growth of that item was impossible. Even if the deputy-chairman's explanation could be accepted as perfectly satisfactory, there remains the question of the policy of giving extended credit to the owners of merchandise coming into the docks. A due alarm at the growth of the credit as indicated by the fictitious amount of the item, would have brought about the *dénouement*. Then, again, there was the practical common-sense test embodied in the question : What proportion does the amount of the outstanding accounts bear to the half-yearly or annual receipts ? As a matter of fact, the proportion was absurdly large, and therefore suggestive of error.

Granted, that directors have a right to be devoid of common sense and to be perfunctory in the discharge of duties for which they are not specially qualified, the consideration remains whether they could not easily from the commencement have adopted an internal system of audit or inspection of accounts. The working operations of the company involved the employment of a large and active staff conducting the bookkeeping at the dock. But the company has a city office, the staff of which is doubtless, to a large extent, independent of the influences which reign in the dock itself. The continuous audit of the dock books could easily have been conducted by the city staff. This is a matter which to our mind is of very great importance, for while we hold little belief in the efficiency of audit from outside, we are profoundly convinced that every considerable establishment should have its own internal audit department, conducted by men who are independent of the operations which furnish the material for the bookkeeping. As matters stand there was practically no audit of the books of the Millwall Dock Company. There was no internal audit, and the so-called public audit appears to have consisted in the checking of the addition of certain columns of figures, in collating the items composing the balance statement with the ledgers, in verifying some of the larger amounts, and in giving a certificate. Of course, highly admirable qualifications may centre in the auditors who do this kind of work, but they cannot do justice to the accounts of a large institution whose operations involve an enormous number of trivial entries, especially when the time allowed them is only a week. The auditors have, however, evidently been uneasy for several years. In 1890 the then auditor, Mr. BETTS, pointed to the magnitude of the amount due to customers. It was about £145,000, but the investigation made recently shows that an overstatement existed at the time of £110,000 to £115,000. The then chairman gave an explanation, and Mr. BETTS' place as auditor found him no more. Questions on the same subject have been occasionally put since 1890, but Mr. BIRT's assurances were always accepted. Against the merely technical form in which the so-called audit so far as it went has been conducted, no reproach is possible. But in this matter of the falsification of the accounts of the Millwall Dock Company, and in various matters that have come under our notice in the colonies, we are convinced that too little attention is paid to the question of the practical business qualifications of public auditors. To master all possible forms of bookkeeping, to have a perfect knowledge of the Companies and the Insolvency Acts, to be versed in a multitude of forms is an excellent thing in its way, but a really able auditor should have had sound business experience, and be possessed of shrewd common sense.

MISCELLANEOUS

UNIFORMITY IN STATING ACCOUNTS

Uniformity in Stating Accounts.

The *Post Magazine* of the 25th November contains a notice of an essay by Mr. Edwin Guthrie, read before the Manchester Society of Chartered Accountants on 20th October last. Peculiar interest attaches to this essay, because it exposes the want of uniformity displayed in the statements of the accounts of 124 insurance companies contained in one volume of the *Post Magazine*.

"Disregarding," says Mr. Guthrie, "one or two cases in which Cash Accounts perhaps properly appear, there are, besides the three headings properly applicable, viz., Revenue Account, Profit and Loss Account, and Balance-sheet, at least eleven other headings used, viz., "Capital Account," "General Balance," "General Statement," "General Statement of Affairs," "General Account," "Income and Expenditure," "Receipts and Payments," "Revenue and Expenditure," "Receipts and Disbursements," "Statement of Revenue," "Statement of Account."

Regarding the placing of the items in profit and loss accounts, Mr. Guthrie remarks:—

"Finally, there appear thirty-six profit and loss accounts, ten of which exhibit the elements of cost on the left and the elements of return upon the right-hand side, and twenty-six the elements of cost on the right and the elements of return upon the left-hand side."

Previously to the reception of the *Post Magazine*, we had read, with much interest, Mr. Guthrie's essay as it appeared in full in the *Accountant*, as well as the record of the discussion and correspondence which followed it. The conclusion we formed was that while Mr. Guthrie had found a fair target for his lance, his own proposals were not calculated to secure a logical uniformity. He would establish uniformity on two remarkable propositions:—First. That "profit and loss " and revenue accounts are identical in " their elements and in their purpose—in " fact, everything but in name." Second.

That in drawing up a balance-sheet the assets should be placed on the left-hand side and the liabilities on the right-hand side. Germane to the second proposition, Mr. Guthrie contends that a balance "is " not an account at all."

Now on the main question as to the desirability of uniformity, we agree with Mr. Guthrie to some extent, not entirely. The form in which the items of a balance-sheet should be stated must be controlled in a large degree by the nature of the business, and by the necessity of studying the capacity of the trader or shareholders for whose information the statement is intended. In the narrow limits of this article we cannot enter fully into the first point, but as a mere matter of experience, all thoughtful accountants know that the same terms are not always well adapted or sufficiently literal to express the same class of items occurring in the balances of various concerns. In fact, the terminology employed by accountants should aim at a simple but logical description of the various elements of an account, and should be precisely adapted to the business treated. The second point is more important than is often supposed. A trader may understand perfectly how to carry on a successful business, but be utterly unable to comprehend the abstractions of a system of accountancy. In such a case we hold that a good accountant will adapt his terms, as far as circumstances will permit, to the comprehension of the trader, whose wish, in plain language, is "to know how he "stands," and not that his affairs should form the subject of, to him, a mystical piece of technicism. For these, and some minor reasons, we are unable to coincide with Mr. Guthrie. He forgets, it seems to us, that there can be no uniformity of treatment without uniformity of conditions.

243

But we admit that in any one department of business, in which the conditions are alike, however numerous the concerns, uniformity should be sedulously sought after.

Turning to Mr. GUTHRIE's propositions, we find that he identifies the profit and loss account with the revenue account, and is positively rude, either from impatience of intellect or of temper, to those who dissent from this judgment. His illustrations, however, are most unfortunate for his contention. He refers to the revenue account of the Gresham Life Assurance Society for the year ended 30th June, 1880, which, according to his proposition, is identical with a profit and loss account. The merest tyro in assurance accounts knows that such an assumption is dangerously erroneous, that without an actuarial valuation there can be no legitimate statement of the real position of a life assurance company, that even a large increase of the life fund may be insufficient to meet the additional liabilities incurred in a given period. Herein we at once get at the essential of a true profit and loss account, which is, that its results shall be dependent upon the element of *valuation*. Valuation of stock, properties, risks, &c., lies at the root of a perfect profit and loss account. But in the example given above there is no valuation of the existing policies, and therefore the account is only what it professes to be—a revenue account. Mr. GUTHRIE also quotes the profit and loss account of the North British and Mercantile Insurance Company for the year ended 31st December, 1880. But it is not a revenue account, as he contends. It contains the heads of revenue and expenditure, it is true, but it also contains three all-important items, which make it a real profit and loss account, viz., on the credit side the "premium reserve account, 1879" and the "balance of profit realised on sale of investments and of company's shares," and on the debit side "premium reserve "account, 1880."

Digressing for a space, we would here call the attention of our readers to the item "premium reserve account," because of its rare occurrence in the statements of colonial fire and marine insurance companies. The North British (see *Record* for June, 1882, page 225) and the Northern (see *Record* for August, page 304) adopt the principle of setting aside one-third of the year's premiums as a temporary reserve, the former office calling the account " pre-"mium reserve" and the latter "premiums " set aside to meet current policies." We presume that practically this rather rough apportionment comes out correct, but we see no reason why an actual valuation of running policies cannot be made at the end of each term. Now it seems to us that colonial companies would do wisely to adopt this practice. It is unquestionably the fact that the common method magnifies the "profits" in the case of young and quickly growing companies and excites unreasonable expectations. The Southern Insurance Company, Limited, may be instanced as rightly using the term revenue and expenditure in place of profit and loss. It also makes a practice of maintaining a balance large enough to cover current risks.

The second proposition laid down by Mr. GUTHRIE requires little notice. It appears to us that a balance is a personal account, and that the almost universal method adopted in England and the colonies of placing liabilities on the left hand side is the only rational one. What is a balance but the statement of the trader's position, and that being so, what more sensible than to debit the trader with his liabilities and credit him with his assets ?

The mental confusion which identifies the profit and loss account with the revenue account is too common. They are distinct, and we believe that in a perfect system of stating accounts both would be included. Perhaps one of the best illustrations of sound practice that we have met is that presented by the recent statement of the

Australian Frozen Meat Export Company (Limited). Excepting one or two slight blemishes that statement is a model of perfection. It exhibits a statement of income and expenditure, a schedule of liabilities and assets, and a profit and loss account which distinguishes the individual items of gain and loss. This statement confutes Mr. GUTHRIE in the most unmistakable manner; for, supposed Mr. GUTHRIE right, then revenue and profit and loss accounts being identical, the balance must be the same. But the former shows a debit balance of £4087 18s. 8d., and the latter a credit balance of £16,825 12s. 8d.! Can anything be more conclusive as to the erroneousness of Mr. GUTHRIE'S proposition?

There is much to be said for uniformity in stating accounts, but on the whole we expect the improvements will come from the accountants of business concerns rather than from professionals.

———◆———

ACCOUNTS OF TRADING COMPANIES

Accounts of Trading Companies.

WE have noticed in the accounts of some trading companies a want of definite information regarding receipts and expenditure, which appears to us unjust, both to shareholders and to the public. The vital part of the business—the turnover and the expenses charged thereto—is often omitted, the balance of the working or manufacturing account only being brought into the profit and loss account, against which the establishment expenses are stated. This practice disguises, and, we are afraid, is sometimes intended to disguise, the operations of the company. Directors adopt it, under the impression that they conserve the interests of shareholders by withholding information. As a matter of business, we doubt the wisdom of such a conclusion, and, beyond that, the practice is of questionable legality. It should always be remembered that limited liability companies do not stand on the same ground as private concerns. Certain privileges and immunities are granted to them by law; but, against these, certain obligations and conditions are rightly attached. One of these obligations is unquestionably the clear statement of all their affairs. The Companies' Statute is explicit on this matter. Sections 79 and 80 of the Second Schedule prescribe :—" Once, at the least, " in every six months, the directors shall " shall lay before the company, in general " meeting, *a statement of the income and* " *expenditure* for the period succeeding that " embraced by the then last statement, &c. ". . . The statement so made shall show, " arranged under the most convenient " heads, *the amount of gross income, dis-* " *tinguishing the several sources from* " *which it has been derived, and the amount* " *of gross expenditure*, distinguishing the " expense of the establishment, salaries, " and other like matters."

We submit that the passages we have italicised do not simply present mere balances of income over expenditure, or the reverse, to be brought into the accounts presented to shareholders, but require the gross figures on either side to be stated. It is to be hoped that more care will be displayed to comply with the spirit of the Companies' Statute in this regard. In one or two instances, lately, shareholders might have been saved from severe loss if the accounts presented to them had been sufficiently copious to bring out the naked fact that the amount of business being done was inadequate, under almost any circumstances, to meet the heavy establishment charges.

Another questionable matter has come under our notice since last issue. The directors of an important company, in a circular to their shareholders, stated, "that it was not advisable, in the " interests of the company, to publish the " June balance-sheet." Yet the articles of association of that company provide that " a printed copy of such balance-sheet and " report shall, seven days previously to such " meeting, be served on the members in " the manner in which notices are herein- " after directed to be served."

It is true that in an earlier part of this circular it is mentioned that on 10th August last, a balance-sheet to 30th June " was submitted, showing a loss on the " working for the half-year about the same " as that of preceding half-year." (This loss, we observe, by reference to the accounts at 31st December, 1882, was £8397.) And we cannot forbear saying, that it is, in our opinion, best for a company to avoid anything wearing the appearance of withholding information. The directors of the company in question are business men of unimpeachable integrity, and we are confident that their action is dictated by no sinister motive. But other cases might arise, where in a company under the direction of men of less assured standing, their example, in not publishing accounts, might be quoted as a justifying precedent. We hold that, sooner or later, the best policy for all companies is to respect the provisions and intention of the statute, by publishing a full and proper statement of all their affairs. And experience has shown that the fuller the information afforded, the larger and the more cordial the confidence and support of the public.

WHAT ARE PROFITS FOR DISTRIBUTION?

What are Profits for Distribution?
COMPETITION not unfrequently forces directors, in the words of a Lord Chancellor, "to make things look pleasant for their "shareholders." A balance-sheet is a common place thing enough, but even a balance-sheet affords some opportunity for imaginative writing. In the case of limited liability companies the influence of imagination is moderated, as far as possible, by legislative enactment. It is in the matter of profits, and by consequence of dividends, that the enthusiasm of directors is so apt to mislead them. As far as concerns the present discussion, the law on this subject admits of a ready statement, but it does not seem to go very far. The statutory regulations for the management of limited companies are given in the second schedule to the Companies Statute 1864. By article 73 "no dividend shall be payable "except out of the profits arising from the "business of the company." This statement, simple as it seems, can scarcely be said to be free from doubt. "Profits," it will be noticed, is an unknown quantity. No definition of the word is furnished, and the sentence must be read by the light of judicial decisions embodying mercantile usage. There is an opinion among business men that the legal view and the commercial view do not always harmonize. This perhaps results from the frequent uncertainty of usage. What, then, are profits in the legal sense? How do judges arrive at a statement of profits for the purpose of declaring dividends? These are questions which have lately pushed themselves into prominence.

The law on the subject is, unfortunately, singularly meagre. The only authoritative statement is to be found in the judgment of SELWYN, L.J., in STRINGER'S CASE (L.R. 4 Ch., 475.) A company was started during the American Civil War, for the purpose of blockade-running to the Southern ports. It had a large capital in ships, and for a time at least was highly successful. In the days of its prosperity the Confederate Government became co-owners with the company in their ships. Two-thirds were to be owned by the Government, who gave a guarantee for payment, and the other third by the company. In a subsequent balance-sheet of the company the Confederate guarantee and a large quantity of cotton lying at a blockaded port were reckoned among assets. The sheet showed a large profit, and a dividend of £25 per cent. was declared and paid with borrowed money. The guarantee, of course, became utterly worthless, and it was sought to impeach this dividend as wholly delusive and improper. The directors, it was contended, were not justified in putting a value upon what they could not then realize—upon what it was very doubtful if they ever would be able to realize. But the Court of Appeal was unwilling to accept this doctrine. The law will never prevent directors putting a fair—and not more than a fair—value on their assets, and a fair value is a matter of opinion. "I think," says Lord Justice SELWYN, L.J., in an exhaustive judgment, "the company was "justified in doing that which, in truth, is "done in almost every business—namely, "taking the facts as they actually stood, and "forming an estimate of their assets as they "actually existed, and then drawing a bal- "ance so as to ascertain the result in the "shape of profit or of loss." The suggestion that there should be money in hand or at the bank to the full amount of the dividend declared was held to be inconsistent with commercial custom. Such a rule would open the door to endless litigation. He was followed in a similar strain by another Lord Justice.

These two judgments, together with an anterior but strengthening *obiter dictum* of V. C. KINDERSLEY, are, we believe, the whole judicial opinion on the method of ascertaining profit for the purpose of dividends. They are followed by BUCKLEY, who adds that the fact that an estimated value was put upon assets which were in jeopardy and were subsequently lost, does not render a balance-sheet fraudulent and delusive. The law, therefore, must be regarded as settled on the lines indicated. At the same time it should be remembered that in STRINGER'S case MALINS, V.C., took the opposite view in the Court below; that the ultimate decision did not hinge on this point; and that an isolated judgment, even of the Court of Appeal, can scarcely be said to place the matter beyond all doubt. Legal guidance is, as BUCKLEY admits, still much needed. It would be impossible to say how considerations which affect not only the pockets of members, but the interests of the public also, might influence later opinion. No doubt the Courts have given expression to established mercantile usage ; but a Court of Equity might be induced to consider such usage unreasonable in the case of companies regulated by Act of Parliament. There is no particular sanctity about the custom of merchants. The matter might be looked at thus :—The Companies Statute 1864, which confers the privilege of limited liability, also imposes certain conditions and limitations. These may be considered the price of that privilege. They are imposed for the protection of the public, for the safety of creditors, and for the benefit of shareholders. The regulation under discussion will serve as an illustration. It may be, as one learned writer remarks, a warning to directors ; but it is a great deal more. Payments out of capital, for instance, are in fraud of creditors ; and, it seems to us, that an unfair and improper method of reckoning profits is a snare for investors, who for the most part walk by the faith of dividend quotations.

Where assets are liable to eccentric variations in value this danger is peculiarly great. A company, for example, is making a revenue profit on a paltry scale. It possesses property which is subject to sudden rises and falls in value. A valuation, not necessarily unfair, but taken at a period of inflation, gives an immense increase in the value of certain assets. A large dividend is declared and the shares rise, and the cause of the rise is soon forgotten. Nothing could give those ignorant of the real circumstances of the case a more misleading impression of the actual position of the company. It is obvious that there is a vast difference between private partnerships and public companies. A method of ascertaining profits, which may be safe in the case of the former, may be unsafe, and even perilous, in the case of the latter. Of the inexpediency and unwisdom of declaring dividends on the basis of unduly inflated assets, no sensible man can have two opinions. In practice such a course is almost invariably avoided. Where a company is honestly administered succeeding valuations should reflect the value of these fluctuating assets. This, we imagine, might be distasteful to shareholders. But, in any event, it is necessary in the interest of those seeking investments, that re-valuations should take place regularly and at the shortest possible intervals. This is not altogether a question of mere expediency.

GOODWILL AS AN ASSET

GOODWILL AS AN ASSET.

THE *Economist* of 3rd April had a pertinent article on business goodwill as an asset, in which it is alleged, on irrefragable grounds, that "it is not right to allow the goodwill to stand as an asset in a company's balance-sheet at the price paid for it." Our contemporary goes even further, and says that as a company's capital must be represented by valid assets in its balance-sheet before dividends can be legally paid, the payment of dividend made where goodwill is an asset is *ultra vires*. We think the *Economist* is right, and have never shrunk from referring pointedly to the item, goodwill, in balance-sheets coming under our notice for criticism. Excepting in two or three instances, goodwill has proved an unsubstantial phantom, and investors should be very chary of buying shares in any company which has for an asset a goodwill exceeding in amount one year's net profit, or uncovered by a reserve fund.

Our contemporary deals with the supposed difficulty of treating goodwill as follows :—

"How, then, are vendors of businesses to companies to be paid for goodwill, so that this item will not appear in the balance-sheet to prevent dividends being legally paid? There are only two ways by which this can be effected. One is by founders' shares, which will entitle the holders to a proportion of the future profits after a certain fixed dividend has been paid to the shareholders. The other way, which is commonly resorted to when private banks are transformed into limited companies, is to allot to the vendors a certain portion of the capital at par, and to offer the remainder to the public at a premium, the money raised by the premium being paid to the vendors for the goodwill. The capital of the company is thus kept intact, and the goodwill does not appear as an asset in the balance-sheet."

One of the best methods we know of was that adopted by the promoters of the Union Mortgage and Agency Company of Australasia Limited, who issued the share capital at a premium, and paid for the goodwill of the acquired business by the premium, the two items effacing one another.

COMPANY LAW IN VICTORIA

The bill to amend the Companies Act of Victoria, brought in to the Legislative Council by Mr. AGAR WYNNE, will, if passed, constitute an important advance on existing legislation. For it is to be remembered that at the adoption in 1864 of the English Companies Statute of 1862 the colony stopped short, and has done nothing since to provide against the perpetration of abuses sure to spring up in the course of twenty-seven years upon a measure which, when it was enacted, was of a tentative character. We hardly think that Mr. WYNNE'S meritorious effort at improving company law will, however, be successful, for the subject is one which in its comprehensiveness should be dealt with by a Ministry. And, moreover, the time is inopportune for enforcing a new enactment, as nothing should be done to artificially increase the difficulties which exist. A year or two hence will suit better, and in the meantime there is no likelihood of any fresh abuse being originated. As in the day of prosperity we urgently pressed for amending legislation, the force of our plea for postponement at the present juncture will be understood. Several of the provisions of Mr. WYNNE'S bill call for comment; but before proceeding to examine them it will be useful to recapitulate the chief English Companies Acts which have been passed since the principal Act of 1862, but have not been imitated in the colony. These Acts are as follows:—

1. *The Companies Seals Act 1864.*—An Act to enable joint-stock companies carrying on business in foreign countries to have official seals to be used in such countries.

2. *The Companies Act 1867.*—This Act amends the principal Act of 1862 in some material points, providing for the adoption of unlimited liability of directors, for the reduction of capital and shares in companies, for the subdivision of shares, calls upon shares, transfer of shares, share warrants to bearer, contracts, meeting, and winding-up.

3. *The Joint-Stock Companies Arrangement Act 1870.*—An Act to facilitate comprises and arrangements between creditors and share-

holders of joint stock and other companies in liquidation.

4. *The Companies Act 1877*, which amends the Acts of 1862 and 1867, as regards the power given for the reduction of capital, &c.

5. *The Companies Act 1879*, which was the outcome of the failure of the City of Glasgow Bank, providing for the conversion of unlimited companies to limited companies, for the unlimited liability of banks of issue in respect of notes, for the audit of accounts of banking companies, &c.

6. *The Companies Act 1880*, which provides that accumulated profits may be returned to shareholders in reduction of paid-up capital, &c.

7. *The Companies Act 1883*, providing that wages and salaries owing by a company in liquidation are to be preferential claims.

8. *The Companies (Colonial Registers) Act 1883*, which authorises companies registered under the principal Act to keep local registers of their members in British colonies.

9. *The Companies Act 1886*, which amends the provisions of the Companies Act 1862 so far as they relate to the liquidation of companies in Scotland.

10. *The Directors' Liability Act 1890.*

11. *Companies (Memorandum of Association) Act 1890.*

12. *The Companies (Winding-up) Act 1890.*

The fifth of the foregoing Acts (that of 1879) has to some extent been followed in the Victorian Banking Companies' Registration Act 1888 and the Banks and Currency Amendment Statute 1887. Two or three others of the Acts enumerated are of local interest. But the remainder should (with the qualification as to time recommended above) be re-enacted in Victoria, with such amendments as may be found necessary, in a consolidated form. Mr. WYNNE'S bill fulfils this desideratum, with the important exception that another bill before the Victorian Parliament, introduced by Mr. ZEAL, adopts the provisions of the now celebrated English Directors' Liability Act 1890. We would suggest that in the event of Mr. WYNNE'S bill being actively taken up for consideration, Mr. ZEAL should withdraw his bill on the understanding that its provisions be adopted by Mr. WYNNE.

The bill lying before us goes further than recent English legislation in some important particulars, which require much consideration. First—The bill provides that trading companies may register as no-liability companies on condition that one-half of the shares shall have been subscribed for. The provision, it will be seen, is a permissory one, and to some extent, therefore, criticism is disarmed. But it is doubtful whether any good purpose will be served by introducing the no-liability principle into trading companies. The life of trade is credit, but how could a company hope to obtain credit which did not even offer the security of the uncalled portion of the subscribed capital? The operations of a no-liability trading company, like those of a no-liability mining company, would be contracted within the limit furnished by the amount of capital actually paid-up. We do not quite understand the tenderness displayed for shareholders in the proposal that they may adopt the no-liability system. The disadvantages of that system are, however, so great that it is doubtful whether it would be often adopted.

Second.—The bill makes provision for the filing of an annual statement of accounts in a schedule form at the Registrar-General's office. The principle that a statement should be filed is heartily to be commended. At present there is no compulsion of the kind, and thus, although shares may be dealt in publicly, no means of ascertaining the position of the company is open to the intending investors. It has always seemed to us that companies availing themselves of company legislation should be required to give more publicity to their accounts than many of them do. As regards the form in which the accounts are to be rendered, while Mr. WYNNE'S desire that definite information on certain points shall be supplied is commendable, yet it is to be feared that no one model can be elastic enough. The text of the schedule is as follows:—

THIRD SCHEDULE.

Statement of assets and liabilities of company

That the liabilities of the company on the day of   were

1. Debts owing to depositors on money deposited at interest, £.
2. Money owing on open accounts.
3. Debts due to bankers and how secured.
4. Debts due on judgment.
5. Debts due on mortgage [*specifying whether to a company or a private person distinguishing same and amounts thereof.*]
6. Amount due on notes or bills.
7. Amount due on simple contracts.
8. Estimated other liabilities [*setting out nature of same*]

That the assets of the company on that day were—

Government or municipal securities [*stating the same*]

Bills of exchange and promissory notes

Cash in hand at bankers.

Real estate [*stating cost price and present value.*]

Debts due to company [*distinguishing good bad and doubtful*]

Money lent on mortgage [*distinguishing amounts lent on first and subsequent mortgages.*]

Money lent on other security [*specifying nature of security.*]

Money lent without security.

I   of   do solemnly and sincerely declare that I am [state official position in company.]

That the above statement is to the best of my belief and knowledge true in every particular. And I make, &c.

Declared, &c.

Third.—The bill provides that no company using the word "bank" is to deal in land, the section (10ᵗʰ) being as follows:—

No company having the word "bank" or "banking" as part of its name or designation shall purchase freehold or leasehold estate except for the purpose of using the same for its offices or business premises and any such company purchasing freehold or leasehold estate except for the purposes aforesaid shall forfeit for every such offence the sum of one thousand pounds such penalty to be recovered by action in the Supreme Court by any person who shall sue for the same.

Everyone will welcome an enactment of this kind, in view of the great uneasiness which has been engendered by the careless use of the term "bank."

Fourth.—Section 11 provides that "no company shall lend or advance money on the security of shares in the company." The practice of advancing money on the security of shares, in order really to float the company, is highly reprehensible, and should be legislated against. But it may reasonably be doubted whether the provision stated above is necessary without some limitation. Plenty of cases occur in which companies whose business it is to lend money may advance to their shareholders on the security of their shares. Not that the security is one to be sought or to be largely taken. The section might, we think, be amended by prescribing—(1ˢᵗ) The proportion of the total capital that may be advanced upon shares in the company; and (2ⁿᵈ), the proportion of the value of the share that may be lent. But the question is a very difficult one to legislate upon, and great caution should be exercised.

Fifth.—Section 14 introduces the principle that deposits and debentures shall be a first charge upon the Victorian assets, its terms being as follows:—

All deposits whether at call or for a fixed term taken, and all debentures issued by any company in Victoria, shall in the event of such company being would up be a first charge on the assets in Victoria of such company, provided always that nothing herein contained shall prejudice or affect—

(1) The charge or lien of any *bonâ fide* holder of notes within the meaning of section 12 of *The Banks and Currency Act* 1890.

(2) Any mortgage or charge expressly made or given in favour of holders of debentures at the time of the issue thereof.

(3) Any mortgage pledge lien charge or other security heretofore given by any company.

This provision must provoke a great deal of discussion. In the first place a definition of the term "deposits" should be supplied. As we have sometimes had occasion to remark, deposit receipts have been issued to pay for real estate. Should "deposits" so constituted be a first charge on assets? If so, then we can confidently express the conviction that the provision will often prove inoperative in practice. Another point that would have to be settled is, whether the Legislature should sanction the principle that Victorian assets, however acquired, are to be ear-marked as security against Victorian liabilities. If this principle should be adopted, a great restriction would be placed, doubtless unconsciously, on the investment of British capital in the colony. The principle might work as follows:—A company, with headquarters in London, has invested British money in Victoria to the extent of say £1,000,000; it has received, say £500,000 on deposit and on debenture in the colony itself; it fails, and its total assets yield say 10s. in the £. But under the 14th section of MR. WYNNE'S bill it would be quite possible for the Victorian depositors and debenture-holders to obtain 20s. in the £, and even interest thereon, with the result that the loss of the English creditors would be increased. We cannot conceive any circumstances in which it would be right to thus give the colonial creditors a preferential claim over the British creditors of a company, and suggest, therefore, the amendment of the section as it now stands.

THE FORMATION AND PRESENTATION OF BANK BALANCE-SHEETS

The Formation and Presentation of Bank Balance-Sheets.

As much interest is now taken in the half-yearly balance-sheets of the banks carrying on business in these colonies, many persons are no doubt struck by the diversity of ways employed in presenting them to the shareholders, and are surprised that a uniform system is not adopted. It has to be recognised that the public are becoming more exacting in matters of this kind, and that those banks which publish clearly and logically arranged balance-sheets will command a preference with a certain class of minds over those which present accounts in a confused form, conveying a minimum of positive information. The reconstruction period of last year afforded an admirable opportunity for recasting the forms of balance-sheets in vogue, and we are inclined to the opinion that the banks might with advantage have conferred together with the object of framing a model for general acceptance, one which would have satisfied the public, and accordingly barred the way to an agitation for an inquisitorial statutory form, such as that followed by the Canadian banks. It is true, however, that several of the reconstituted banks have improved the forms in use by the old banks. The Bank of New South Wales has also remodelled its form in such a way that it is now one of the best employed by the colonial banks. It is as follows :—

LIABILITIES.

Notes in circulation ... ...
Deposits and accrued interest ...
Bills payable and other liabilities (which include reserves held for doubtful debts and amount at credit of officers' fidelity guarantee and provident fund) ... ...

Paid-up capital ... ...
Reserve fund ... ...
Profit and loss ... ...
Contingent liabilities — Outstanding credits and endorsements, as per contra ... ...

ASSETS.

Coin, bullion, and cash balances ...
Government securities ... ...
Treasury notes ... ...
Notes of other banks ... ...
Due by other banks ... ...
Bills receivable, bills discounted, and remittances in transit ... ...
Loans and advances to customers ...
Bank premises ... ...
Liabilities of customers and others on letters of credit and drafts, as per contra ... ...

Without being prolix or giving unessential details, this form gives a sharp and clear outline of the business of the bank.

Of the forms adopted by reconstructed banks, we will select two, of which one is that of a bank having its head office in London, and the other is that of a bank having its head office in the colonies. First, the form used by the London Bank of Australia Limited is as follows :—

LIABILITIES.

Notes in circulation ... ...
Bills payable and other liabilities ...
Fixed deposits of old bank ... ...
Current accounts and new deposits...
Capital paid-up ... ...
Balance of contingency account held in reserve, pending realisation of assets of the old bank ... ...
Profit and loss ... ...

ASSETS.

Cash in London and the colonies ...
Investments, bills of exchange, loans and other assets in London ...
Bills discounted, loans and other securities in the colonies ...
Bank premises ... ...
Open policies and stamps ... ...

In the preceding form the arrangement of the liabilities leaves little to be desired. But the arrangement of the assets—the form used by the old bank having been retained—is not so satisfactory. Investments, for instance, might with advantage be stated separately; bills of exchange and bills discounted might be separated from loans and advances, just as in the balance-sheet of the Bank of New South Wales; and the minor old-fashioned item, "open policies and "stamps," might be merged in other accounts, stamps, perhaps, being included with the cash items.

We take as our second illustration the form adopted by the Australian Joint Stock Bank Limited. It is as follows:—

LIABILITIES.
Notes in circulation ... .
Bills in circulation and balances due to other banks... ... ...
Deposits—
　Current accounts not bearing interest ... ...
　New fixed deposits ... ...
　Fixed deposits of old bank extended for long periods ...
　Inscribed stock deposits ...
Interest accrued on deposits and stocks ... ...
Capital paid up ... ...
Reserve fund ... ...
Profit and loss ... ...
ASSETS.
Coin and bullion ... ...
Cash at London bankers ... ...
British consols ... ...
Treasury notes ... ...
Notes of other banks ... ...
Cash balances in hands of agents, and remittances *in transitu* ... ...
Bills receivable and bills discounted current ... ...
Loans and advances to customers ...
Bank premises ... ...

This form is the fullest and clearest in detail yet adopted, and is worth the study of other institutions.

It will be readily seen from a comparison of other forms in vogue with those given above, that important divergences occur in the treatment of deposits and lendings. Should deposits be stated *en bloc*, or as current accounts and deposits fixed for periods? Should the lendings be stated simply as "Bills "receivable and all other advances" or as "discounts" and "loans and advances?" We advocate the subdivisions, although we have to admit that the precedents amongst the English banks for the

separation of current accounts from fixed deposits are by no means numerous, although on the other hand discrimination between discounts and loans and advances is almost invariable. We take for illustration the forms of Lloyds' Bank and the London and County Bank, as follows:—

LLOYDS'.	LONDON AND COUNTY.
Debts owing to sundry persons by the company— On current and other accounts. On deposit accounts at notice.	Due by the bank on current accounts, on deposit accrued, circular notes, &c.
Bills of exchange— Advances to customers, promissory notes, and other securities.	Discounted bills current —Advances to customers at the head office and branches.
Liabilities of customers for bills accepted or indorsed by the company as *per contra*.	Liabilities of customers for drafts accepted by the bank, as *per contra*.

Some of the differences of practice amongst colonial banks could be made to disappear with little trouble, particularly the methods of dealing with the figures of the branches in London and outside Australia. Nearly all the banks having their head offices in the colonies include in their half-yearly balance their London office figures of a much earlier date. Would not a more exact statement of the position be shown if these banks adopted the practice pursued by one of the Sydney banks (The Commercial Banking Company of Sydney Limited) in obtaining the figures of the London office at the exact date of the half-yearly balance by cablegram? By an arrangement of ciphers this is by no means an expensive proceeding, and we learn that it costs the bank alluded to something under £15 each half-year. It is expected in a balance-sheet that all accounts comprised therein shall be closed to one date, or as near thereto as possible, It, therefore, strikes one as extraordinary to find in the balance-sheets published by some banks that the London figures included therein are of three months' earlier date, whilst the course of post between London and Australia is little more than one-third of that time. The employment of such figures involves the inclusion of many transactions amounting to very large amounts that have run off long before the date of the balance-sheet, which fact should induce the banks to exhibit the balance more in accordance with the spirit of the times by calling in the cable to their aid in the manner indicated above.

Leaving the subject of the arrangement of the accounts, the question of the date of submitting the balance-sheet to the shareholder deserves consideration. It would appear that an unnecessarily long time is taken by those banks having their head offices in London in issuing their half-yearly reports. In some cases over five months elapse between the date of balancing and the date of the meeting. Could not this period be considerably abridged? The practice is a survival from the old days of slow transit between Australia and England, when the delay was perhaps unavoidable, but with the existing speedy means of communication surely the period could be much shortened. Banking statistics, as derived from balance-sheets, would then be enhanced in value. With regard to the periodicity of balance-sheets, two or three banks still publish annual statements only. But would it not be well for them to adopt the now almost general practice of stating their position half-yearly?

———————◆———————

"'RESERVE FUND' AND 'RESERVES'"

"Reserve Fund" and "Reserve."

SEVERAL months ago a discussion was conducted in the columns of the London *Times* on the meaning of the term "reserve," and the functions of a reserve. The discussion was started by a remark of the city editor of the *Times* that a reserve is not a true reserve when it is employed in the business or locked up in bricks and mortar. Thereupon " C.A." expressed the opinion that " a reserve " is simply profit due to shareholders, "which is not paid to them." Mr. A. E. WEBSTER (a Fellow of the Institute of Bankers) considered "C.A.'s" proposition to be rather too narrow, and held that—

As exceptional profits may arise from exceptional circumstances, and should be held under the law of averages against exceptional losses in the form of a reserve, and this reserve is really divided into three parts and should be so stated as follows : -
1. Reserve as provision against loss of capital.
2. Reserve for equalisation of dividends.
3. Reserve as extra security held out to creditors.

Mr. WEBSTER expressed his conviction that in none of these cases can a reserve with strict propriety be used in the business and maintain its true character. The *Times* interposing at this point, insisted that it is the duty of boards of directors, when they decide that a reserve is necessary for any purpose, to see that if not kept in cash it is properly invested. Mr. T. A. WELTON, a leading London accountant, then joined in the discussion, saying that—

Many managers of companies would gladly use another word for undivided profits if " reserve be improper. . . but if it be contended that a reserve employed in the business (*e.g.*, in paying off creditors) disappears as much as if it had been distributed, then you will not find much support amongst practicalmen."

Mr. FRANK HYLAND, A.C.A., contributed the following *dicta* : —

Limited trading companies, like private individuals, find that they cannot prudently spend all their income. Part of it must be devoted to the development of their businesses to keep pace with the times and to provide for bad ones. The fund used for these purposes has, by custom, been called a reserve, and may be quite properly tied up in bricks and mortar.

Mr. G. H. JEFFARES put the matter differently from the previous disputants, asking—

Is not the recent discussion due to the indefinite use of the words "rest" and "reserve?" The former is a liability to the proprietors of the company, which would appear after all other liabilities had been liquidated and all assets realised. The "reserve" is an asset which should be composed of cash or liquid securities.

He referred to the Bank of England weekly statements, in which both terms are employed. Mr. WEBSTER, replying to Mr. WELTON, remarked—

I do not think anyone would contend that where profits had been capitalised they had disappeared "as much as if they had been distributed," but they thereafter are liable to the same influences as the capital ; and, should difficulty arise and the latter become lost or locked-up, the former would infallibly encounter a similar experience. A real "reserve," on the contrary, would be removed from such eventualities and would be directly available in time of need.

Mr. WELTON, rejoining, wrote as follows :—

Mr. Webster states in plain terms that a real reserve would be removed from the eventuality of being lost or locked-up, and yet would be directly available in time of need. I have seen vague remarks before which implied doctrines like these, but I think they have never before been stated so plainly. I think it will be out of the power of any company so to treat its reserves as to place them outside the risk of being lost or locked-up until some new law is passed. I shall be glad to see what arguments can be adduced for enabling shareholders to ear-mark and put out of reach of their creditors any portion of their company's assets. And, further, I shall be glad to know what Mr. Webster means by "directly available in time of need." Hitherto it has been well understood that reserves, or "capitalised profits," if that term be preferred, are subject to all the fluctuations and contingencies of ordinary capital. They form a first line of defence, the capital itself being the second line, and both must be lost before the creditor can suffer.

Mr. WEBSTER, unnecessarily, became rather prolix, but we quote the following passages from his reply to the foregoing :—

In answer to Mr. Welton, I would point out that it is not pleaded that shareholders should " ear-mark and put *out of reach* of their creditors any portion of their company's assets," but that they should so ear-mark them as to place them constantly *within the reach* of the creditors, and this is effected by the process of rendering them " directly available in time of need" by investing them in some permanently and readily marketable security, as illustrated in the case of the bank alluded to immediately above, which has a "real reserve" invested in a large holding of 2¾ per cent. consols at 95. This leads to the point of difference between " reserves" and " capitalised profits ;" the former should be invested similarly to those just alluded to ; the latter are merely added to and used as capital in the business. A real "reserve" must be a fund absolutely beyond the resources supplied by the general funds or liquid assets ordinarily held for the conduct of business, and one which creditors or others interested may see at a glance is additionally available. Excess of assets over liabilities cannot be construed as constituting a reserve unless the assets embrace a special, easily-convertible security held solely against the "reserve," otherwise the excess is simply a "margin" subject to realisation.

Towards the close of the discussion, Mr. PRIDEAUX SELBY intervened with a letter, from which we take the following :—

It appears to me that the public, and even you yourself, as well as most of your recent correspondents, fail to distinguish clearly between a reserve properly so-called and a reserve fund. The former is a part of the general resources of the company, from whatever source derived ; the latter is undivided profit. Reserve must be in cash or in securities readily and promptly convertible into cash, its object being, as you rightly contend, to insure the ability of the company to meet promptly unusual or unforeseen demands from creditors. It is, in fact, another name for liquid resources, and is often--in the case of banks I might say always—much larger than the so-called reserve fund. The reserve fund, on the contrary, whether set apart directly from profit or indirectly from premium on shares sold, is a portion of the profits of the company so set apart to protect the capital from depletion in the event of unusual or unforeseen losses, and to equalise dividends. In many cases, whether from failure to appreciate the essential distinction between reserve and reserve fund, or in deference to popular views, some part of the reserve is set aside as a special investment of the reserve fund. In such cases it may often be found that the reserve, including reserve fund investments, is no greater than the reserve alone of other prudent companies doing similar business, but employing the reserve fund, quite legitimately, I contend, in their trade. If the trading assets be good assets no claim can fall on the reserve fund, but trading assets may be perfectly good, yet the company fail, from insufficient reserve, to meet its engagements punctually. Otherwise stated, the essential difference between reserve fund and reserve is shown by their appearing on opposite sides of the balance-sheet. Reserve fund as a security to creditors is equivalent to an increase of the capital of the company, yet no one says that capital should not be employed in the business of the company.

It will be seen that the controversy was conducted chiefly by one of the younger school of accountants, a stickler for precision in the use of terms, by an older accountant of great experience, and by a shrewd practical banker. But the best contribution of all, in our opinion, was that of the outsider, Mr. G. H. JEFFARES. A "reserve" in banking practice is just what Mr. JEFFARES and Mr. SELBY held it to be, and is not necessarily, either in whole or in part, the same thing as a "reserve fund." It is, however, hardly, as Mr. SELBY puts it, "another name for liquid resources," unless, indeed, those liquid resources are

ample to prevent the bank from being depleted. Even here, again, there must be further qualification, for by ample liquid resources should be understood an amount bearing such a proportion to liabilities as has been shown to be adequate by a long and wide experience. Modern Australasian banking dates from just after the gold discoveries in Victoria, say 1852, and the largest percentage of liquid resources which has ensured safety during that period (the crisis of 1893 included) might fairly be adopted as the approximate reserve for the future, whenever banking affairs resume their normal condition. It is unsafe, however, to dogmatise upon this point, so many considerations existing which can only be known to the management of the individual banks. No hard and fast rule need be observed, although the principle readily suggests itself that the general resources of a bank should be sufficiently well in hand to admit of the rapid strengthening, or at least the maintenance of the normal amount of the reserve in time of·need.

The amount of the banking reserve, then, has no necessary connection with that of the reserve fund. There may be no reserve fund at all, and yet the reserve may be adequate. Even if the rule were adopted of holding the reserve fund in cash or public securities, bank managers, properly desirous of utilising within the lines of safety the resources at their command as far as possible, would probably adjust their cash reserves accordingly and hold not a pound more or less than if they altogether ignored, in this connection, the existence of the reserve fund.

As regards the expression "reserve fund," it is not accurate, and the inaccuracy has probably given rise to the confusion of ideas illustrated in the course of the discussion. It may be considered as the excess of assets over liabilities and capital, or as the aggregate of undivided profits, or as reserved profits. The term "rest," as employed by the

Bank of England, although old-fashioned, seems to be the best, meaning what remains after deducting liabilities from assets. Possibly, the use of the term "reserve fund" has wrought mischief in leading the public to adopt the belief that it was something that should be kept inviolate, untouched by the vicissitudes of business, and ear-marked in some mysterious but really impossible manner for the benefit of creditors. The run attendant upon a crisis, however, speedily dispels illusions, and merges assets into one common fund available for the whole body of creditors.

The question of locking up money in bricks and mortar is one altogether apart from that of the distinction between a reserve and a reserve fund, and unless a balance sheet explicitly states that the reserve fund is invested in buildings, there is nothing at all to fix bricks and mortar as a lock-up of what should be kept immediately available. At the same time, we have always been careful to point out in our periodic reviews of bank balance-sheets that bank premises (adapted as they are only to one specific purpose) constitute a deduction from working capital resources. Thus, in June, 1893, we stated the capital paid up, reserve fund, and undivided profits (as at 31st March) of the Australasian banks at £24,004,779, but deducted amount invested in premises, &c., £6,162,283, calling the balance of £17,842,496 the "effective working capital."

Beyond suggesting the desirability of a more logical term than "reserve fund," the immediate object of the discussion in the *Times* was practically *nil*. Its value consisted chiefly in bringing out the true distinction between the reserve against liabilities and the so-called reserve fund, or, more properly speaking, the "Rest."

THE ITEM DEPRECIATION

A QUESTION in connection with the periodic statements of companies' assets of some importance has lately suggested itself. It is that of the treatment of the charge for depreciation. That charge ought unquestionably to be made regularly in the profit and loss account, or the working account, and should not be postponed. But it is to be feared that the habit of ignoring or deferring it, and therefore of publishing an inaccurate and misleading balance-sheet, is growing. The item depreciation either does not appear or is quite inadequate, especially when it is found that its inclusion would make the payment of a dividend impossible. It is, of course, to be admitted that where the valuation of securities is concerned considerable latitude has to be allowed in times when criteria of value are temporarily hidden by a cloud of depression. But we are not referring to such a case, but to the charge that ought to be made for ordinary wear and tear of plant and machinery, vessels, and other movable property. The necessity for scrupulousness in this matter is really much greater in the colonies than elsewhere, because obsolete machinery is being run (particularly in Melbourne, where protection favours the continuance of the use of antiquated appliances as well as methods) which may at any time finally become quite useless. Suddenly the directors find that they have to make provision for "special depreciation." Even then it may occur that the provision is not made where it ought to be—in the profit and loss or working account statement—but forms a deduction *after* the so-called profit balance is ascertained. The point we have glanced at is a part of the great question of the proper valuation of properties and stock in the framing of balance-sheets. Upon the soundness of valuation the position of the company really hinges.

ACCOUNTANTS AND AUDITORS

ﻫ ﻫ ﻫ

HE following is a summary of lecture delivered by Mr. W. O. Strangward, F.I.A.V., before the Bank Officers' Students' Society on 29th inst.

Book-keeping is the art of recording, in the plainest and simplest form, the financial records of a business or undertaking. Many people have an erroneous idea as to the value of book-keeping; they look upon it as a necessary evil, as something to be reduced to its smallest compass,—as an encumbrance, in fact. On the contrary, I think that a reasonable amount of time devoted to keeping intelligible accounts will prove quite as profitable as the labour expended in a man's own occupation. Of this I am certain, that if proper books of account were universally kept, there would be fewer disputed business transactions, and the work of the Insolvency Court greatly reduced. Those who are acquainted with the working of this Court are perfectly aware that most men who fail in business have neglected to keep adequate books of account. Many traders go from year's end to year's end calculating their profits by the "rule of thumb," until suddenly the doors of the Bankruptcy Court open to their astonished gaze. As long as their bank balance is in a satisfactory condition, they are apt to think they are making profits, whereas a rational system of book-keeping might have shown them that in place of their capital being intact, they had, for some years past, been living upon their creditors' money.

Roughly speaking, there are two systems of book-keeping,—double and single entry. Nearly everybody is familiar with keeping books by single entry, but double entry is to many people a sort of "*terra incognita.*" As a matter of fact, the difference is very slight. In single entry every item is posted to some account in the ledger ; in double entry it is posted *twice*, either in detail or in total. For example, under the simplest system, if you sell on credit £100 worth of goods to fifty customers, you will debit the respective amounts to each customer ; but under double entry you will, in addition, post the total sales each month or half-year to the credit of a "goods" or "sales" account. If, on the contrary, you *buy* goods on credit, you will, in addition to crediting the seller, debit your "goods" account. This, then, is the basic principle of double entry,—that every amount shall be posted on *each* side of the ledger.

The results are very valuable, because if your postings are correctly made, your ledger will balance; and in addition to your customers' accounts showing their transactions with you, the ledger will exhibit what are known as "Impersonal" or "Statistical" accounts. Thus, your "sales" account will inform you as to the total sales for the period under review. Your "discount" account will show the total discount received and allowed, and so on. Of course, in actual practice, there are many more complicated entries than the above, but the principle of dealing with them is precisely similar,—*every debit has its corresponding credit.*

In a merchant's business there are usually six distinct books of account, whose uses are as under :—

The Cash Book records all items of cash actually received and paid, showing in separate columns the discount received and allowed, and amounts paid to and drawn from the bank.

The Day or Sales Book contains entries of all sales to customers.

The Invoice or Purchase Book is used to enumerate particulars of goods purchased.

The Bill Book is a specially ruled book to record the details of each bill received or given.

The Journal is a book essential to double entry. In addition to collecting the totals, etc., of the other subsidiary books, it records every entry which cannot properly find a place in any of the books before mentioned.

The duty of the **Ledger** is to collect in concise form every entry which appears in the other books. It thus exhibits a bird's eye view of the business. No entry, save additions or balances, should appear in the ledger except as a posting from some other book of account.

In banking, the system followed is exactly the same in principle, although, owing to the multiplicity of money transactions, it is necessary to greatly increase the number of books kept. Still, the totals are all incorporated into the private books, and reach the ledger as in a merchant's business. Many bank officers, who are not aware of the way in which their totals are brought into the accountant's books, are apt to think they are not working at a double entry system at all, whereas the underlying rules are exactly the same.

There are many reasons why bankers should have a fair knowledge of mercantile book-keeping. In the first place, bank officials (especially in the country districts) are generally looked upon as financial experts, and as such are often called in to advise as to making up balance sheets and the dreaded income tax returns. Unless they have at least a passing acquaintance with the art, they cannot undertake the responsibility with such confidence as they otherwise would [do. Besides, the ability to take an intelligent interest in a client's affairs will do much to gain their respect, and I know many instances where such expert knowledge, and the ability to explain a balance sheet, have been the means of gaining a good supporter to the bank. Then, again, a bank official in the country will be elected, often without his previous consent, to act as auditor to the local hospital or charitable institute accounts, and will be expected, generally without any "cash insult," to append his name to the district Agricultural or Tennis Club accounts as a guarantee of their accuracy. Considering the great amount of moral responsibility thereby incurred, it is not too much to urge that such honorary auditors should know their work.

Apart, however, from these reasons, the uncertainty of banking appointments should impel all to ground themselves in a knowledge of accounts. One never knows when retrenchment, closing of branches, etc., may result in one's retirement, and a banker suddenly hurled from his groove, and compelled to seek occupation in some other walk of clerical life, is a man to be pitied. To be cast into the ocean of unemployed clerical labour, which too often engulfs even those who have made themselves expert swimmers, is a calamity to anyone, but unless a knowledge of mercantile book-keeping be possessed, his position will be infinitely worse.

Suppose you were called in to prepare a merchant's balance sheet. You first see that every entry is posted, that the list of ledger balances (called a trial balance) shows the same total on each side of the ledger. You will then take a sheet of ruled foolscap, and head it, John Smith & Co., Ltd. Balance Sheet at 31st Dec., 1899. On the left hand side will be enumerated the "Liabilities"; on the right, the "Assets." A reference to the "*Pro forma*" balance sheet which you have in your hand will explain the class of entries which will appear. Then you open a "Trading" or "Manufacturing" account, to which you debit the stock on hand at 1st January, 1899, and the cost of *producing* the goods intended for sale. No item incurred *after* the completion of the goods will be debited here. On the Credit side you enter the gross sales, whether paid for or not, as well as the stock on hand at date of balance sheet. The credits will probably be the greater, in which case the difference will be entered on the Dr. side as gross profit and transferred to the Cr. of a profit and loss account, which you now proceed to compile. The profit and loss account contains as debits the cost of administering the business and all expenses incurred (whether already paid or not) in the sale and delivery of the goods. The surplus again will, in every well-conducted business, be on the credit side, and the amount thus required to balance is the nett profit for the year under review.

The object of these separate statements is to show, from every standpoint, the progress of the undertaking. The liabilities and assets will testify as to whether the trader is solvent or not; the trading account will exhibit the amount of gross profit upon the manufacture of goods; and the profit and loss account proves whether that gross profit has, or has not, been swallowed up in the cost of management.

You will notice in the accounts which I have prepared a "Statement of Receipts and Disbursements." This requires a little explanation, as it is a constant source of bewilderment to shareholders. It is simply a summary of the cash book, and shows the whole of the cash operations for the period. Very often it is almost identical with the profit and loss account, and is then often confused with it. The differences, however, may be very great. For example, the profit and loss account has nothing whatever to do with cash or bank balances or, expenditure upon plant, etc; whilst the receipts and disbursements take no cognisance of expenses *incurred*, but not actually paid, or profits earned, but not actually *received*. Thus, in the profit and loss account you observe Directors' and Auditors' fees, £160. Whilst this was evidently incurred it has not been *paid*, and will not, therefore, appear in the cash statement. Similarly, the former account shows that the rents due for the year amounted to £100, whilst the latter statement of accounts shows £150 as having been *received*. It is plain, then, that the other £50 must represent rents *received* during the year, but which fell *due* some time prior to the 1st January, 1899.

As a rule the receipts and disbursements' statement is only adopted by mining companies, as the profit and loss account is usually of far more value in showing the position of the undertaking.

Having prepared your balance sheet, make ready for the auditor by having the totals inked in, balance brought down and ruled off. Stock sheets certified to by some responsible person must be at hand. The bank pass book must be made up, and a reconciliation balance showing the cheques outstanding prepared. Vouchers should be arranged in order of the cash book, so that no time need be lost by the auditor in comparing them.

Now, transform yourself into that important personage, the auditor. Your first action is to look over the books and see that they are properly balanced, ruled off, etc., and, if possible, don't make a start until they are in "apple-pie" order. Then make a list of the books, and a memo of each detail of work to be done. You will find this very useful, even in small

.audits. Your next duty is to call for the original prospectus and articles of association, etc., and see that all matters concerning money or shares are ·correctly recorded in the journal. The articles will inform you as to any special duties devolving upon you as auditor. It will be advisable to obtain ɾthe last audited balance sheet, and to see that the books correctly exhibit the position as at that date. Then commence the checking work, comparing the entries, as far as possible, with the original source from which they came. You must cultivate the faculty of viewing every entry—every voucher with suspicion—as something concealing possible fraud. It is also advisable to complete each portion of the work at one sitting, so that when you have finished it you are certain that that part of the audit, at any rate, is correct : if you cannot complete it the same day, take a memo of the position. I came across a case where a pair of auditors fell into serious disgrace through the neglect of this simple precaution. The secretary of a large building society was accustomed to present his vouchers without any regard to their order in the cash book ; consequently, at the close of the day, the auditors had passed many items for which they had not yet seen vouchers. During the night, the secretary placed an honest-looking tick opposite each of the items which represented his defalcations, and thus, at the conclusion of the audit, the auditors were able to compliment him upon the excellent manner in which his vouchers had been obtained. A little care would have saved the auditors from being deceived by such a simple expedient. It is a good idea to adopt a distinctive tick, because, after a lengthened period of use, you are able to distinguish your own mark amongst others—and, for the same reason, a coloured ink, if possible, differing in shade from any easily obtainable by other persons. The checking of the postings, verification of pass book, additions and vouchers, etc., is usually mere mechanical work, and they will probably be found correct. It would be a very simple defaulter who was detected by an error in additions or postings. It is always advisable for an auditor to satisfy himself of the identity of the bank pass book by personal enquiry at the bank, or by obtaining a certificate as to the balance at the date of the balance-sheet Many a careful auditor's reputation has been tarnished by the acceptance of a fraudulent pass book. In some instances, F.D.R., payable to a number in place of a name, will be presented as vouchers. The auditor will requɪre to convince himself that such securities really refer to the institution whose accounts he is auditing. Some years ago defalcations were successfully cloaked up by the same deposit receipts being submitted to two sets of auditors, the cash representing one of the deposit receipts having been misappropriated.

Care must be exercised that all items properly chargeable against profit and loss account are so dealt with instead of being capitalised. For instance, if repairs to plant be debited to the plant account, it will obviously affect the net profit and the company's solvency.

Having satisfied yourself that the accounts, as presented, are correct, you certify to the balance sheet. In all but companies under Part i. of the Companies Act, "audited and found correct" will usually be all that is necessary, but if you cannot give an unqualified certificate, the reservations you make must be *distinctly* shown in your certificate. Avoid all ambiguous certificates as being both dangerous and contemptible. It will not be sufficient for the auditor to give a clearance and then to report his objections to the directors. Such a course is probably only informing the offending party or parties of their wrongdoing. Instances are frequent of an auditor being held personally liable for failure to exercise reasonable care and vigilance, and particularly if loss occurs through his neglect to report his doubts to the shareholders. An auditor was recently held liable for dividends paid out of capital, although he had drawn the directors' attention to the impolicy of such a proceeding. At the same time, it is reassuring to know that there is no case on record where an auditor was held liable after having ably and conscientiously done his duty. The failure to discover fraud will not, of itself, personally recoil upon the auditor, provided he has not been lax.

Having briefly sketched some of the mental qualifications required by an accountant and auditor, I will rapidly enumerate his statutory requirements. There is no restriction at present as to what persons can act as auditors to private firms or mining companies, but Legislative action in this direction will probably soon be taken.

Companies Accounts under Part i. (except Proprietary Cos.) must be certified to by one or more licensed auditors, whose licenses are obtained from the Companies' Auditors' Board by examination in book-keeping, auditing, and the Companies Acts. The 1896 Act prescribes a special form of certificate, which is shown on my specimen balance sheet. It also compels the auditors to file with the Registrar-General a sealed envelope containing a private balance sheet, which shows the details upon which the shareholders' balance sheet is based. This envelope can only be opened by order of the court.

Municipal Accounts are vouched for by two auditors, one of whom, the "local auditor," is elected by the ratepayers. He requires no auditorial qualifications. The second is a Government nominee, who must possess a certificate, obtained by passing an examination in book-keeping, auditing, and the Local Government Act.

I cannot too strongly urge upon all in clerical occupations to qualify themselves for one of the accountants' institutes. The Victorian Institute is usually considered the best. Whilst insisting upon the highest qualifications, its policy is to open its doors to all who are willing to show their ability. Students may, for a nominal fee, borrow books from a library replete with works upon every subject which will come under the notice of a professional accountant. Free monthly lectures are held, and capable coachers obtainable at a moderate fee. I am often asked how long it would take to pass the examinations. Of course the reply to this query will vary according to the previous experience and perseverance of the student, but to the man of average ability, and who is willing to devote himself closely to his object, eighteen months or two years should be amply sufficient. Unless the degrees were somewhat difficult to obtain, they would be worth nothing, but, setting aside the added stock of knowledge, I am certain that every successful candidate will reap a great monetary advantage from his labours, no matter what line of clerical occupation he follows.

I have been requested to prepare a few questions upon accountants and auditors, answers to which may be sent to the hon. secretary of your society for correction. These questions will be published in the columns of the BANKERS' MAGAZINE this month.

1. Explain the desirable results attained by keeping books by double entry as compared with single entry.

2. Outline what work a bank auditor should do.

3. Suppose you considered the assets of a company greatly overvalued, what course of action would you as auditor adopt ?

4. Prepare a liabilities and assets, trading and profit and loss accounts from the following brick-making business figures :—

Capital at 1st January, 1899, £5,000
Total Purchases, £5,000
Total Sales, £25,000
Stock on Hand, 1st January, 1899, £3,000
Do., 1st January, 1900, £4,000
Wages at Works, £2,000
Book-keepers' Salaries, £200
Directors' and Auditors' fees, £100
Rent of Offices, £100

Cartage Outward, £490.
Interest on Overdraft, £100
Bank Overdraft, £1,000
Plant Account, £1,000
Sundry Creditors, £1,000
Sundry Debtors, £16,030
Bills Payable, £500
Bills Receivable, £1,000
Cash in Hand, £5
Freehold Buildings, £2,500

Printing, Advertising, and Stationery, £20

Bad Debts, £250

Cartage Inward, £500

Rents Received, £50

Discount allowed, £225

Repairs to Machinery, £120

JOHN SMITH AND CO.

BALANCE SHEET AT 31ST DECEMBER, 1899.

LIABILITIES.				ASSETS.			
To Capital (1st Jan., 1899)	£15,000	0	0	By Stock, 31st Dec., 1899...	£5,000	0	0
„ Sundry Creditors ...	5,000	0	0	„ Sundry Debtors ...	1,900	0	0
„ Bills Payable ...	1,000	0	0	„ Plant and Machinery...	13,000	0	0
„ Bank Overdraft ...	2,000	0	0	„ Freehold Buildings ...	5,000	0	0
„ Balance Profit (from P. and L. Account) ...	2,000	0	0	„ Cash in Hand ...	100	0	0
	£25,000	0	0		£25,000	0	0

TRADING ACCOUNT, YEAR ENDING 31ST DECEMBER, 1899.

To Stock at 1st Jan., 1899	£2,500	0	0	By Sales Account ...	£13,700	0	0
„ Purchases	10,000	0	0	„ Stock at 31st Dec., 1899	5,000	0	0
„ Wages	1,200	0	0				
„ Balance, Gross Profit carried to P. and L. Account	5,000	0	0				
	£18,700	0	0		£18,700	0	0

PROFIT AND LOSS ACCOUNT FOR YEAR ENDING 31ST DECEMBER, 1899.

To Salaries	£450	0	0	By Balance from Trading Account ...	...£5,000	0	0
„ Rent Rates and Taxes	150	0	0	„ Rents, etc.	100	0	0
„ Discount and Allowances	500	0	0				
„ Bad and Doubtful Debts	690	0	0				
„ Repairs to Machinery	1,000	0	0				
„ Bank Interest ...	150	0	0				
„ Directors' and Auditors' Fees	160	0	0				
„ Balance, Nett Profit (carried to Balance Sheet)	2,000	0	0				
	£5,100	0	0		£5,100	0	0

BANKERS' MAGAZINE OF AUSTRALASIA
[NOVEMBER 30, 1899, pp.218-26]

JOHN SMITH AND CO.
STATEMENT OF RECEIPTS AND DISBURSEMENTS, YEAR ENDED 31ST DECEMBER, 1899.

RECEIPTS.		DISBURSEMENTS.	
To Sales Account ...£14,000 0 0		By Bank Overdraft, 1st	
„ Rents 150 0 0		Jan., 1899 ... ... £3,375 0 0	
, Overdraft at Bank 31st		„ Purchases 9,000 0 0	
Dec., 1899 ... ... 2,000 0 0		„ Wages 950 0 0	
		„ Salaries 175 0 0	
		„ Repairs to Machinery 1,500 0 0	
		„ Plant Purchased ... 1,000 0 0	
		„ Bank Interest ... 50 0 0	
		„ Cash in Hand ... 100 0 0	
£16,150 0 0		£16,150 0 0	

SPECIMEN OF AUDITOR'S CERTIFICATE UNDER PART I. COMPANIES ACT, 1896.

I hereby certify that I have examined and compared the Books, Accounts, and Securities of the Company for the year ended 31st December, 1899, and that so far as I am in a position to form an opinion, the Balance Sheet and Accounts have been drawn up in accordance with the provisions of the Companies Act, and present a correct view of the state of the Company's affairs at that date.

I further certify that I have not observed, nor become acquainted with, during the audit, any breach of the Companies Act committed by the Company, or any Director, Manager, or Employee, Auditor or Shareholder thereof.

I also certify that all my requisitions as Auditor in connection with the Private Balance Sheet have been complied with.

WILLIAM BROWN,
1st Feb., 1900.   Licensed Auditor.

BANKERS' MAGAZINE OF AUSTRALASIA

[NOVEMBER 29, 1900, pp.210-16]

BANKERS' BOOKS AS COMPARED WITH TRADERS

ॐ ॐ ॐ

Lecture by C. M. HOLMES, F. I. A. V., on November 28, 1900.

OOK-KEEPING has been described as an "art," but it may be much more accurately classed as one of the applied sciences. It treats only of wealth and indebtedness, and is, briefly, the science of recording transactions so as to show their effect on the financial position of the person primarily concerned in a complete and convenient form ; the entries should be susceptible of proof as to their accuracy, and so clear and full as to need no explanation other than that they contain.

The transactions which it is the province of book-keeping to record are various. They may be summarised under four heads, as those relating to, (1) goods ; (2) money; (3) use; and (4) personal service. It may be accepted as an axiom that each transaction tends in itself to the creation of a liability by one of the parties to the other, and the principle involved in this axiom is applicable even where the transaction is not one in which two persons are concerned but where abstractions are manifest, such as in the following instances : Goods Dr. to Freight, and Manufacturing Account Dr. to Wages.

The precursor of the one scientific system of book-keeping was known as the Italian system, and dates back to the fifteenth century. The widely-spread commerce of the Italians of that age is doubtless responsible for their pre-eminence in the matter of accounts, and for the fact that their methods of book-keeping spread, with their commerce, to other lands. The Italian system, as illustrated by the journal, exhibits a confusion of entries from which the modern journal of our double entry system is absolutely free. By way of illustration I will refer you later on to the specimen entries on one of the diagrams with its accompanying correction, according to present-day usage. It will, perhaps, be a surprise to some to be told that there are journals kept in Melbourne to-day showing this same confusion of thought and expression, having only one money column—an entry consisting of one amount which serves alike both for debit and credit.

An application of the principles of double entry to public accounts is reported to have been made by direction of Prince Maurice of Nassau, and the treatise of Stevinus, published in the Dutch language in 1544, is said to have been the first to show the applicability of double entry to other than mercantile accounts. The sixteenth and seventeenth centuries witnessed the

272

publication in England of several books of book-keeping, in which the double entry method was taught, if not elaborately expounded ; but in 1796 Mr. Edward Thos. Jones, of Bristol, " devised " a plan for keeping accounts correctly, and published the first edition of Jones' System—since followed by numerous editions, the last which I have seen being the twentieth, edited and enlarged by Theodore Jones, the son of the originator of the system. There can be no reasonable doubt that Jones' system is the foundation of present-day methods.

In all accounting and book-keeping the related terms " debit " and " credit," " debtor " and " creditor," are of primal importance. Debit is literally something owed, being derived from the Latin verb *debeo*, I owe ; " debtor " is strictly the person owing, but the term is frequently inter-changeable with " debit." " Credit," also derived from the Latin, signifies trust or confidence, which obviously exists in the mind of the person who sells his goods or lends his money on the understanding that payment, though not made immediately, will be made at some future date. The personal term in this operation is, of course, " creditor," which, as an expression, is often synonymous with the word "credit." The following quotation from Dawson's " Accountant's Compendium " defines the terms, debit and credit, and their relation to each other, so concisely that I cannot do better than give the exact words :—

" The term debit is applied to all entries corresponding with, or opposed to, the credit entries. The placing of an amount to the debit of a personal account either implies a right to demand such amount from the particular person, or serves to satisfy an equivalent cross demand. The universal rule in book-keeping is to place all debit items on the left-hand side of the various books of account, the credit entries being placed upon the right-hand side.

" With regard to items placed upon the debit side, such as will ultimately be received or continue to be enjoyed (*e.g.* book debts and lands purchased) are to be considered as assets, and those which will not be recovered (*e.g.* trade expenses) represent losses or charges against profits. Conversely, items placed upon the credit side, which will ultimately have to be paid (by the person whose accounts are under review) must be treated as liabilities, whilst the credit items which do not involve a liability (*e.g.*, commissions received) are to be treated as profits."

Every transaction has thus two sides. When John Smith sells £50 worth of goods to William Brown, the transaction appears in Smith's books as a debit to Brown, while in Brown's books a corresponding entry is made to the credit of Smith. Thus far the relation of debtor to creditor is easily seen in the respective account books of the two parties; but there is another and closer connection between the debit and the credit in the case of each of the parties. When Smith (an importer) sells his goods to Brown he does not create fresh wealth (except so far as the possible profit is concerned, with which we are not now dealing), as the debit to Brown's account in the ledger might lead us to suppose. This out-going of goods actually lessens Smith's stock in hand, and concurrently with the debit to Brown there is required a credit to goods account, by means of which the book-keeping equilibrium is maintained. To give effect to the process indicated, the entry may be stated thus—in Smith's journal :—

William Brown	Dr. £50
For 10 tons of flour at £5	
To goods	£50

Here, William Brown, a *personal* account, is the debtor, and goods, an *impersonal* account, is the creditor. This entry is an illustration of the dictum, which is the basis of double entry or scientific book-keeping, that " every debit has its corresponding credit."

Other illustrations of a different nature may be given showing the relation between debits and credits, into which the personal and impersonal elements are introduced. For example :—

(1) H. ROBINSON   Dr. £400
     For sale of land at
     Footscray Allotment 13
     Section B, Parish of
     Cut-paw-paw 800 ft. at
     10/-
    To THOMAS JONES £400

and again—

(2) THOMAS JONES   Dr. £10
     For commission on sale of land
     To H. Robinson—2½% on £400
    To COMMISSION £10

In the first of the transactions, our friend Smith acts as an agent, and sells an allotment of land to H. Robinson on account of Jones for £400. There is no difficulty in seeing that by this operation Robinson owes Smith (as Jones' agent) £400, with which he is properly charged or debited; while, simultaneously, Jones, whose land has been sold, has become Smith's creditor, and is accordingly credited with the same amount. By this stroke of business Jones becomes indebted to Smith for a commission on the sale, and his account is debited with £10, but Smith cannot credit himself—no man can keep an account with himself—the corresponding credit takes the form of commission account.

Single entry is the negation of this law : under its method (if such an empirical device may be called a method) only personal accounts are posted into the ledger, all other accounts being absolutely disregarded, and so what is known as balancing the books is an impossibility. To the student who is curious to learn what may be said in support or elaboration of the practice of single entry book-keeping, there is a " Guide " by Dr. Brewer. The following is an extract from the preface to a school book, from which I was given my first lessons in book-keeping. I doubt if to-day such foolish words would find a publisher :—

" Amidst a variety of forms for keeping accounts, as suited to particular businesses and professions, they may be all resolved into two general methods, viz., BOOK-KEEPING by SINGLE ENTRY and BOOK-KEEPING by DOUBLE ENTRY.

" For the common purposes of retail trade, *single entry* is deemed sufficient, and even among merchants, where double entry is used, it becomes almost essential that the scholar should first be made familiar with the forms of book-keeping by single entry, as it will tend to unfold the general principles and facilitate his acquisition of the nature of accounts, however intricate.

" How happens it that the knowledge of book-keeping has not hitherto been made a regular branch of school business at some period of a boy's education, unless it be because the treatises on the subject have been drawn up in a manner so perplexing and voluminous, and that both scholars and masters have shrunk from the arduous task ?"

A complete set of books for a trader can consist of many books, but may be compressed into three : cash book, journal, and ledger. Thirty or forty years ago doubts might have been expressed as to the necessity of a cash book, except as a rough book. To-day, it can only be in antiquated offices that the cash book is not an integral part of every set of books. The development of the modern cash book will be dealt with later on. The rulings given in the diagram of these three books are purposely in the most elementary forms, and yet they will suffice for the accurate recording of the largest and most ramified transactions (although not the best adapted to such), simply because they are right in principle. The cash book is to be used to record every item of money received and disbursed, as and when the transaction occurs, and for no other purpose. The one test for a cash book entry is this : " Has the transaction an actual cash settlement ?" If any element of credit or deferred payment enters into it, the cash book is not the book to be used. The journal is for all other transactions : purchases, sales, transfers between one account and another, and, generally, for recording every piece of business that is not an actual cash transaction. It may be, and is, freely used for the detailing of cross transactions, the balance of which is settled in cash—the settlement *only* appearing in the cash book.

It will be convenient to consider the relation of the trader's cash book and journal to his ledger before we proceed further. The two former are the chronological and continuous record from which the classification which the ledger accounts give is derived. While the journal, with only two columns, will answer for all transactions excepting cash, it is usual and desirable to exclude details of purchases and sales, bills receivable and bills payable, from the journal. By some writers these separate books are regarded as sub-divisions of the journal. There are, of course, businesses which do not consist in the purchase and sale of goods ; for instance, the Trustee Companies, Financial, Agency and Insurance Companies. For any of these, the subdivision of the journal, where desired, may be effected by the introduction of the Columnar or Tabular system. An illustration of the use of this method is embodied in the columns provided in the sales book of a produce merchant doing an export business, a specimen of which is shown in one of the diagrams, to which I will refer more fully later on. The ledger is susceptible of similar subdivision to that of the journal. Take the case of a trader who has transactions with two principal classes of persons, those from whom he buys and those from whom he sells. If the business is of such a size as to necessitate the employment of a staff of clerks, it will certainly be well to keep at least two, or possibly three, ledgers ; first, the private ledger, and second, the trade ledger. The first should contain capital, profit and loss, stock, plant, buildings, and bank accounts, and, generally, all accounts of an impersonal character ; while the trade ledger is for all personal accounts with merchants and customers. In some cases, as already stated, this book is divided into two, when purchase and customers' ledgers take the place of the single volume known as trade ledger. Alphabetical and geographical subdivisions of trade ledgers are frequently met with, such as A to L, and M and Z ; town, country, and intercolonial ; and wholesale and retail. Other examples of subsidiary ledgers may be seen in the loan ledgers of financial institutions, where separate columns for principal and interest are often used ; borrowers' and investors' ledgers of building societies, and the current account ledgers of bankers. In the illustrations I have shown rulings for trade accounts suitable to both plans. The cash book, it will be observed, has columns for two ledgers only, trade accounts and private accounts. The journal has also the same provision, contained in four columns, Trade Accounts Dr. and Cr., and Private Accounts Dr. and Cr. The headings of the purchase journal and sales journal, it will be observed, do not quite correspond, the personal column in the former being headed Merchants', and in the latter Customers' Accounts. In each case the transactions should be posted item for item into the trade ledger. Where the trade ledger is divided into two parts, the former would be posted into the purchase ledger, and the latter into the customers' ledger. Where a private ledger is kept with one or more subsidiary ledgers, the private ledger should balance in itself. This involves the keeping of an account for each subsidiary ledger in the private ledger, to which account there should be posted the monthly totals of the purchase journal, sales book, bill books, and the totals of the special columns for trade or merchants' and customers' accounts in the journal and cash books. The great advantage of this plan is that the private ledger (which is the key of the position of a business) can be balanced independently of the Trade or Subsidiary Ledgers, and that it supplies in its Trade Account (or Merchants' and Customers') the figures with which the balance of these Subsidiary Ledgers must agree. In Jones' plan this advantage is wanting ; the private and trade ledgers are made complementary one to the other, and the balances of both books have to be added together to ensure a balance. Should the aggregate debit and credit balances not agree, it is not possible to locate the error ; whereas in the plan I have outlined (which is very generally known and adopted), should the private ledger balance, and the balances of the trade ledger, or ledgers, be out of harmony with their corresponding accounts in the private ledger, it is known at once where the error lies, and the work of searching for its source is accordingly reduced to a limited area. I must now ask your attention to the details of the several books, specimen rulings of which are displayed. [The lecturer then explained the use of the columnar cash book, the purchase journal, the sales book, and the journal by means of diagrams, showing their applicability to the transactions of several businesses having special features.]

I have deferred, until this stage, reference to one of the greatest merits of Jones' system, a feature that is very rarely adopted, but which, when used, affords one of the best checks that can be imagined. It will be found in the last page of his valuable book, and consists of what he terms the Balance Book and the Abstract Book. The object which the balance book accomplishes is to show a summary of the postings of each ledger account for the period under review, as well as the balance at balancing time. The abstract book shows the totals for the same period abstracted from the journal (into which the totals of all transactions, *including cash*, have been entered), and the aggregate of the operations of the various ledger accounts, as shown in the balance book, must agree with the aggregate of the abstract book, if the books have been accurately kept. As I have already said, I regard Jones' method of taking cash book totals into the journal undesirable, especially as the manner in which he performs the operation involves what has been called one-legged entries for the two monthly entries affecting cash.

It is more than idle to find fault with the details of any plan unless one is prepared with a substitute for that which is objected to.

The method I would advise to reach the same desirable end is the following : At the foot of the closing entries in the journal, and below the ruling off of the addition, make a summary consisting of two sets of figures only. First, the total receipts and disbursements as shown in the private ledger columns of the cash book; and, second, the journal totals. The addition of these sums should prove to be the total of the transactions posted into the private ledger. To test this summarising, it will be necessary to take out not only the balances of the private ledger but also the transactions. This can easily be done by subtracting from the additions in each account at the close the total of the transactions prior to the month or period with which you are concerned. The transactions columns used in the extraction should, of course, be both debit and credit. The suggested plan is actually in vogue in the banks, and will be seen in the illustration of the weekly balance book of a branch bank in the diagram to which I invite your attention. We pass from these weekly transactions and balances to the re-statement of the balances as a balance sheet and profit and loss account, so far as profit and loss can be shown during the course of a banker's half-year. I regard this and the general cash book as the specially good features in bank book-keeping, conforming exactly to correct double entry principles.

The general cash book illustrates the essential element of double entry, which every cash book possesses, but which is not so obvious in any cash book I am acquainted with, as in the general cash book, or journal, or accountant's cash book as it is sometimes called of a bank. [The lecturer referred at some length to two diagrams, one exhibiting the weekly abstract embodying the transactions and balances of a branch bank, and the other the general cash book showing one day's transactions.]

BANKERS' BOOKS AS COMPARED WITH TRADERS.'

⚜ ⚜ ⚜

Lecture by C. M. HOLMES, F.I.A.V., on November 28, 1900.

WE were able to get nearly the whole of the text of this most instructive lecture into our last issue just as it was going to press. Mr. Holmes closed his remarks by showing on an enormous diagram, which everyone could easily see, the returns required by the Government from the banks trading in Victoria. The form of the weekly abstract is dictated by the Banks' and Currency Act 1890, sec. 4. The reference to the second Schedule to this Act showed that its particulars are practically contained in the Abstract (shown in the diagram). The reason for the Weekly Statement which bankers are required to make up to the close of business on each Monday is to be found in section 5 of the same Act, which directs that a quarterly statement of the average amount of the assets and liabilities shall be made up to the date of the last Monday in March, June, September, and December of each year. The quarterly statement, verified by oath, is published from time to time in the " Government Gazette."

This concluded a memorable lecture.